T0306072

Mauritius: A Successful Small Island Developing State

The economic upturn and performance of Mauritius is a far cry from predictions made in the 1960s. The island's remarkable economic performance since the 1980s can be attributed to a multitude of factors instrumental to the success of the economy, including structural reforms, outward-looking export-orientated strategies, diversification in the manufacturing, tourism and financial services sectors among others, sound economic governance and institutions, and significant investment in human capital.

This book attempts to provide a detailed analysis of the various key ingredients which have helped to propel Mauritius to its current status. The various chapters are essential reading for both academics and policymakers, with the final chapter providing key policy strategies which the government needs to implement in order to help Mauritius to graduate to the next level of development, namely to that of a high-income economy and, in moving out of the middle-income trap, laying the foundations for future growth and shared prosperity in the light of both domestic challenges and global constraints.

Boopen Seetanah is an Associate Professor at the University of Mauritius with research interest in tourism and transport, international trade and finance and development economics. He is currently the Co-Chair of the WTO Chair and the Director of Research at the International Centre for Sustainable Tourism and Hospitality at the University of Mauritius.

Raja Vinesh Sannassee is a Professor in the Department of Finance at the University of Mauritius. He holds a PhD in Economics from the University of Reading, UK. Sannassee served as Dean of the Faculty of Law and Management between 2014 and 2017.

Robin Nunkoo is an Associate Professor in the Faculty of Law and Management at the University of Mauritius; a Visiting Senior Research Fellow in the Faculty of Management at the University of Johannesburg, South Africa; and an Adjunct Professor at Griffith Institute for Tourism, Griffith University, Australia. He holds a PhD from the University of Waterloo, Canada.

Europa Perspectives: Emerging Economies

The Europa Emerging Economies series from Routledge, edited by Robert E. Looney, examines a wide range of contemporary economic, political, developmental and social issues as they affect emerging economies throughout the world. Complementing the *Europa Regional Surveys of the World* series and the *Handbook of Emerging Economies*, which was also edited by Professor Looney, the volumes in the *Europa Emerging Economies* series will be a valuable resource for academics, students, researchers, policy-makers, professionals, and anyone with an interest in issues regarding emerging economies in the wider context of current world affairs.

There will be individual volumes in the series which provide in-depth country studies, and others which examine issues and concepts; all are written or edited by specialists in their field. Volumes in the series are not constrained by any particular template, but may explore economic, political, governance, international relations, defence, or other issues in order to increase the understanding of emerging economies and their importance to the world economy.

Robert E. Looney is a Distinguished Professor at the Naval Postgraduate School, Monterey, California, who specializes in issues relating to economic development in the Middle East, East Asia, South Asia and Latin America. He has published over 20 books and 250 journal articles, and has worked widely as a consultant to national governments and international agencies.

Argentina's Economic Reforms of the 1990s in Contemporary and Historical Perspective
by Domingo Cavallo and Sonia Cavallo Runde

Handbook of Small States
Economic, Social and Environmental Issues
edited by Lino Briguglio

Pakistan at Seventy
A handbook on developments in economics, politics and society
edited by Shahid Javed Burki with Iftekhar Ahmed Chowdhury and Asad Ejaz Butt

Mauritius: A Successful Small Island Developing State
Edited by Boopen Seetanah, Raja Vinesh Sannasee and Robin Nunkoo

For further information, see https://www.routledge.com/Europa-Perspectives-Emerging-Economies/book-series/EPEE.

Mauritius: A Successful Small Island Developing State

Edited by
**Boopen Seetanah, Raja Vinesh Sannassee
and Robin Nunkoo**

LONDON AND NEW YORK

First published 2020
by Routledge
2 Park Square, Milton Park, Abingdon, Oxon OX14 4RN

and by Routledge
52 Vanderbilt Avenue, New York, NY 10017

Routledge is an imprint of the Taylor & Francis Group, an informa business

First issued in paperback 2021

Europa Commissioning Editor: Cathy Hartley

Editorial Assistant: Lucy Pritchard

British Library Cataloguing-in-Publication Data
A catalogue record for this book is available from the British Library

Library of Congress Cataloging-in-Publication Data
Names: Seetanah, Boopen, editor, author. | Sannassee, R. V., editor,
author. | Nunkoo, Robin, editor.
Title: Mauritius: a successful small island developing state / edited by
Boopen Seetanah, R.V. Sannassee and Robin Nunkoo.
Other titles: Europa emerging economies.
Description: First edition | New York : Routledge, 2019. |
Series: Europa emerging economies
Identifiers: LCCN 2019023459 (print) | LCCN 2019023460 (ebook) |
ISBN 9781857439717 (hardback) | ISBN 9780429262357 (ebook)
Subjects: LCSH: Economic development--Mauritius. | Mauritius--
Economicpolicy. | Mauritius--Economic conditions--20th century. |
Mauritius--Economic conditions--21st century.
Classification: LCC HC79.E44 M38 2019 (print) |
LCC HC79.E44 (ebook) | DDC 338.96982--dc23
LC record available at https://lccn.loc.gov/2019023459
LC ebook record available at https://lccn.loc.gov/2019023460

ISBN: 978-1-85743-971-7 (hbk)
ISBN: 978-1-03-208569-2 (pbk)
ISBN: 978-0-429-26235-7 (ebk)

Typeset in Times New Roman
by Taylor & Francis Books

Contents

Figures

Tables

Boxes

Contributors

Boopen Seetanah is an Associate Professor at the University of Mauritius (UoM) with research interest in tourism and transport, international trade and finance and development economics. He is currently the Co-Chair of the WTO Chair (UoM) and the Director of Research at the International Centre for Sustainable Tourism and Hospitality at the UoM. Seetanah is an editorial board member and a reviewer for numerous highly regarded journals. He is a consultant for the Mauritius government and also for numerous international organizations including UNEP, UNDP, UNCTAD, the World Bank, the ADB, the ILO and the Regional Multi-disciplinary Centre of Excellence (RMCE).

Raja Vinesh Sannassee is a Professor in the Department of Finance at the University of Mauritius (UoM). He holds a PhD in Economics from the University of Reading, UK, and currently lectures on International Business at both undergraduate and postgraduate level. Sannassee served as Dean of the Faculty of Law and Management (4,000 students) between 2014 and 2017. In addition, Sannassee has contributed to several publications in the areas of finance, economics and trade. He is also the Director of Programme for the MSc in Social Protection Financing, a joint initiative by the UoM and the ILO, and funded by the IDRC. Sannassee is also a Co-Chair of the WTO Chairs Programme. Finally, he has also acted as a consultant for various international organizations including the World Bank, UNDP, UNCTAD, UNECA and the AfDB.

Robin Nunkoo is an Associate Professor in the Faculty of Law and Management at the University of Mauritius; a Visiting Senior Research Fellow in the Faculty of Management at the University of Johannesburg, South Africa; and an Adjunct Professor at Griffith Institute for Tourism, Griffith University, Australia. He holds a PhD from the University of Waterloo, Canada, a Master of Philosophy in Tourism, a Master's degree in Tourism Management, a Master's degree in Development Administration, both from the University of Westminster, UK, and a degree in Economics from the University of Mumbai, India. He is the Associate Editor for *Annals of Tourism Research*, the *Journal of Hospitality Marketing and Management*, and *Tourism Review*. He has published widely in leading journals such *as* the *International Journal of Information Management, Annals of Tourism Research, Tourism Management*, the *Journal of Travel Research*, the *European Business Review* and *Government Information Quarterly*, and has edited books on research methods and tourism planning. He is an editorial board member of several leading journals. Nunkoo has research interests in quantitative methods, public trust, sociology of knowledge and sustainable tourism. In 2015 Nunkoo received the Emerging Scholar of Distinction Award from the International Academy for the Study of Tourism.

L. Amédée Darga is a former member of parliament in Mauritius. He was first elected at the age of 26, when he served as Minister of Housing and Lands. He also served as Mayor of the second most important town in Mauritius. He is a trustee of the Southern and Eastern African Trade and Information Network (Seatini), a member of the African Association of Political Science since 1977 and a former executive member of the organization. He was a member of the task force of the OAU for the drafting of the African Nuclear Weapon Free Zone Treaty. Darga acted as resource person for the preparation of the Africa Governance Reports and was a lead consultant for the ECA study on the State of Good Governance in Mauritius as well as leading a National Survey on the Perception of the State of Corruption in Mauritius. Darga has long-standing expertise on issues of African economic development strategies and on regional and international trade issues. He has widely researched and published on democracy, governance and economic development issues. He served recently for six years as a member of the Bureau of the Committee on Human Development and Civil Society of the UN Economic Commission for Africa. Since October 2005 he has been the chairperson of Enterprise Mauritius and is the Managing Partner of StraConsult, a management and economic development consulting firm. He is a Fellow of the Institution of Engineers in Mauritius.

Pierre Dinan was a Senior Partner at De Chazal Du Mee for 20 years until he retired in June 2004. He was also a Director of Multiconsult, a global business management services company, for 12 years. He is currently a director for a number of public companies in the manufacturing and financial services sectors, respectively. He was the founder Chairman of the Mauritius Institute of Directors. He is a former independent member of the Monetary Policy Committee of the Bank of Mauritius. He has been a director of the Sugar Industry Pension Fund board since 2012 and the Chairperson of the Audit Committee since 2016. Dinan is an economic observer and regularly writes in the Mauritian press on economic matters.

Sheereen Fauzel is a senior lecturer at the University of Mauritius. Having completed a PhD in International Economics at the University of Mauritius, along with a Master's degree in Banking and Finance and a Bachelor's degree in Economics and Finance, her areas of expertise are international economics, development economics and related areas. She has participated in international conferences and has published in several notable international journals covering business, economics and tourism. Fauzel is a reviewer for a number of refereed journals including *Current Issues in Tourism* and the *Journal of Hospitality Marketing and Management*, among others.

Saileshsingh Gunessee is an Associate Professor in Economics in the Business School at the University of Nottingham Ningbo China, where he also is the School's Director of Research Development. His research broadly spans the areas of spatial economics, economics of international business, experimental and behavioural economics and China-related economics. His research has been published in Clarivate Analytics' Social Sciences Citation Index, Chartered Association of Business Schools and Australian Business Deans Council listed journals, including *Environment and Planning A*, the *International Journal of Operations and Production Management*, the *International Small Business Journal* and *Review of World Economics*. He has taught mostly in the area of Microeconomics and Methods (i.e. Statistics and Econometrics).

Shashi Jeevita Matadeen is currently a lecturer at the University of Mauritius in the Faculty of Law and Management. She has completed the CFA programme and has recently completed her PhD. Her research interests include economic development, financial development and stock markets.

Rafael Muñoz Moreno is the World Bank's Program Leader for Equitable Growth, Finance, and Institutions for Brazil since August 2017. Moreno joined the World Bank in 2005 as part of the Young Professional Program. He has worked in the office of the Vice President of the Economic Department and has served as Country Economist in the Africa region. In addition, he was the Country Economist and Resident Representative in Mauritius and coordinated the World Bank work programme with Mauritius and Seychelles. In his previous assignment in the Bank, Moreno led the macroeconomic and fiscal policy dialogue between the government of Malaysia and the World Bank. Previously, Mr Muñoz worked in the Spanish embassy in Tokyo as an economist and in the European Commission as Operations Officer in charge of budget support projects in Latin America. Moreno holds a PhD in Economics from the University of Louvain (Belgium) and a European Doctoral Program in Quantitative Economic after attending the London School of Economics and Political Sciences. He has published several research papers, mostly on macroeconomic policies, labour economics and business cycles.

Harris Neeliah currently manages the Research and Projects division at the Human Resource Development Council, which he joined in 2013. He holds a Master's degree in Agricultural Development Economics and a PhD in Applied Economics, both from the University of Reading, UK. He was previously employed as a Research Coordinator for the Mauritius Research Council (2006–2013). Prior to that he was consulting in applied development economics projects, for both local and international clients. From 2004 to 2005 he was employed as Marketing Manager on the Agricultural Marketing Board. He has also extensively lectured in both the UK and Mauritius, principally in applied economics, quantitative methods and research methods. His current research interests are in the role of human capital in economic development and innovation strategies at the corporate and national level.

Kesseven Padachi is an Associate Professor in the field of Accounting and Finance at the University of Technology, Mauritius. He holds a PhD in small business finance and is a Fellow of the Chartered Association of Certified Accountants, UK. He is the Chapter Secretary/Finance for the OSSREA Mauritius Chapter. He joined the university in June 2001 after spending some 10 years in the private and public sector as a professional accountant/auditor. He has acquired widespread practical experience in the field of accounting and auditing. He has also been involved in the design and delivery of training in the area of financial management and is very much involved in the Entrepreneurship Development Programme. Padachi has developed a research interest in small firms and his current research area is on short-term financial management practices of small and medium-sized enterprises. He also has research interests in corporate governance, e-banking and corporate finance, particularly issues relating to capital structure. He has published a number of papers in international refereed journals and has presented papers at numerous international conferences.

Rama Sithanen's professional career spanning over 40 years is split between public sector, private sector and international consultancy and advisory work. He has held senior positions in the private sector as an economist, a partner in a consulting firm and a group strategist in a large conglomerate in Mauritius. He was Minister of Finance between 1991 and 1995 and was instrumental in shaping policies to diversify the economy and laid the foundation for the emergence of Mauritius as an international financial centre. Sithanen was Deputy Prime Minister and Minister of Finance between 2005 and 2010. He introduced bold institutional, policy and fiscal reforms, moving Mauritius from dependence on trade preferences to global competitiveness. He has acted as international consultant and adviser, working in Africa and the Indian Ocean, advising governments and public sector bodies on public policies. He worked as Director of Strategy at the African Development Bank in Tunis, Tunisia, in 2011. Since 2011 Sithanen has been Chairman and Director of International Financial Services (now Sanne Mauritius), one of the largest management companies in Mauritius, engaged in providing fund administration services for capital market and private equity/venture capital funds to global corporates, institutions and family offices. He was Chairman of the Rwanda Development Board between 2013 and 2017. Sithanen is Chairperson of 4 Sights, an international technology company. He currently chairs Thomas Cook (Mauritius), a company engaged in foreign exchange transactions and tourism-related activities, and sits on other corporate boards. Sithanen holds a BSc in Economics and an MSc in Economics from the London School of Economics and Political Science, UK. He also has a PhD in Political Science from Brunel University, UK.

Brinda Sooreea-Bheemul is a lecturer in Economics in the Department of Economics and Statistics at the University of Mauritius. She is an international macroeconomist with teaching and research areas spanning international trade, economic development, international business strategy, and applied macroeconometrics. She has particular expertise and interest in foreign direct investment, trade, economic policymaking and governance in developing countries and emerging markets. Before joining the University of Mauritius, she taught extensively in the UK at Lancaster University, the University of Kent, and London Metropolitan University. Her work has been published in several international peer-reviewed journals such as the *International Journal of Business and Emerging Markets*, the *Journal of International Business Research*, and the SCMS *Journal of Indian Management*.

Riad M. Sultan is a Senior Lecturer in Economics at the University of Mauritius. He followed his specialized courses on environmental and natural resource economics at the Centre of Environmental Economics and Policy in Africa, University of Pretoria, South Africa. He holds a PhD in Economics from the University of Cape Town, South Africa. He has conducted research on areas such as green jobs assessment, green industry, energy and bioethanol, and ecosystem valuation in Mauritius. He has wide experience in socioeconomic issues and policymaking and was also involved as the Research Coordinator for the African Peer Review Mechanism project in Mauritius for the African Union. He is currently researching on natural resource accounting and bioeconomic modelling of fisheries and marine protected areas in the Indian Ocean.

Verena Tandrayen-Ragoobur is Associate Professor in Economics in the Department of Economics and Statistics at the University of Mauritius. Her research areas are international trade, labour markets, gender and development. She has published in the *Review of Development Economics*, the *Journal of African Business*, the *Journal of Chinese Economic and Foreign Trade Issues, Equality, Diversity and Inclusion: An International Journal and Journal of Economic Research*, among others. She has been involved in a number of research projects and consultancies funded by international and regional institutions, including the Centre of Environmental Economics and Policy, the African Economic Research Consortium, Trade and Industrial Policy Strategies, UNCTAD, the ILO and the World Bank.

Foreword

When Mauritius gained independence in 1968 it faced a number of chronic issues, namely a high population density, an unemployment rate of approximately 20 per cent, and per capita gross domestic product (GDP) that reached barely US $225. To make matters worse, the local economy was over-reliant on sugar as a source of export revenue; the country had no exploitable natural resources; its geographical location was not conducive to fostering a growth in exports; it lacked the requisite technological know-how and human capital; and the small size of its domestic market severely hampered any incentive to adopt an inward-looking stance. Taken together, these elements led to the Nobel prize-winning economist James Meade painting a rather dismal picture of the island's future prospects. In 1961 he opined that 'Mauritius faces ultimate catastrophe'.

Five decades later, the island's economic upturn and performance is a far cry from what Meade predicted. Mauritius has successfully managed to register average annual GDP per capita growth in excess of 4 per cent over the last three decades, with the island being categorized as an upper-middle-income economy, with a per capita income of US $10,500 dollars at current exchange rates or $22,500 on a purchasing-power parity basis in 2017, which is approximately six times higher than the average in Sub-Saharan Africa (SSA). The Mauritian economy can now be considered as one of the fastest growing and best performing in SSA. Eminent scholars and economists have often rereferred to the economic performance of the island as the 'Mauritian miracle' and the 'success of Africa'.

Such a remarkable economic performance has been attributed to a multitude of factors which include the implementation of structural reforms designed to sustain long-term growth, the government's gradual introduction of more outward-looking, export-oriented strategies, diversification of the textile and tourism sector while developing a vibrant financial and ICT sector, sound economic governance, and the implementation of institutional reforms as well as an effective state-business relationship. In this regard, it is undeniable that there has been a successful diversification of the economy following timely and effective policy reforms and the adoption of market-oriented strategies, along with strong commitment from the private sector. This structural transformation has necessitated macroeconomic reforms such as fiscal discipline, outward-oriented development strategies, significant investment in human capital education, and health and public infrastructure. Undoubtedly, the adoption of an outward-looking strategy geared towards fostering the delineation of comparative advantages has been instrumental to the economic success of Mauritius.

With this in mind, this book attempts to provide a detailed analysis of the various key ingredients which have helped to propel the island to its current status. The various chapters are essential reading for both academics and policymakers.

The first chapter highlights the development strategy of the island following independence. It identifies and discusses some key elements which have been instrumental to the island's growth trajectory, namely sound diversification policies, an outward-looking philosophy, strong and competent political governance, and a firm institutional framework. Dinan also provides key pointers for the various stakeholders which are crucial to sustaining economic growth.

Chapter 2 mainly relates to an assessment of the drivers of growth during the period 1990–2015 using the standard growth accounting framework. Seetanah *et al.* then provide a policy-oriented perspective on savings and capital and their relative importance for the island's development.

Chapter 3 examines the interplay between the role of institutions and their impact on the island's economic performance. To that end, Darga discusses the sound and balanced political governance that is necessary for fuelling economic prosperity. This would free up the social factors which are crucial for wealth creation, namely an indigenous entrepreneurial class and the promulgation of the requisite human capital.

Chapter 4 emphasizes the unequivocal importance of the adoption of an outward-looking approach by successive governments in their drive to augment economic prosperity. Incentivizing the establishment of export-oriented enterprises has been key to boosting export figures and this has significantly helped the island's diversification process.

Chapter 5 investigates another key driver of the island's economic success, namely the financial services sector. Using rigorous econometrics modelling, Matadeen and Fauzel investigate the interplay between financial development and economic growth in Mauritius during the period 1988–2016. Interestingly, however, the authors also attempt to highlight certain factors which could potentially be harmful to the sector's future growth prospects.

The underlying objectives of Chapter 6 are two-fold. First, it presents the historical facts and figures relating to the development of the tourism sector in Mauritius and then it examines the impact of tourism development on the Mauritian economy, based on past empirical evidence. Finally, it also identifies and briefly discusses the future challenges which the sector may be faced with.

Chapter 7 documents and evaluates the role of foreign direct investment (FDI) – inbound and outbound – on fostering economic growth in Mauritius.

It narrates chronologically inward FDI's continued role in the island's economic progress, with the particular role played by the FDI policy framework. The chapter also highlights the growing importance of outward FDI as a key ingredient for future economic growth, even more so in light of the small size of the local market and the need to sustain competitiveness.

Chapter 8 highlights the importance given by successive governments to promoting human capital as a key ingredient for economic success. Using rigorous quantitative analysis, this chapter brings additional credence to the existing literature on the link between human capital and economic growth, and also adds to the empirics within the endogenous growth paradigm. More importantly, it also confirms the importance of human capital in the Mauritian economic growth, and supports the views regarding the macroeconomic pay-off to historical investment in human capital.

Chapter 9 delineates the linkages between the development path of Mauritius and the consequences of carbon dioxide emissions over the last five decades. It answers an important question on whether the economy-environment interaction for Mauritius corresponds to the Environmental Kuznets Curve hypothesis whereby economic development eventually leads to a drop in per capita carbon dioxide emissions. A detailed description of the economic transformation that took place between 1970 and 2014 is provided to seek insights on the trend of carbon dioxide emissions and the extent to which it is 'coupled' or 'decoupled' with economic growth.

The benefits that can be gained from membership of a regional initiative are well documented in the literature, most notably with respect to trade creation. In this regard, Chapter 10 analyses the trade potential and performance between Mauritius and the African continent with particular emphasis on countries within two regional blocks, namely SADC and COMESA. Furthermore, Tandrayen-Ragoobur provides crucial insights into key ingredients for enhancing trade between Mauritius and the region. For instance, the study highlights the need for Mauritius to make more effective use of its bilateral trade agreements with and membership of African trading groups by diversifying its export products and markets; to that end, investment in research and development, knowledge creation and innovation will help to generate higher value added activities and improve the level of sophistication of exports.

The final chapter provides some key policy strategies which government needs to implement to help Mauritius to graduate to the next level of development, namely to that of a high-income economy. Sithanen argues that although Mauritius has witnessed a significant period of transformation and has achieved substantial economic and human development four decades after gaining independence in 1968, nevertheless the island is finding it hard to achieve a high growth momentum and this has adverse implications for employment creation and the quality of life of its people. A new economic paradigm is called for, and Mauritius must articulate a bold development strategy for moving out of the middle-income trap and for laying the foundations for future growth and shared prosperity in the light of both domestic challenges and global constraints. There is a dire need to reignite the engines of the old economy to make it more dynamic and competitive; it should bolster growth in the emerging sectors and it must identify new pillars of growth that will pursue the diversification and transformation of the economy.

1 Mauritius

Developmental perspectives, 1968–2018

P. Dinan

Introduction

In the literature devoted to the process of economic development, the case of Mauritius is generally referred to as being a success story (Subramanian, 2009; Frankel, 2010; Darga, 2011; Subramanian and Roy, 2003). This is due to the relative rapidity with which the island graduated from being a mono-culture based on sugar cane production to a multi-sectoral economy, characterized by light manufacturing industries for export markets and by export services, namely tourism, a freeport, cross-border finance, and information and communication technologies. This begs the question: is the economic development model of Mauritius unique or is it replicable? Are there any lessons to be drawn from the development process which the country experienced during the first 50 years of its existence after achieving independence?

In order to answer this question, one must first recall the characteristics of the economy of Mauritius before it took off, how it achieved that major step, and finally where it is heading now. The answers to these questions will constitute the next three sections of this chapter, and the lessons to be drawn from that experience will make up the conclusion.

Yesterday

When Mauritius became an independent country on 12 March 1968, the population numbered 800,000, resulting in a high population density equivalent to 430 persons per sq km. With an average annual income of only US $200 per head, Mauritius was a poor country, forming part of what in those days used to be termed the 'third world'. Unemployment was high at 20 per cent.

The newly independent country was characterized by a monocrop economy, with cane sugar accounting for 96.2 per cent of exports. In January and February 1960 two successive violent cyclones struck the island, destroying the cane sugar crop. In the wake of this disaster, the then colonial power sought the advice of international experts about the socio-economic future of Mauritius, particularly because on the political front claims for the granting of sovereignty and independence were becoming more and more vocal.

Professor James Meade (see Meade *et al.*, 1961), who was appointed to study the economic situation and make recommendations, quite rightly emphasized that it was enormously risky for Mauritius to rely on a single export industry. One of his recommendations was that an export tax of 5 per cent should be levied on sugar exports as a disincentive measure, in the hope that economic operators would find other avenues for their activities. However, by the time that independence had been achieved in 1968, the benefits of such recommendations had not filtered through the economy of Mauritius.

Meade also suggested that other industries should be set up, such as the manufacture of soap, jewellery and fabrics made out of artificial fibres, while arguing for the introduction of protective import duties and tax holidays. The establishment of an Industrial Development Board was also recommended. Elements of these recommendations would form part of the strategy of import substitution which Mauritius was to adopt in the 1970s. Another of Meade's recommendations was not to proceed with the construction of a first-class hotel in the north of the country, because he did not envisage that many people would be attracted 'to a place so far off the beaten track' (Meade *et al.*, 1961). On this latter point, subsequent developments would prove him wrong.

Seen through Meade's eyes the scene was a rather dismal one. It was not desperate, but no one at that particular time could have imagined that, five decades later, Mauritius would, according to the International Monetary Fund (IMF), achieve the status of an upper-middle-income country, which in 2017 had a population of 1.26 million, an average annual per head income of US $10,500, and a low level of unemployment totalling 7 per cent.

In order to capture the socio-economic situation at that time, it is appropriate to take note of a number of facts and figures pertaining to that period. Simultaneously, comparative facts and figures for the present time will be set out, thus giving us an opportunity to assess the progress which the country has made since 1968.

In as far as the structure of the economy is concerned, in 1968 the primary sector, mainly agriculture, accounted for 24 per cent of gross domestic product (GDP), with the secondary sector, mainly manufacturing, at 25 per cent and the tertiary sector, mainly services for the local market, at 51 per cent (Dinan, 1979). Comparative figures for 2018 are 4 per cent, 19 per cent and 77 per cent, respectively. The lion's share goes to services, particularly the export-oriented ones, such as tourism, cross-border financial services and Information and Communication Technologies (ICT). Such modifications in the respective percentages reflect the extent of the transformation of the economy of Mauritius over the past five decades (see Sannassee *et al.*, 2014).

In 1968 the labour participation rate was 83 per cent for males and 21 per cent for females. The comparative figures for the present time are 74 per cent and 46 per cent, respectively. The increase in the female participation rate is particularly striking and is mainly attributable to the development of tax-free zone enterprises which were based on a model of cheap labour for the transformation of imported raw materials.

In 1968 only 23 per cent of houses had cyclone-resistant concrete walls and roofs; today, the percentage is equal to 92 per cent. Gas is now used for cooking by 98 per cent of households; in 1968 only 1 per cent of households had access to gas. Likewise, only 65 per cent of households had access to electricity in 1969; now all households have electricity. These figures the rate of progress that has has taken place, the economy has been transformed in a relatively short space of time, and the standard of living of the average Mauritian citizen has improved.

How did it all happen? This is the subject-matter of the next section.

The present day

It is convenient to analyse the causes of the transformation of the economy of Mauritius in terms of both external and internal factors. The external factors which contributed to the economic development of Mauritius are as follows:

- The signing of a series of agreements that were beneficial to external trade, such as the Commonwealth Sugar Agreement since 1951, the Yaoundé Convention, the Lomé Convention and the Cotonou Agreement.
- The paramount importance of the Sugar Protocol annexed to the Lomé Convention.
- As a consequence of the above, Mauritius benefited, in its traditional markets in Western Europe (e.g. Britain, France, Germany and Italy), from preferential quotas and prices for sugar, ready-to-wear garments and textiles.
- The consequential ability for Mauritius to pay for its imports. It must be borne in mind that the international trade of Mauritius (i.e. the sum of its imports and exports of goods and services) has been consistently greater than its annual GDP over the years (by more than 30 per cent at times).
- The take-off of manufacturing for exports during the 1980s, facilitated by the preferential environment. This was coupled with significant improvements in terms of trade, due to the depreciation of the US dollar by 25 per cent from 1985 to 1988, the index having jumped from 102 to 143 during that period.
- The contribution of the technical and marketing know-how of the Chinese diaspora towards the launching of manufacturing units for exports.
- The contribution made by foreign specialists from France, South Africa and India. This was facilitated by the use of two international languages, English and French, and by the multicultural profile of Mauritius.

In addition, a number of internal factors were at play throughout this period. They are as follows:

- The observance of democratic principles (except during the state of emergency from 1972 to 1976). Mandatory general elections have been

held every five years. The rule of law prevails, and there is an independent judiciary.
- There is a vibrant written press and widespread ownership of private radios.

The operation of those two internal factors has been, and still is, essential for the maintenance of a peaceful climate wherein economic activities can flourish and investments can be fruitful.

In addition, Mauritius has benefited from a successful demographic transition over the past five decades. Population growth has averaged 1.1 per cent per year, while economic growth has averaged 9.3 per cent per year. As a consequence, per head income has increased by 8.1 per cent per year. It is noteworthy that the fertility rate, which in 1968 stood at 4.6 total births per woman of child-bearing age, had fallen to 1.4 in 2018, i.e. it is below the replacement rate of the population (Statistics Mauritius, 2018)

The structural adjustment

While keeping in mind the factors – both internal and external – discussed above, one must acknowledge that one of the main contributions to the transformation of the economy in the 1980s was the structural adjustment programme prescribed by the IMF in the wake of the two devaluations of the local currency in 1979 (to 29.6 per cent) and in 1981 (to 20 per cent). When Mauritius was forced to devalue its currency in September 1979, its FOREX reserves had, in the preceding month, fallen to a mere 1.5 days of import equivalent.

Before the contents of the structural adjustment are examined, it is worth considering why the economy was in such dire straits at the end of the 1970s. This period was marred by a combination of negative factors in Mauritius. On the political front, from 1976 there was a very weak coalition government in power with a slender majority and an opposition party whose popularity was increasing. The government was so weak that it could hardly resist the numerous claims coming from lobbies of all sorts. A good example of such a situation is the increase in the number of public holidays, to twenty-eight per annum, towards the end of the decade. Thankfully, in the early 1980s, the list of public holidays was reviewed by a committee comprising representatives of both the public and private sectors, and the number of annual public holidays has, since then, been fixed at 15.

To make matters worse in the 1970s, the economy suffered two shocks originating from abroad. The first shock had its roots in the exceedingly high world market price for sugar, due to an imbalance between demand and supply. Mauritius benefited greatly from this situation, prompting both the public and private sectors to behave as if Mauritius had achieved prosperity. As should have been realized, supply to the world sugar market was soon to increase in response to the high prices, and by 1976 the sugar boom had petered out.

The second shock originated from the depreciation of the pound sterling to which the Mauritian rupee was still attached at the time. In 1976 there was a severe sterling crisis, which culminated in a request by Britain for a bailout by the IMF. Sterling took a downward path, taking the rupee along with it. This caused an unusual influx of depreciated rupees into the local economy, making it a hard task indeed for the government to resist increasingly vocal demands for populist measures (Dinan, 1979). And, finally, to make matters worse, the island was struck by severe cyclones in 1975, 1979 and 1981.

In such circumstances, the need for two devaluations, and a Structural Adjustment Programme, is not surprising.

The nine IMF policy reform prescriptions

There is a saying that every cloud has a silver lining. That may be said of the obligation, in the early 1980s, for Mauritius to apply the IMF's nine policy prescriptions of the IMF in return for a foreign currency bailout. Had it not done so, it would have been impossible for Mauritius to transform its economy given the conditions that had prevailed in the country since the 1970s. The Mauritian government and its citizens deserve merit for the way in which they accepted the imposition of these new conditions and for putting them into immediate effect.

The IMF's prescriptions were as follows:

- reduce the budget deficit (13.7 per cent of GDP in 1980–1981);
- reduce salary compensation (53.5 per cent of GDP in 1980);
- reduce consumption (89.5 per cent of GDP in 1980);
- channel more bank credit to business enterprises as opposed to the public sector;
- liberalize imports and interest rates, and discourage excessive government intervention;
- adopt export promotion policies, as opposed to previous import substitution policies;
- work towards a reduction in the rate of inflation;
- diversify the economy through the promotion of manufacturing in export processing zones (EPZ) and of the tourism industry;
- create jobs in new enterprises.

While each of these prescriptions was worthwhile in themselves in order to place the economy on the right track, it must be emphasized that two of them were of a strategic nature. One called for the adoption of export promotion policies, as opposed to the previous import substitution policies. As mentioned above, there had been a recommendation since the 1960s for a recourse to the levying of protective duties, and indeed during the 1970s such policies had been applicable side by side with the nascent support of the EPZ industries through fiscal incentives. The co-existence of two opposing strategies proved to be ineffective, and this is why the IMF gave a clear indication that the path to be followed was export promotion policies.

The second prescription of a strategic nature concerned the diversification of the economy. This was an obvious path, given the island's over-reliance, up until then, on a single export industry. The prescription was fully applied; not only was there recourse in the 1980s to diversified export activities in manufacturing and tourism, but in the ensuing decade, the diversification process was extended to the development of a freeport, cross-border financial services and ITC.

The structural adjustment era came to an end before 1990, by which time Mauritius had repaid in full some US $500 million to the IMF and to the World Bank.

Meaningful economic indicators

The following macro-economic indicators reflect the situation in Mauritius during the 1980s.

- Unemployment fell from a high of 20 per cent in 1983 to a low of 2.7 per cent in 1991.
- After falling from US$1,197 in 1980 to $1,014 in 1985, per head income increased throughout the rest of the decade to reach $2,361 in 1990.
- The growth rate of the economy averaged 5.9 per cent per annum between 1981 and 1990.
- Taken together public and private consumption fell from 89.5 per cent of GDP in 1980 to 71.5 per cent in 1986.
- Inflation, which stood at 15 per cent in 1981, fell to a record low of 0.6 per cent in 1987, before rebounding. During the next decade, it hovered at around 5 per cent.
- The budget deficit, which had reached almost 14 per cent of GDP in the financial year 1980–1981, decreased steadily thereafter, reaching a low of just over 1 per cent in 1987–88.
- The share of salary compensation was in free-fall up to 1986 when it stood at 45 per cent, having recorded 53.5 per cent in 1980.
- The share of bank credit to the public sector had averaged some 55 per cent during the first five years of the decade; it then started to fall, hovering at around 25 to 30 per cent for the rest of the decade.
- The local currency, which had been linked to the IMF's Special Drawing Rights in the early 1970s, was now linked to a unspecified basket of currencies, selected according to the international trade profile of Mauritius.
- Foreign currency reserves moved up gradually in terms of the value of a week of imports of goods and services, reaching 18 weeks in 1990, and 24 weeks in 1992.

These indicators show that sound economic policies were put in place by the government, boosted particularly by proper control over public finances and sound monetary policy. Success would not have been so resounding if the population had not played the game, agreeing, *inter alia*, to moderation in the share of salary compensation and to a lower appetite for consumption. In return, the population at large was gratified with the creation of thousands of new jobs.

Looking ahead

The first two sections of this chapter have emphasized the success achieved by the economy of Mauritius over the last half century (1968–2018) as it graduated from a poor country deprived of resources into an upper-middle-income country. Is past success a guarantee for future success? This is the subject-matter of the present section. Turning our back on the past, we shall first take stock of the present situation with the help of relevant facts and figures. That exercise should throw light on the challenges the economy of Mauritius has to grapple with and the opportunities it has to seize.

The present situation in a nutshell

In 2018 GDP amounted to around US $13 billion, equivalent to $10,500 per head for a total population of 1.26 million. Unemployment stood at 6.9 per cent, and the annual inflation rate at 3.7 per cent. Consumption was high at 89.3 per cent of GDP. The gross national savings rate was equivalent to 16.1 per cent when expressed as a percentage of gross national disposable income. At 17.3 per cent of GDP, investment was on the low side, as it had been for several years. Foreign exchange reserves amounted to an import equivalent of 9.7 months, but the deficit on the current account of the balance of payments was equivalent to 5.8 per cent of GDP.

A mixed bag, overall, reflecting a rather comfortable picture, but with an alert on the international trade front, particularly when it is known that, year in year out, exports of goods and services are lower than imports. The deficit is made good by surpluses on the capital account of the balance of payments, where net investments by cross-border investors are an important source of financing. Thanks to a favourable Double Taxation Agreement (DTA) between Mauritius and India, the latter have been particularly active since the launch of the export-oriented financial services sector in 1992. The DTA has now been modified in such a way that the tax benefit advantages accruing to the cross-border investors have been significantly curtailed; it is reasonable, therefore, to expect that the net income streams recorded every year on the capital account may no longer be a regular feature, with risks of lower or vanishing overall balance of payments surpluses. The situation may become even more challenging, following the implementation by the Organisation for Economic Co-operation and Development of comprehensive measures targeted against countries that impose low tax rates to the detriment of its member states, thus giving rise to base erosion and profit shifting.

Still on the topic of international trade, it is pertinent to highlight a geographical imbalance between the import and export of goods. The latter is Eurocentric, since the share of exports to Europe stood at 63 per cent in 2018, with South Africa, Madagascar and Réunion together accounting for 13 per cent and the rest of Africa a meagre 3 per cent. Imports are Asia-centric, with Asia at a level of 52 per cent, Europe 27 per cent, South Africa 8 per cent and the rest of Africa 4 per cent. Such percentages point to the adoption of strategies for the development of exports of goods and services to the neighbouring Mascarene Islands, and further away, certain countries in Asia such as India and the People's Republic of China. There are 21 Agreements for the Protection and Promotion of investments in place with countries on the African continent, but 14 of these were still awaiting ratification in 2019. However useful such Agreements may be, they are just tools which must be supported by proactive joint marketing efforts by the public and private sectors. Mauritius lives by its exports; hence, the inescapable obligation for its export industries to be constantly on the alert to identify new markets and to develop new products.

But success in finding new markets depends on the degree of competitiveness of Mauritius as reflected in the price and quality of its products. While Mauritius can pride itself as being ranked first in the global competitive index for sub-Saharan Africa, worldwide it ranked only 49th out of 137 countries in 2018. Competitiveness is a function of productivity. During the period 2007–2018 capital productivity recorded an annual average fall of 0.1 per cent, indicating the island's failure to use its installed capacity to the best of its ability. Labour productivity recorded an annual average increase of 2.6 per cent, but the compensation of employees rose by an annual average of 5.5 per cent. The message to be drawn from these indicators is that there is a need for improvement in productivity throughout the economy if Mauritius is to capture new export markets, let alone hold on to its existing ones. In this context, there is an inescapable fact: as pointed out already, during the first three decades after independence, Mauritius benefited from various types of protection for its exports to a number of European countries. Not only have these facilities come to an end, but in the new era characterized by the launch of the World Trade Organisation in 1995 and the subsequent disappearance of the Multi-fibre Agreement, liberalization is the order of the day. It is indeed in the context of liberalization that Mauritius became a member of a number of regional organisations, including the Southern Africa Development Community, the Common Market for Eastern and Southern Africa and the Commission des Etats de l'Océan Indien, whereby recourse to import and export taxes is minimized and trade facilitation measures are put in place. The success of such arrangement depends, of course, on the observance, by all member states, of the rules and regulations.

Another cause of concern is the unemployment rate for females and young people, respectively. The overall unemployment rate of 6.9 per cent is, in fact, a weighted average of the respective rates for the male workforce, at 4.6 per cent, and the female workforce, at 10.5 per cent. The picture worsens further when the respective activity rates for men and women are compared; in 2018 they stood at 74.4 per cent and 45.8 per cent, respectively. One wonders what the unemployment rate for females would be if they were as economically active as men. The overall lesson to be derived from those indicators is that the economy of Mauritius is not benefiting fully from its female workforce. In addition, over the past few years youth unemployment has become a serious problem. In 2018 there were 19,300 unemployed youth, equivalent to 24.9 per cent of the workforce and 47 per cent of the unemployed population. It is no excuse that this is a world phenomenon. The situation calls for an active search for long-term remedies. Not only is the country failing to reap the rewards of the resources which it has invested in educating its youth, but the latter risk losing all their energy and enthusiasm for the world of work. It is common knowledge that there is a mismatch between demand and supply in the labour market. This raises the question of whether the current education system is geared towards providing the youth, over and above the essential academic knowledge and civic values, with the skills needed for steering modern Mauritius. An example is the ICT sector which could do with a larger qualified local workforce, made up of new entrants to the labour market, equipped with the right skills for the digital world.

The imbalances in the workforce cannot be taken lightly. This is because the workforce is a major resource in Mauritius, having such particular characteristics as cultural diversity, the ability to understand, if not to speak, two international languages, and adaptability to the changing circumstances, as was indeed demonstrated in the 1980s. Owing to an ongoing decline in the fertility rate (1.4 total births per woman is the current average), the population of Mauritius is expected to start decreasing by the 2030s. Furthermore, due to improved health care, average life expectancy has risen to 78 years for women and to 71 years for men; consequently, the ageing population is increasing. Such trends – a persistently low birth rate, below the replacement rate of two children per woman of child-bearing age, coupled with longer life expectancy – will, over the next few decades, significantly modify the shape of the population pyramid of Mauritius: the wide base will start to narrow, while the peak will start to widen. In the middle of the pyramid, the population of working age people will start to dwindle. This will impact negatively on the availability of a workforce that is large enough to carry out the economic activities of the country. In addition, that reduced workforce may well be faced with having to foot a larger tax bill, following an inevitable rise in old age pensions coupled with higher hospital bills for the ageing population. In such circumstances, if Mauritius intends to pursue its development path over the next few decades, it will need to encourage immigration, signs of which are already apparent. The social consequences of immigration, if practised on a large scale, will have to be assessed, and the local population will need to be properly trained in order to ensure a smooth transition to a new profile of the local environment.

To complete the list of challenges affecting the economy as a whole, one must mention deficiencies in the island's infrastructure. Gridlock is becoming a common feature of road traffic, particularly in towns. It remains to be seen whether the new metro services, due to link the towns of Curepipe, Rose-Hill and the capital, Port Louis, from 2019, will alleviate road traffic. It will be of paramount importance that daily commuters modify their travelling habits, failing which the government would be well advised to introduce a toll system, similar to that practised in many developed economies. The port has to grapple with severe competition from neighbouring countries, a continuous water supply is still equivalent to wishful thinking, and electricity supply, in spite of recent improvements, is still highly dependent upon imported fossil fuel.

Selected sectoral challenges

The mature industries of Mauritius are up against a number of problems which must be tackled with determination.

- The sugar cane industry has lost the last trade preferences to which it was entitled in its traditional European markets. It is now faced with having to sell sugar at prices much below the production cost. Apart from supplying niche markets with the so-called special sugars, the cane industry has no alternative but to use its immense knowledge, acquired over the centuries, to focus its research capabilities on alternative uses for cane, such as a provider of green energy for the national grid and of a mixture of ethanol with petrol for the running of motor vehicles. This is the time for the launching of studies in those fields, in order to establish their engineering and financial feasibility, or otherwise.
- Non-sugar agriculture and fishing have always played second fiddle to the sugar cane industry. Their role must now be enhanced, if only to contribute to the food security and requirements of the inhabitants of Mauritius and of the visitors to the island. A reduction in the import bill for food would also be an advantage. It is common knowledge that too few people work in agriculture, and the younger generation is unable to envisage a future in this industry. This is why a renewed interest in such activities is a must. One proposal that has been mooted is the establishment of a School of Trades and Technology to provide the youth of Mauritius with the opportunity to learn, *inter alia*, modern agricultural and fishing techniques. This, coupled with the provision of adequate financing, would modernize both non-sugar agriculture and lagoon fishing, and would go some way towards providing the younger generation with jobs of value.
- The once triumphant EPZ enterprises have lost some of their lustre, as noted above, in light of a reduction in exports of textile products. Apart from the possible provision of further fiscal incentives, the time has perhaps come for a thorough review of the activities of that sector. Could there be a dose of innovation as regards the type of products offered on the world market by the Mauritian manufacturers? In other words, how can the country

distinguish itself from its competitors, particularly those with lower production costs? Also, serious consideration needs to be given to securing direct contacts with foreign retailers, in order to try to bypass foreign wholesalers and capture their margins. There are indications that recourse to the facilities of digital technology would be helpful in that connection.

- The hotel industry has been doing well for the past few years, particularly since the opening of the skies. This has led to a welcome diversification of the tourism market, which previously was excessively Eurocentric. Markets, particularly those in some Asian countries (e.g. mainland China and India), are now active. However, there is no room for complacency. Diversification must also be applied to the products on offer. Asian tourists do not necessarily have the same leisure requirements as European tourists. For instance, while so far Europeans have been fully satisfied with the all-inclusive type of beach resort tourism on offer, provision should be made for the development of interior tourism. This would have the unique advantage of enabling foreign visitors not only to enjoy the natural beauty of the island, but also to admire its cultural diversity. In that connection, Mauritius' town centres are in urgent need of an uplift, together with the provision of well-kept gardens and the introduction of leisure facilities.

- The more recent sectoral additions are (a) financial services for cross-border operators and (b) ICT. Problems pertaining to their operation have already been alluded to. For the financial services, the challenge is to modify the model and to provide value added services to the foreign investors, instead of limiting oneself to tax optimization formulae. As regards ICT, its continued success depends on the availability of sufficient bandwidth and of an ample provision of trained operators. In this regard, it is noteworthy that the successful adaptability of Mauritius to the digital revolution depends on what a reformed education system will be able to deliver. Rote learning and exam cramming will have to give way to creative thinking and an interest in innovation. Also, the excessive wastage which characterizes the present educational system must be addressed. Currently, 37 per cent of students fail to progress at primary level, while only 17 per cent of the student cohort reach tertiary level. Furthermore, there is unhealthy competition for the relatively restricted number of academic scholarships that are available, although some improvements have been made recently in offering assistance to economically disadvantaged students.

How can Mauritius escape from the middle-income trap?

While the steps described above should help the respective sectors to deal with the identified challenges, there is reason to believe that it may take an unduly long time for the reforms to enable Mauritius to make that quantum leap lifting it to the top status of an upper-income country. This is why Mauritius must find the key that will provide it with the ability to escape from the middle-income trap in which it is currently mired.[1]

That key is the proper development of the maritime resources of Mauritius. Those resources are made up of an exclusive zone of 1.9 million square kilometres, to which must be added a co-partnership with the Seychelles for a further 0.4 square kilometres. In itself, the area of that exclusive zone is impressive. When compared to the puny size of mainland Mauritius, (1,900 square kilometres), it is immense. Mauritius cannot, on its own, carry out the studies required to identify the potentialities of that vast maritime zone. Nor would it have the muscle needed to finance such research projects. But Mauritius is a respected member state of the international community of nations, as well as a member of a multilateral institution, namely the World Bank, which has recently issued a report on the maritime zone. There are also friendly countries, particularly in Europe, which could carry out studies, financed by, say, the European Investment Bank. What seems to have been lacking so far is the adoption of a clear and forceful strategy for a rational economic development of the maritime resources of Mauritius, such as stocks of fish, potential sources of energy, port services, and support for the emerging sectors of technology and internet communications. If the potentialities are identified, feasibility studies carried out by competent experts, and financing requirements marshalled, Mauritius would then be putting to work it's by far largest economic resource and would be on its way to achieve the status of an upper-income country.

Conclusion: lessons of experience

It was stated in the introduction to this chapter that its purpose was to highlight the lessons to be drawn from the economic experience of Mauritius over the first 50 years since it achieved national sovereignty. At the end of the 1960s Mauritius was a poor country, with few, if any, development prospects. Thanks to a very smart strategy of sectoral diversification, the economy took off during the mid-1980s. The chapter has highlighted the challenges which now confront the economy if it is to stay on course, let alone improve its performance.

In this context, some plain truths bear repeating. As investment professionals like to point out, past success is no guarantee for the future. So it is for the economy of a country. Past success will not be repeated automatically. Indeed, the success which characterized the last two decades of the twentieth century in Mauritius was the result of the combination of several critical factors: the sound economic strategy of diversification, the emphasis on exports of goods and services, strong and competent political governance, leading to a well-managed public sector, a responsive local private sector, reinforced by foreign entrepreneurs and, last but not least, citizens determined to improve their standard of living through the implementation of economic activities, instead of rent-seeking through wasteful political lobbying.

As discussed above, Mauritius is now facing economic challenges which are a world apart from those experienced over the previous decades. Solutions must and can be identified. In the final analysis, however, success will depend on two principal factors: sound and intelligent political governance, in favour of inclusive socio-economic development, coupled with a positive attitude, devoid of selfishness, on the part of every citizen. While it is true that the economic well-being of Mauritius requires the active support of friendly countries and of multilateral institutions, ultimately, success will depend on the population itself, the political and economic leaders, the researchers, the innovators, and its diverse workforce. Further socio-economic development will depend on the active contribution of all the citizens of Mauritius.

A well-known saying sums up this situation well: *where there's a will, there's a way.*

Note

1 See also 'Stuck in a Middle-Income Trap', *The Economist* (2015). Available at http://country.eiu.com/article.aspx?articleid=213440405&Country=Mauritius&topic =Economy&subtopic=Forecast&subsubtopic=Policy+trends.

References

Darga, L. A. (2011) 'The Mauritius Success Story, Why Is this Island Nation an African Political and Economic Success?', in Moeletsi Mbeki (ed.) *Advocates for Change: How to Overcome Africa's Challenges*, Johannesburg: Picador Africa.

Dinan, P. (1979) *Dix Ans d'Economie Mauricienne, 1968–1977*, Port Louis: Editions IPC.

Frankel, J. A. (2010) 'Mauritius: African Success Story', NBER Working Papers 16569, Cambridge, MA: National Bureau of Economic Research.

Meade, J. E.et al. (1961) *The Economics and Social Structure of Mauritius: Report to the Government of Mauritius*, London: Methuen.

Rojid, S., Seetanah, B. and Shalini, R. (2010) 'Are State Business Relations Important to Economic Growth? Evidence from Mauritius', Discussion Paper 36, London: IPPG.

Sannassee, R. V., Seetanah, B. and Lamport, M. J. (2014) 'Export Diversification and Economic Growth: The Case of Mauritius', in M. Jansen, M. S. Jallab and M. Smeets (eds) *Connecting to Global Markets—Challenges and Opportunities: Case Studies Presented by WTO Chair-Holders*, Geneva: World Trade Organization, pp. 11–23. Available at www.wto.org/english/res_e/booksp_e/cmark_full_e.pdf.

Statistics Mauritius (2018) Port Louis: Statistics Mauritius. Available at http://statsma uritius.govmu.org/English/Pages/default.aspx.

Subramanian, A. (2009) 'The Mauritian Success Story and Its Lessons', Research Paper No. 2009/36, Helsinki: UNU-WIDER.

Subramanian, A. and Roy, D. (2003) 'Who Can Explain the Mauritian Miracle: Meade, Romer, Sachs, or Rodrik?', in D. Rodrik (ed.) *In Search of Prosperity: Analytic Narratives on Economic Growth*, Princeton, NJ: Princeton University Press.

The Economist (2015) 'Stuck in a Middle-Income Trap'. Available at http://country. eiu.com/article.aspx?articleid=213440405&Country=Mauritius&topic=Economy& subtopic=Forecast&subsubtopic=Policy+trends.

2 An analysis of the sources of growth in Mauritius

*R. M. Moreno, B. Seetanah, R. Sannassee and
V. Tandrayen-Ragoobur*

Introduction

Eminent economists including Romer (1993), Frankel (2010) and Stiglitz (2011) have referred to Mauritius' economic performance since independence in 1968 as the 'Mauritian miracle' and the 'success of Africa'. Indeed, Mauritius in its early years of independence was confronted by a number of constraints related to (i) being a low-income monocrop (sugar) exporter; (ii) sizeable terms of trade and output shocks; (iii) the scarcity of capital and raw materials; (iv) limited technical knowledge (with the exception of sugar); (v) a limited domestic market; (vi) the country's remote location;, (vii) high population growth; and (viii) ethnic tensions. James Mead (Nobel Prize-winning laureate in economics), who led an economic survey mission to Mauritius in 1960 and taking into account all the above, famously predicted 'In the author's opinion, Mauritius faces ultimate catastrophe' (Meade, 1961).

Despite these early constraints, the island successfully evolved into an upper-middle-income economy, with annual average real gross domestic product (GDP) growth of 5 per cent between 1969 and 2017 compared to annual average growth of approximately 3.5 per cent during the same period for Sub-Saharan Africa (SSA). In terms of GDP per capita, the island grew by 4.4 per cent on average compared with just 1.5 per cent for SSA. Income per capita in 2013 was US $10,500 dollars at current exchange rates or $22,500 on a purchasing-power parity basis, which is about six times larger than the average of SSA. Since independence the Mauritian economy is been one of the fastest growing and best performers in SSA. It developed from a low-income, agriculture-based economy to a middle-income diversified and resilient economy with growing industrial, financial, and tourism sectors. Over the 50 years since independence, the government has gradually adopted an outward-looking, export-oriented strategy leading to the diversification of the economy and carving out niches in the textile industry and the tourism sector as well as developing a vibrant financial services sector. Emerging sectors such as Information and Communication Technology (ICT), seafood, real estate and property development have also contributed to sustaining economic growth. Alongside the diversification strategy, aggressive policy reforms implemented during the past decade have been instrumental in building resilience against external economic shocks (Sannassee et al., 2014; Tandrayen-Ragoobur and Kasseeah, 2017).

The remarkable performance of the Mauritian economy can be attributed to a number of factors[1] and includes reforms to sustain long-term growth, sound economic governance as well as effective state business relations. The economy has successfully diversified following timely and effective policy reforms and the adoption of market-oriented strategies, along with strong commitment of the private sector. This structural transformation has necessitated macroeconomic reforms such as fiscal discipline, outward-oriented development strategies, mass investment in human capital education and health and public infrastructure (Romer, 1993; Sachs and Warner, 1995; Subramanian and Roy, 2003; Zafar, 2011). Overall, the economy has become more globalized and open to foreign investors. The country also ranks highly in terms of competitiveness, its investment climate and governance[2] and has solid economic fundamentals. It is also worth noting that in terms of its institutional framework, Mauritius has been able to demonstrate its ability to maintain political stability complemented by social harmony with commendable institutional quality and good governance.

Mauritius embarked on a multi-sector reform agenda in 2006 with the objective of improving the competitiveness of the economy. These reforms had considerable success in accelerating the rate of growth, reducing unemployment and speeding up the pace of diversification of the economy through the development of new sectors. The reforms created fiscal space to allow the authorities to perform a comprehensive, targeted and temporary counter-cyclical policy in early 2009 to mitigate the negative impact of the global financial crisis. The fiscal stimulus contributed to absorb the shock of the 2007/2008 global crisis, which was reinforced in August 2010 by a second stimulus package to cushion the impact of a weaker euro. However, during 2013 both the public and the private sectors appeared to have lost their momentum. After three consecutive years of sub-par economic growth, the need to overhaul the economic engine and enhance investment attractiveness had become imperative.

In recent years, the economic strategy has focused on the objective of turning Mauritius into a high-income country. Following a change of government in 2014, a new initiative known as Vision 2030 was introduced to effect a second economic miracle and to propel the country to high-income status. However, the question of whether Mauritius will be able to achieve this will depend on its ability to improve the skill set of its labour force, the quality of the country's infrastructure, and the speed at which it adopts new technology (Svirydzenka and Petri, 2014). In addition, improvements to the business environment will be essential to attract foreign direct investment (FDI) into the country, generate domestic investment, and maintain and improve Mauritius' image as an open, stable and well-functioning country with which to do business. Finally, reforms to the pension system, public enterprises, social benefits, and the tax system should make the public sector more efficient, while macro policies to increase public and private savings can create opportunities for further productive investments (ibid.).

Given the economic success of the island, this chapter first attempts to empirically assess the drivers of growth in Mauritius during the period 1990–2015 using the standard growth accounting framework. Second, since the transformation of an initial growth spurt into a sustained process of output expansion and prosperity requires the accumulation of capital and its corresponding financing, the chapter subsequently provides a policy-oriented overview of savings and capital and their importance for a small island developing economy. It examines the major factors that may explain both variables for the Mauritian economy, reviewing the trend of capital formation and technical progress over the years and the constraints that the country is currently facing.

Sources of growth and the growth accounting framework

A standard growth accounting technique (see Bosworth and Collins, 2003) is employed to break down the economic growth rate of Mauritius to show contributions from capital, labour and total factor productivity. The latter is computed as the residual of the growth in GDP, once capital and labour contributions are removed. A constant return to scale using the Cobb-Douglas aggregate production function is assumed as follows:

$$Y_t = A_t K_t^\alpha L_t^{1-\alpha} \tag{1}$$

The aggregate production function links output (GDP) Y_t in period t to two factors of production, the capital stock K_t and the size of the labour force L_t. Total factor productivity A_t is also reflected in equation (1) above. Since there are three factors affecting GDP in this production function, this framework will allow us to break down observed growth rates into contributions from capital, labour and productivity. Since productivity serves as a residual in this sense, it is computed from the production function (1), as opposed to being inferred from some other sources. Solving (1) for A_t, we obtain:

$$A_t = A \frac{Y_t}{K_t^\alpha L_t^{1-\alpha}} \tag{2}$$

Under the assumption of perfect competition, the capital share is a measure of the parameter α. Once capital and labour shares have been estimated, productivity values can be computed for any given year. We assume that growth rates can be computed as natural log differences so that the growth rate of output in a given year can be computed as $\log Y_{t+1} - \log Y_t$. The growth rate of output can therefore be expressed as:

$$\ln Y_{t+1} - \ln Y_t = \ln A_{t+1} - \ln A_t + \alpha(\ln K_{t+1} - \ln K_t) +$$

$$(1 - \alpha)(\ln L_{t+1} - \ln L_t) \tag{3}$$

Nonetheless, a central element in the above process is to estimate the appropriate share of capital (α) and labour (1-α). Indeed, estimating the capital shares assumes the traditional constant return to scale using the Cobb-Douglas production function in per capita form and to measure the relative contribution of factor accumulation and productivity the following regression can be estimated (see Bosworth and Collins, 2003).

$$\Delta \log\left(\frac{Y_{it}}{L_{it}}\right) = \lambda_i + \alpha_i \Delta \log\left(\frac{K_{it}}{L_{it}}\right) + \varepsilon_{it} \tag{4}$$

The slope α represents the capital share in output, Y real output, K the capital stock and L labour. We use the above regression model to estimate the country's share of capital individually and these findings are presented in Table 2.1. The results confirm that the capital share for Mauritius is on average 0.6, which is consistent with previous estimates obtained by Rojid and Seetanah (2011), Bosworth and Collins (2003) and Senhadji (2000) who estimated the capital share to be around 0.5 for a sample of countries.

Once the capital and labour shares have been calculated, the contributions of capital, labour and TFP to the growth rate of GDP are then computed for the period 1990–2015. Output is measured by GDP at constant prices and labour is approximated by total labour force. The perpetual inventory methodology is used to estimate the value of capital stock for Mauritius. This uses current price estimates of gross domestic fixed capital formation (GDFCF) and price indices over the years to estimate values of gross capital stock at constant and current prices by accumulating past expenditures on GDFCF, while accounting for inflation.

The results from growth accounting exercises during the period 1991–2015 are provided in Table 2.1.

The table above shows that the Mauritian economy has been growing at an average rate of 4.9 per cent during the period 1991–2015. With an average contribution value of 2.3 (the growth rate of capital remained more or less stable annually with slightly decreasing rate in 2015), capital growth is seen to be the major driver of economic growth in Mauritius, as opposed to labour with an average contribution of 0.7 (with varying volatility during the period under study). TFP growth remained positive in most years, averaging a contribution of 1.9 in the average GDP growth rate. The results demonstrate that the growth rates experienced by Mauritius over the last 25 years have been driven more extensively by its capital component rather than by labour growth, with total factor productivity playing an increasingly important role.

Table 2.1 Growth decomposition

Year	Growth rate	Capital	Labour	TFP
1991	4.24	1.81	0.75	1 68
1995	5.13	1.70	1.82	3.52
2000	9.88	3.02	0.45	6.41
2005	2.66	2.45	0.20	0.01
2010	4.16	2.80	0.89	0.47
2015	3.2	2.0	0.4	0.8
1995–2015	4.9	2.3	0.7	1.9

Source: Authors' computation.

In fact, capital-driven growth has overtaken labour growth as the main contributor to economic growth since 1990s, partly explained by the decline in the role of labour, and coupled with a slowing population growth and increasing unemployment. The dominance of capital accumulation followed the country's expansion of its capital base after diversifying into textiles and later into the higher-end and more capital-intensive brackets of the sugar and textiles markets, resulting in a boost to capital. It is noteworthy that capital accumulation was initially textile-driven in the 1970s, slowing in the subsequent decade as underutilized capacity was ploughed back into production following the 1980–81 crisis. Interestingly, by the end of 1980s an increase in both public and private investment was noted, with private investment nearly doubling from around 11 per cent of GDP in 1982 to 20 per cent in 1991. Subramanian and Roy (2001) posited that the reinvestment of profits from sugar and textiles played a critical role in sustaining high levels of investment in the Mauritius, emphasizing the role of domestic rather than foreign savings in financing investment during the growth boom. Indeed, with the disappearance of the profits from sugar and textiles in the 2000s, Mauritius relied increasingly on FDI inflows to finance investment. However, the results obtained may also reflect a growth in dependence of the Mauritius economy on capital accumulation, perhaps because returns to capital are high due to preferential market access in some industries (e.g. the garment industry) or the market power of other industries, which allow for additional mark-up (e.g. high-end tourism).

In terms of total factor productivity, the island's performance is in line with other successful nation-states and reflects the careful reallocation of resources towards growth-enhancing sectors. This reflects the shows great lead when comparing to the rest of Africa continent. A sector disaggregate analysis confirmed that growth in output is essentially driven by growth in capital stock in most sectors with total factor productivity being relatively higher in the services sector, it was quite low in the manufacturing sector, while agriculture recorded negative productivity.

How has the Mauritian growth been financed? Through domestic savings or through FDI?

Although a number of explanations have been provided to explain Mauritius' growth performance, it is important to analyse how this growth has been financed. A critical element of that performance is to view the key role of domestic savings and foreign savings.

The good years

The early 1970s saw a rise in the average savings rate which culminated in a peak of 34.1 per cent in 1974. This was primarily the result of an improvement in the terms of trade as sugar prices more than trebled between 1972 and 1975. However, by 1976 the uptrend in world sugar prices was reversed and in the face of serious economic difficulties in the latter half of the 1970s the average savings rate experienced a constant decline (see Figure 2.1). Thus, in 1980, following dramatic negative economic growth, the average savings rate reached a historic low, at 10.4 per cent of GDP. This was also followed by lower investment, constrained by the lack of available financing and poor external conditions. The two devaluations in 1979 and 1981 and the adoption of the Structural Adjustment Programme reversed this situation. As a result, from a low base of around 10 per cent in 1980–1981, the savings rate improved to 28 per cent in 1986–1988.

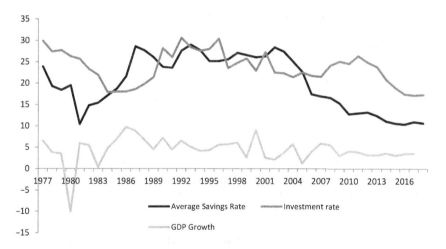

Figure 2.1 Savings rate, investment rate and GDP growth rate in Mauritius (1976–2017)
Note: Savings rate is gross national savings as a share of GDP (%). GDP growth rate is GDP annual growth rate (%). Investment rate is the share of investment to GDP (%).
Source: Authors' compilation, taken from Statistics Mauritius (2018).

The trend in investment is also closely linked to domestic economic conditions. During the period 1970–1976 the investment rate more than doubled, increasing from 12.2 per cent in 1970 to 27.4 per cent in 1976. Resources from the sugar boom served to finance the development of the export processing zone (EPZ) and the tourism sector. Substantial investment in infrastructure was also made during this period. A downtrend in investment followed thereafter. On the back of the economic crisis of the late 1970s and the start of the 1980s, the investment rate reached 17.9 per cent in 1982. Investment picked up after the adoption of the Stabilisation and Structural Adjustment Programme and maintained robust growth between 1983 and 1990 when it peaked at 30.6 per cent.

These relatively high savings and investment rates were sustained thanks to a number of liberalizing reforms enacted in the financial sector after 1987. These included the liberalization of interest rates through the abolition of the minimum deposit rate and the maximum loan rate guideline; the issuing of two Bank of Mauritius savings bonds to non-financial institutions; the introduction of tax-free savings bonds by the Mauritius Housing Corporation and the creation of the Stock Exchange of Mauritius.

The savings rate fluctuated within the range of 23 and 29 per cent during the 1990s, averaging a respectable 26.4 per cent of GDP during the decade. A significant positive and robust relationship between the savings rate and the investment rate that remained around 29 per cent of GDP was observed. Furthermore, this virtuous cycle was reinforced by high GDP growth that increased income, savings and investment, which in turn further increased economic growth.

In fact, the high savings rate in the 1980s and 1990s can be explained by substantial revenues accruing from the export sector. Mauritius has enjoyed preferential access to the markets of its major trading partners, namely the United States and especially Europe. This access has affected two important products that together have accounted for over 90 per cent of Mauritian exports. Mauritius has also enjoyed preferential access for its exports of textiles and clothing.[3] According to the calculations of Subramanian and Roy (2003), revenue obtained in Mauritius from preferential access for sugar and clothing together amounted to about 7 per cent of GDP in the 1980s and to about 4.5 per cent of GDP in the 1990s. These substantial revenues accruing to exports ensured that resources were not diverted away despite the attractiveness of the protected import-competing sector. From a macroeconomic perspective, moreover, these revenues played a crucial role in sustaining high levels of investment and explain the fact that during the growth boom in Mauritius domestic rather than foreign savings (see Figure 2.2) financed domestic investment (ibid.). Economic growth was largely led by investment and although foreign investment, both direct and portfolio, has grown in recent years most of this total investment was financed domestically.

However, since then, the investment rate has declined considerably, reflecting a worsening of economic conditions caused by the ending of trade

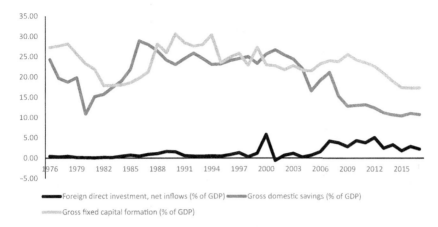

Figure 2.2 Gross domestic savings as a share of GDP and FDI as a percentage of GDP in Mauritius (1976–2017)
Source: Authors' compilation, taken from the World Development Indicators, World Bank (2018).

preferences at the start of the 2000s and the enduring economic uncertainty and slowdown in the aftermath of the 2008/09 global recession. It averaged 22.5 per cent during the period 2000–2015 and, in particular, it fell consistently between 2009 and 2015 when it stood at 17.5 per cent. In 2017 it stood at 17.3 per cent, the lowest level attained since 1972.

Meanwhile, the savings rate has declined in recent years and stood at 10.7 per cent in 2017. This can be attributed to a number of reasons, namely the high indebtedness and over-indebtedness of Mauritian households (Sobhee *et al.*, 2016), a low rate of interest on savings and poor financial literacy among the population. In fact, the rising cost of living has also made it difficult for households to save as the major share of their income is spent on consumption and the repayment of loans and existing debts. Such reduction is problematic in that it may increasingly signal inadequate capacity to fund future investment, thus undermining the future growth potential of the Mauritian economy.

In addition, another major contributor to growth has been the transformation over the last two decades of the economy from a monocrop to a diversified one with flourishing manufacturing and service sectors (see Figure 2.3).

Structural change

Mauritius has undergone structural change over time, reflecting a successful economic diversification strategy. The primary sector has been declining since independence. Its contribution to GDP has fallen from 22.5 per cent in 1976 to 3.7 per cent in 2017 (see Table 2.2). This is mainly explained by the contraction of the sugar industry which has faced difficult challenges with the ending of the EU Sugar Protocol. In order to ensure its survival, there have been important reforms under the

Table 2.2 Main sectors, 1976–2017 (percentage distribution of gross value added by industry group at current basic prices)

Sector of economic activity	1976	1980	1985	1990	1995	2000	2005	2010	2015	2016	2017
Agriculture, forestry and fishing	22.5	12.4	15.3	12.9	10.4	6.5	5.7	3.7	3.5	3.6	3.5
Sugar cane production	17.8	8.1	11.1	8.0	5.7	3.3	3.0	1.2	0.9	0.8	0.7
Manufacturing	15.2	15.2	20.6	24.4	23.0	22.5	19.2	18.0	14.7	13.9	13.4
Sugar	5.5	2.4	3.2	3.4	1.6	0.8	0.8	0.3	0.2	0.2	0.2
Food	–	–	–	–	–	3.9	4.9	6.3	5.1	4.9	4.7
Textiles and clothing	2.6	4.3	9.5	12.0	11.5	11.5	6.8	5.1	4.6	4.1	3.8
Construction	8.0	7.6	5.6	6.7	6.4	5.3	5.4	6.9	4.4	4.2	4.3
Wholesale and retail	11.3	14.2	13.2	13.0	12.8	11.5	11.9	11.8	12.0	11.9	12.1
Hotels and restaurants	1.8	2.3	2.4	3.9	5.1	6.0	7.1	7.0	7.4	7.8	7.3
Transport, storage and communications	8.5	11.3	10.9	10.4	11.4	12.7	11.9	9.5	6.2	6.3	6.1
Financial intermediation	5.7	5.0	4.7	4.9	6.5	8.8	9.2	10.0	12.0	12.1	11.9
Real estate, rental and business activities	10.2	12.7	11.1	8.9	8.5	8.4	9.8	8.4	5.0	4.8	5.9

Source: Authors' computation, taken from Statistics Mauritius (2018).

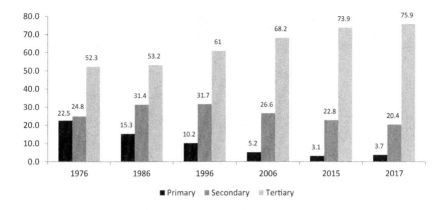

Figure 2.3 Sectoral composition of GDP from 1976 to 2017
Source: Authors' compilation, from Statistics Mauritius (2018).

Multi Annual Adaptation Strategy to reduce costs, enhance competitiveness and diversify into high value-added activities such as the production of special sugars, ethanol and spirits, and electricity generation from bagasse. The share of secondary sector output rose from 24.8 per cent in 1976 to 31.7 per cent in 1996 but fell to around 20.4 per cent in 2017. The performance of the secondary sector is closely linked to the performance of the EPZ sector whose growth averaged 17.5 per cent annually between 1977 and 1986 before declining to 6 per cent in 2011 and to 0.3 per cent in 2017. This decline is attributed mainly to the ending of the MFA along with the closure of factories, increased labour costs and increased competitive pressure from emerging countries.

In fact, as labour and other resources shifted from less productive to more productive sectors, there has been a growth-enhancing structural change boosting the overall productivity of the economy. As a result, overall productivity has increased as labour and capital have shifted towards higher value-added economic activities. Following the work of McMillan and Rodrik (2011), an analysis of the end-of-period relative productivity of sectors vis-à-vis the change in the sectors' share of employment between 1995 and 2015 was conducted with data obtained from Statistics Mauritius. Results show that Mauritius has experienced growth-enhancing structural change over the years as labour has primarily moved from the agriculture and manufacturing sectors, which accounted for around 45 per cent of total employment in 1990, towards higher value-added sectors of the economy, including real estate and financial intermediation. It is observed that a fall in the employment share for the agriculture and manufacturing sectors resulted in a fall in the relative productivity of these sectors. However, because labour productivity in these two sectors is lower than the relative productivity in the majority of other sectors and resources are actually moved to other sectors overall productivity increases.

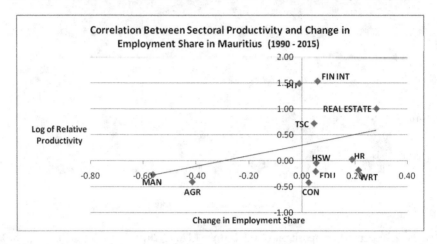

Figure 2.4 Correlation between sectoral productivity and change in employment share (1990–2015)
Note: AGR – agriculture, hunting, forestry and fishing; MAN – manufacturing, CON – construction; WRT – wholesale and retail trade; HR – hotels and restaurants; TSC – transport, storage and communications; FIN INT – financial intermediation; REAL ESTATE – real estate; EDU – education; HSW – health and social work.

Mauritius shares striking similarities with other emerging economies in East Asia where capital accumulation has been more important than total factor productivity in the economic take-off process. Furthermore, based on the findings presented above, it could be argued that the Mauritian case bears many similarities to a number of countries in Asia, particularly India, Hong Kong and Thailand (see McMillan and Rodrik, 2011), which have experienced significant growth-enhancing structural change since 1990. Indeed, it was observed that labour in these countries has moved predominantly from very low productivity agriculture to more sophisticated sectors of the economy.

Can Mauritius' growth model be sustained without higher savings?

From the analysis above it appears that economic growth, which has been driven mainly through capital accumulation, will require sustainable high savings and investment rates. However, since 2001 the strong relationship between investment, savings and growth has diminished and the savings rate of 28 per cent recorded in 2001 coincided with a GDP growth rate of 2 per cent, its lowest figure since 1982. Furthermore, from 2001 onwards the savings rate began a downward trend, reaching 17.1 per cent and 13.9 per cent in 2006 and 2009, respectively. The savings rate has declined even further in recent years and stood at 10.7 per cent in 2017.

This is mostly explained by the ending of the system that worked success-fully during the two previous decades. Behind this are the significant changes that the dismantling of the MFA in 2004 and the EU sugar reforms in 2005 from which it followed that the preferences enjoyed by Mauritius on its major exports markets no longer prevail. For instance, as a result of the loss of MFA clothing preferences low-wage manufacture displaced textiles and apparel in Mauritius and the sector suffered a 30 per cent decrease in output and a 25 per cent decline in employment (Frankel, 2010). Adverse terms of trade worsened following an increase in global prices of oil and food during the period 2003–08. The balance of payments deficit, the budget deficit and unemployment have all deteriorated over the past decade.

Meanwhile, the savings rate has deteriorated continuously so that it reached 15.4 and 15.2 per cent in 2010 and 2011, respectively, comparable to the low savings levels witnessed in the early 1970s and 1980s. While the investment rate also deteriorated up until 2005, substantial economic reforms to further liberal-ize the economy and to open it up to FDI had reinvigorated it. This trend, however, was halted in 2008 and is now starting to decline, particularly in private investments. Finally, because the savings rate is below the investment rate, this exerts demand pressure on prices and has broadened the balance of payments' current account. The resource gap, which is the difference between GDFCF and GNS, has stabilized at Rs 27.7 billion in 2011, down from Rs 27.9 billion in 2010. This is, nevertheless, far from the Rs 8.8 billion gap of 2007.

In order to gain a better explanation for the falling savings rate, we break down the savings by economic agents (Table 2.3). Domestic saving in Mauritius is divi-ded into two parts – public saving and private saving, the latter being divided between household saving and corporate saving. Overall, there has been an improvement in Mauritian savings rates since 2001 with a considerable change in the contribution to savings of each economic agent. First, savings from non-financial corporations in total saving have more than doubled between 2002 and 2007. Second, while savings from financial corporations have been stable over the years, they increased more than 50 per cent, to Rs 7,162 million, in 2007. Third, public savings were reduced between 2002 and 2004 but improved dramatically from 2005 reflecting efforts in fiscal consolidation to contribute around 7 per cent of total savings (compared to the contribution of dissaving in 2003).

Finally, the most noticeable trend has been a negative rate of household savings from 2002 onwards, reaching Rs 20,472 million in 2005 (i.e. households required around 40 per cent of total domestic savings). While the negative rate of household savings decelerated in 2007 it still absorbed 7 per cent of total domestic savings. This process of disinvesting by Mauritian households raises the question of the sustainability of household finance in the medium term. In an effort to explain the dissaving behaviour of Mauritian households, a microeconomic model was tested in order better to understand the structural factors that affect saving behaviour in Mauritius. Income plays an important role in determining household saving as the desire and ability to save depends on having more than the resources dedicated basic needs (Carpenter and Jensen, 2002). On the other hand, household size

Table 2.3 Savings decomposition by economic agents (2002–2015)

	Total conomy	Non-financial corporations	Financial corporations	General government	Households
2002	39,000	26,861	4,848	1,649	5,642
2003	39,580	42,428	2,658	–686	–4,819
2004	39,702	47,383	3,954	256	–11,890
2005	32,189	46,807	4,620	1,235	–20,472
2007	52,445	45,600	10,286	1,554	–4,995
2008	47,249	42,015	7,752	8,169	–10,688
2009	39,299	38,549	8,036	1,181	–8,466
2010	46,475	42,510	13,031	–778	–8,289
2011	46,775	39,413	13,536	1,848	–8,025
2012	49,582	34,051	20,826	3,491	–8,786
2013	46,286	33,592	20,881	–4,638	–3,550
2014	34,864	25,331	17,062	–2,880	–4,648
2015	42,180	29,331	21,583	–5,140	–3,594

Source: Authors' compilation, taken from Institutional Sector Accounts, Statistics Mauritius (2015).

affects savings negatively as additional household members force parents to deplete their savings owing to higher household consumption. The lifecycle hypothesis, which assumes that age impacts household saving behaviour, is reinforced as evidenced by the decreased level of saving in households headed by retired people. Self-employed people have fewer savings, which may reflect their difficulty in obtaining finance from smaller firms. Finally, female heads of households tend to save more than their male counterparts.

Declining savings has often been associated with increased debts. Household indebtedness has always been viewed by economists as the *raison d'être* for consumption by households, especially those who are mostly constrained by lack of liquidity (Sobhee *et al.*, 2016). It is customary for consumers to borrow against their future stream of income in order to finance current consumption; they then automatically become indebted. However, the rationality which underpins such behaviour becomes untenable when household indebtedness crosses borrowing limits and turns into over-indebtedness. In Mauritius, it has been observed that higher income breeds higher indebtedness, and that household debt levels vary significantly across different income levels. It has also been reported that consumers as households were found to be more indebted when their income is low. In a similar vein, since educational attainment is found to be correlated with income, the more educated the respondents, the higher the amount of debt contracted. Out of the total number of 400 households surveyed, 83 per cent were found to be indebted (ibid.). The highest proportion of debt contracted by individual borrowers pertains to the banking sector followed by commercial enterprises through hire purchase credit.

Which factors may explain low savings?

We elaborate on three alternative explanations for the low savings rate in Mauritius: the end of the demographic dividend; reliance on the welfare system; and financial factors.

The end of the demographic dividend

The evidence from estimated growth models has shown that age structure has a significant impact on the growth of the economy. However, the mechanisms through which demographic transitions influence economic growth vary across countries (Mason, 2003). The demographic dividend represents a window of opportunity in the development of a nation that opens with fewer younger dependents, due to the declining fertility rate, and fewer older dependents, with the largest segment of the population being of productive working age. Thus, the dependency ratio declines leading to a demographic dividend that necessitates an increase in the savings rate to support growing investment at a time of rapid economic growth.[4]

The two determining factors for the demographic dividend in Mauritius have been the decline in the fertility levels, and the improvement in the health of the population as evidenced by the increase in life expectancy. Figure 2.5 and Table 2.4 show the declining fertility rate and the increasing life expectancy of the Mauritian population.

The fertility rate has been declining over the past five decades, from 6.2 per woman of child-bearing age in 1960 to 4.0 in 1970 and to 2.3 and 1.4 in 1990 and 2016, respectively. One of the main reasons for this marked decline is the increase in the number of women in employment in Mauritius and a regressing

Figure 2.5 Fertility rate (1960–2016)
Source: Authors' compilation, taken from the World Development Indicators, World Bank (2018).

Table 2.4 Life expectancy by gender from 1960 to 2016

Year	Life expectancy at birth, female (years)	Life expectancy at birth, male (years)	Life expectancy at birth, total (years)
1960	60.6	57.0	58.7
1970	65.6	60.8	63.1
1975	68.1	60.9	64.4
1980	71.1	63.0	67.0
1985	72.2	64.7	68.4
1990	73.4	65.6	69.4
1995	74.3	66.6	70.3
2000	75.3	68.2	71.7
2005	75.9	69.1	72.4
2010	76.7	69.5	73.0
2015	77.8	71.1	74.4
2016	77.8	71.2	74.4

Source: Authors' compilation, taken from the World Development Indicators, World Bank (2018).

mean marriage age during the same period. With an increase in life expectancy (see Table 2.5) and a declining fertility rate, the age structure of the population changes, with a greater proportion of the population falling into the older age group. The Mauritian population is now 'getting older', not only as a result of unprecedented improvements in life expectancy, but also as a result of very sharp declines in fertility. Both trends are likely to continue, and together will have a profound impact on the age structure of the population.

The demographic transition is determined by the level and pace of mortality and fertility changes. The age structure of the population has been further classified according to the lifecycle stages and their impact on the economy: young (age 0–14 years), youth (15–24 years), prime working age (25–49 years), middle working age (50–64 years) and elderly (65+ years).

The demographic transition in Mauritius was completed in a very short space of time. The ageing process has and will continue to be almost equally precipitous

Table 2.5 Age structure of the Mauritian society (1990–2030) as a share of the total population, %

Age structure	1990	2000	2010	2015	2030
0–14 (young)	29.67	25.21	21.60	19.75	16.96
15–24 (youth)	18.91	18.07	16.05	15.65	11.81
25–49 (prime working age)	36.49	39.33	38.90	37.39	35.49
50–64 (middle working age)	9.56	11.07	16.20	18.63	19.95
65 and above (elderly)	5.37	6.32	7.25	8.57	15.79

Source: Authors' compilation, taken from Statistics Mauritius.

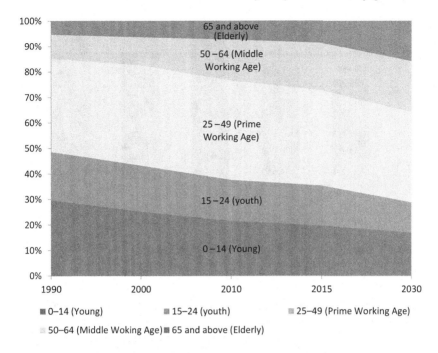

Figure 2.6 Age structure of the Mauritian society (1990–2030)
Source: Statistics Mauritius (2018).

and dramatic. As a result of the fertility decline in Mauritius, the proportionate share of population under 15 years of age has declined from 30 per cent in the 1990s to 22 per cent in 2010. The trend will continue in the future and the share of the child population in Mauritius is expected to reach approximately 17 per cent in 2030. Mauritius experienced a youth bulge (around 19 per cent of the share) in the 1990s but this declined to 16 per cent in 2010. The share of the youth population is expected to decline to 12 per cent in 2030 (see Table 2.5).

The relative share of the prime working age population (25–49 years) has declined from 2000 onwards but overall the working age population will increase from 50.4 per cent of the total population in 2012 to 55.4 per cent of the total population in 2030. It will be a challenge to generate sufficient employment opportunities to meet the projected growth in the labour force, while accommodating a declining youth population and a growing elderly population, which is expected to dissave.

Reliance on the welfare system

Another factor behind the low savings rate in Mauritius is the provision of public services and a national pension system that helps to reduce uncertainty

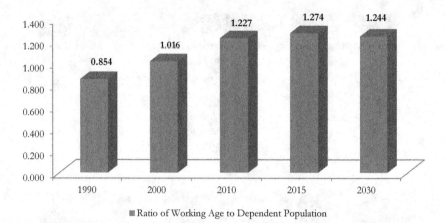

■ Ratio of Working Age to Dependent Population

Figure 2.7 Ratio of working age to dependent population
Source: Authors' compilation, taken from Statistics Mauritius (2018).

about the future and lessens the incentive to increase private savings for retirement. In fact, government expenses are strongly influenced by trends in spending in the social security, welfare, health and education sectors. Figure 2.8 shows the rise in the share of government expenditure on health and on education as a share of GDP from 1999 to 2004. There has been massive government investment in educational infrastructure, namely the construction

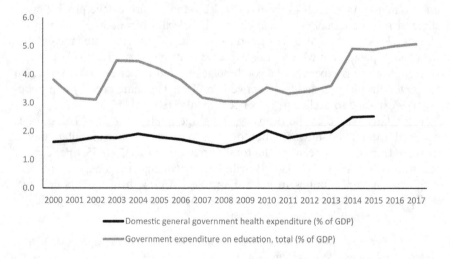

━━Domestic general government health expenditure (% of GDP)

━━Government expenditure on education, total (% of GDP)

Figure 2.8 Government expenditure on health and education as a share of GDP (%)
Source: Authors' compilation, taken from the World Development Indicators, World Bank (2018).

of new schools in different parts of the island. From 2004 there was a decline in government expenditure on education which peaked in 2009 to reach 3.0 per cent of GDP before increasing again to 5.1 per cent in 2017. Similarly, the GDP share of public expenditure on health services has experienced a slightly declining trend from 2007 onwards; nevertheless it has increased in the past decade to reach 2.5 per cent of GDP in 2015.

However, the Household Budget Survey 2017 shows that 'education' saw a strong increase in household expenditure (34.6 per cent) followed by 'health' (16.0 per cent) and 'communications' (39.1 per cent) (Statistics Mauritius 2017). This shows that the average Mauritian household still devotes a considerable share of its expenditure to education and health. In addition, government expenditure on social security and welfare has experienced a considerable increase over the years. From 5.3 per cent of GDP in 2004/2005 to around 7 per cent in 2010, it can be said that social aid has been a major share of government expenditure in recent years (up from 26.4 per cent in 2010 to approximately 29 per cent in 2017). Total government expenditure on social protection as a share of GDP has accelerated over the years in tandem with the rise in the ageing population and the changing economic structure of the island. Increasing longevity and declining fertility rates contribute to rising dependency ratios. In fact, rising pension expenditure in Mauritius reflects rising dependency ratios (World Bank, 2018).

The government of Mauritius funds a wide range of social assistance programmes designed to improve the lives of individuals and households living in vulnerable conditions. These schemes are administered and implemented by various ministries and institutions, and include the Basic Retirement Pension; the Enhanced Basic Retirement Pension; the Basic Widow's Pension; the Basic Invalid's Pension; the Carer's Allowance; the Basic Orphan's Pension; the Guardian's allowance, and Social Aid and Industrial Injury. Furthermore, following the enactment of the Social Aid Act (1983), whereby payments are now means-tested, financial assistance is provided when a claimant is temporarily or permanently incapable of earning an adequate livelihood due to any physical or mental disability or sickness or accident. Beneficiaries of social aid are also entitled to free spectacles, hearing aids, wheelchairs, free bus passes in order to attend medical appointments; funeral grants; payment of examination fees for their wards; and allowances for the purchase of rice and flour; allowances are also made to victims of fire, cyclone refugees and flood victims. All these different schemes and programmes are available to men and women living in difficult circumstances and help to reduce their vulnerability. Given the generous welfare state provision, the household's incentive to save may actually decline over time.

Furthermore, the impact of public spending on private consumption and savings depends ultimately on the degree to which consumers treat government debt as net wealth. According to the conventional (Keynesian) view, the private sector perceives government bonds as net wealth and the stimulating effects of fiscal deficits is based on an assumption that consumers are too myopic or fiscally constrained to account for the future fiscal policy implications of current debt accumulation. The Ricardian equivalence hypothesis stands in sharp contrast to this view by arguing that government deficit financing merely generates the private savings necessary to absorb the additional government debt, leaving national savings unaltered. In other words, the Ricardian equivalence hypothesis maintains that a decrease in the government deficit will be exactly offset by a decrease in private sector savings. Therefore, budget deficits should not cause a deficit on the current account.

By the mid-1980s the revival of the country's economic fortunes brought about a significant improvement in the budgetary outturn. Between 1985 and 1994 the yearly overall budget deficit as a percentage of GDP stood at a low 2.6 per cent on average. The budget deficit as a percentage of GDP has declined over the years from 6.1 per cent in 2002 to 2.5 per cent in 2012 which based on the Ricardian equivalence hypothesis this could partly explain the reduction in private savings in the economy at large. The budget deficit between 2008 and 2014 averaged 3.5 per cent of GDP, while overall government expenditure was 24 per cent of GDP and overall government revenue was 21 per cent of GDP.

Financial factors

Economic theory suggests that financial development may influence saving behaviour in ambiguous ways[5] (Bandiera et al., 2000). The ambiguity comes from the net effect of several simultaneous channels through which financial development could affect saving. For example, it is well established in the literature that financial repression through its below market (repressed) interest rates does exert a negative impact on the intermediation of financial resources and consequently have a negative effect on the savings rate (Shaw, 1973). However, financial liberalization enriches the availability of instruments for saving, and leads to increasing interest rates (compared to a repressed situation) and it enhances access to capital, which in turn encourages consumer spending and housing lending, and of course it also increases savings by raising interest rates.

Furthermore, one of the purposes of borrowing is to allow people to maintain smooth consumption in the face of shocks. However, consumption will follow more closely the current income level of people with low incomes because credit constraints are more binding at these income levels. In contrast, for those with higher permanent (or expected) incomes their consumption is likely to reflect this also at a higher level. It is worth noting that although in the cross-country evidence the simple unconditional correlation between financial depth and domestic saving is positive, the marginal contribution of financial depth (or deepening) on saving is often found to be negative (for example, Loayza et al., 2000). One interpretation of this is that financial liberalization and deepening initially reduces saving, because constraints on credit-constrained households and small and medium-sized enterprises are lifted, and then, over the long term, increases saving indirectly through higher growth.

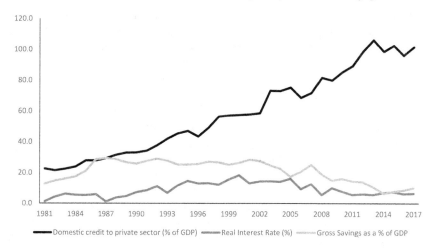

Figure 2.9 Domestic credit to private sector (% of GDP), savings and real rate of interest (1981–2017)
Source: Authors' compilation, taken from World Development Indicators (2018).

Moreover, final consumption expenditure as a share of GDP has shown a rising trend over time. Since 2001 consumption expenditure has been rising, especially with the Hire Purchase and Credit Sales Act being amended in 2000. The Hire Purchase Act provides for two types of credit sale agreements: the 'Credit Sale Agreement' and the 'Hire Purchase Agreement'. Under the Credit Sale Agreement, a buyer may make a payment for 50 per cent of a product and repays the balance in 12 monthly instalments. In addition, the customer becomes the owner of the product once the deposit is made. Under the Hire Purchase Agreement, the customer can make a deposit according to his or his ability to repay the loan – even a zero deposit is allowed. The maximum repayment period is 30 months. The interest rate in both cases is 19 per cent, calculated as the system Annual Percentage Rate or on the remaining balance. It should be noted that the Hire Purchase Act provides, in case of delay in the repayment of monthly instalments, a penalty of 8 per cent of the amount due. Ignorance of this provision may result in the buyer spiralling into debt. As a result, in 2017, consumption expenditure as a share of GDP reached approximately 89.3 per cent. Pyramid selling has gained momentum in recent years, owing to the lack of a legal framework for this type of credit sales. The prevalence of high inflation rates eroded the purchasing power of households and curtailed slightly real consumption growth. As part of efforts by the government to reform the income tax regime, the effective rate of income tax was reduced to 15 per cent from July 2007. Tighter credit conditions resulting from a hike in interest rates coupled with high inflation do not seem to have hurt consumption growth.

In Figure 2.10, we can observe the evolution of inflation from 2001 and the increase after 2006 sparked mainly by rising food and energy prices. We have plotted a scatter to see the behaviour of the real interest rate as a result of inflation and note a negative relationship between the two variables. This may actually show that dissaving is a rational household behaviour to take advantage of negative interest rates.

It is thus believed that in such a scenario more labour (L) and particularly more total factor productivity will be required as compensating factors. While Mauritius is increasingly relying on foreign labour (which is not without it associated problems), total factor productivity remains essential. Productivity gains can be achieved at the aggregate level through the implementation of a successful adjustment policy and more efficient macroeconomic management. Second, improved productivity can result from structural changes, which induce allocation of factors to new, more productive, activities. As an example, Lucas (1993) argued that the creation of the 'Asian miracles' relied on structural changes leading to the production of increasingly sophisticated product mixes. Total factor productivity gains in the above lines still rest on increases in savings and investment rates.

Using some relatively basic calculations based on averages and trend analyses and assuming that the island will experience an ongoing low level of growth accumulation (based on past evidence), it is estimated that in order to achieve an growth rate of 5.5 per cent (the average growth rate in the 1990s), the contribution of labour and total factor productivity (based on recent trends) to growth (from the growth accounting framework) will have to be increased by at least 60–70 per cent. This surely represents a considerable and probably unrealistic challenge for the country, especially in the case of labour which may subsequently require an even higher contribution from total factor productivity.

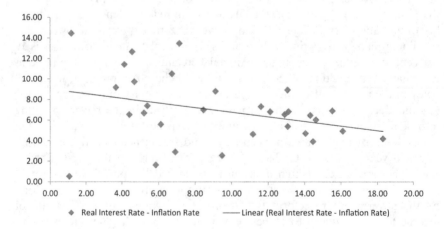

Figure 2.10 Real interest rate and inflation rate
Source: Authors' computation.

Conclusion and policy measures

This chapter first assessed the drivers of growth in Mauritius during the period 1990–2015 using the standard growth accounting framework and, second, it provided a policy-oriented overview of savings and capital and their importance for the island's prosperity. It also examined the major determinants of those variables, reviewing the trend of capital formation and technical progress over the years and the constraints that the country is currently facing.

The growth accounting analysis revealed that the growth rates experienced by Mauritius over the last 25 years have been driven more extensively by its capital component rather than by labour growth, with total factor productivity playing an increasingly important role. Out of an average growth rate of 4.9 per cent during the period 1990–2015, capital growth was observed to be the major driver of economic growth in Mauritius, as compared to labour with total factor productivity growth maintaining a positive contribution. Interestingly, as labour and other resources shift from less productive to more productive sectors, there has been a growth-enhancing structural change (boosting the overall productivity of the economy), resulting in an overall productivity increase as labour and capital have shifted towards higher value-added economic activities.

Since economic growth has been found to be driven mainly through capital accumulation, this implies the need for sustained high savings and investment rates. However, it has been observed that since 2001 the strong association between investment, savings and growth did not hold any more and the 28 per cent savings rate recorded in 2001 coincided with a 2 per cent GDP growth rate, its lowest figure since 1982. Moreover, from 2001 onwards the savings rate initiated a downward trend even reaching 17.1 per cent and 13.9 per cent in 2006 and 2009 respectively, and declining further in recent years to reach 10.7 per cent in 2017.

The low and declining savings rate was observed to be primarily due to a plunge in household savings, with most low- and moderate-income households barely being able to make any savings which makes them vulnerable to economic downturns as well as making their ability to sustain their standard of living when they retire very difficult. Furthermore, an ageing society is bound to put greater pressure on fiscal sustainability. While income is among the most prevalent determinants of saving behaviour in Mauritius, income alone cannot explain the declining trend in household savings. Other factors do influence the low household savings rate, including the real interest rate and the inflation rate and the opportunity for debt-financed consumption as a result of financial liberalization as low- and moderate-income households gain greater access to credit. However, given the low domestic savings rate, the key policy question for Mauritius is how to finance its growing economy in the medium term. There is no doubt that the challenge of boosting savings is of great importance if Mauritius wishes to sustain the its current growth rate and increase its investment rate. A stable and enabling macroeconomic environment, which builds on the island's robust macroeconomic policy performance over the past decade, is thus important to raise domestic savings by increasing incomes.

There are a number of policy tools that can help to promote higher and longer-term household savings. There could be high returns on policies that (1) raise awareness about the benefits of savings, particularly in the long term; and (2) elevate the level of financial literacy of households. Because households do not generally plan to save, they may end up suffering from an income gap later in life and become unable to sustain their standards of living. A national financial literacy strategy would establish a framework for a systematic approach towards increasing the level of financial literacy among the population. Increasing the financial capability of households, starting early in the lifecycle, and helping them make informed financial decisions could boost savings.

On the supply side, the intermediation role of financial markets is central. There are three types of policy option to enhance intermediation: (1) making better use of existing products (e.g. private pensions, corporate bonds), including, but not limited to, taxation of different instruments; (2) investing more in product innovation and improving regulations; and (3) designing special saving schemes. Besides raising household awareness about planning for retirement, making the private pension scheme more attractive could help the sector to generate more and longer-term savings. One option to consider is increasing the tax exemption limit and different parameters (for tax exemption) could be determined in order to maximize the possibility of attracting new savings into the private pension system, with participation from the relevant public and private agencies. Efforts to promote savings would be most effective if they are complemented by reforms to increase the overall development level of the financial markets. The Mauritian financial system remains heavily dominated by the banking system. Mauritius will benefit from a more diversified financial market which can mobilize and allocate savings more effectively and at a lower cost. Further development of the corporate bond market is one potential policy option. More generally, the level of financial development seems to play an important role in channelling savings to growth-enhancing activities. The experiences of Malaysia and Thailand, which both have well-developed financial markets and high saving rates, may be relevant for Mauritius. Special saving schemes, based on successful examples elsewhere, could be instrumental in attracting new savings. The Saving Gateway and the Child Trust Fund in the United Kingdom and the 529 plans in the United States (developed for covering children's future education expenses) are good examples of voluntary savings schemes. Attracting moderate-income households is important for account efficiency because they are more likely to increase savings when given the opportunity to invest.

Savings do not automatically generate investment and a sound enabling environment is critical, particularly for the corporate sector. Additional policy measures could be considered to enhance internal fund generation of the corporate sector, including enhancing operating profits and retaining profits within firms. Hence, it is critical to enable firms to grow and innovate and for labour to be used more productively. Improving work skills, enhancing competitiveness, improving the business climate, and discouraging informality will all help to boost savings.

Sound macro policies to increase incomes and further reduce economic vulnerability would also complement other attempts to promote domestic savings. Rapid credit expansion also suppresses savings to the extent that they are not channelled into productive activities and pushes low-income households into dissaving. Thus, it is essential that monetary and exchange rate policies be designed to control credit growth and excessive appreciation. In particular, policies and measures intended to limit the growth in credit card and consumption loans that encourage growth in consumption could be effective in promoting saving.

Notes

1 For previous analysis of Mauritius's performance, see Romer (1993), Subramanian (2001), Subramanian and Roy (2001), Frankel (2010), Stiglitz (2011), Zafar (2011).
2 According to the World Bank's *Doing Business* report, in 2018 Mauritius' global ranking rose from 49th position in 2017 to 25th position (World Bank, 2018). Mauritius has also achieved a remarkable performance in many other rankings and is considered a regional leader. The Mo Ibrahim Index of African Governance 2018 shows that since 2007 Mauritius has remained the highest ranking country in Africa. Mauritius achieved the highest overall score (79.5) out of a total of 54 African countries.
3 Foreign investment in the clothing sector, which originated largely in Hong Kong SAR, was motivated partly by the need to circumvent the quotas on textiles and clothing that were constraining clothing exports from Hong Kong SAR. The international regime then in place, known as the Multi-Fibre Arrangement (MFA), was an attempt by the United States and the European Union (EU) to limit imports into their own markets. These limits were achieved by awarding country-specific quotas for the different textile and apparel exporting countries. One of the effects of these quotas was to redistribute production between exporting countries, away from low-cost towards high-cost sources of production. Thus, high-cost-producing countries gained an advantage relative to low-cost producers, resulting in higher production than would otherwise have taken place.
4 Higgins and Williamson (1996, 1997) have estimated the relationship between a country's age composition and savings rate. Their study provides an explanation for the 'East Asian miracle', and suggests policies that facilitate the demographic transition by lowering fertility rates and are responsible for opening a 'window of economic opportunity' and yielding a 'demographic dividend' driven by the changing age composition of the population, which is causally related to increasing savings rates and economic growth rates (Birdsall *et al.*, 2001; Mason, 2001).
5 Interest rate fluctuations can impact saving through two separate channels (the income channel and the substitution channel), with opposite effects on agents' saving behaviour. The net impact on saving will depend on the relative size of the each of the effects. The former works as follows: a real interest rate increase makes individuals more prone to consume than to save, as this would positively affect individual disposable income. The latter, however, suggests that higher effective interest rates would increase saving if individuals are willing to postpone current consumption for high returns, and thus would provide the incentive to save. If the real interest rate affects saving negatively, the income effect will be to exert more influence than the substitution effect, and vice versa.

References

Bandiera, O., Caprio, G., Honohan, P. and Schiantarelli, F. (2000) 'Does Financial Reform Increase or Reduce Savings?', *Review of Economics and Statistics* 82: 239–263.

Birdsall, N., Kelley, A. C. and Sinding, S. W. (eds) (2001) *Population Matters*, Oxford: Oxford University Press.

Bosworth, Barry P. and Collins, Susan M. (2003) 'The Empirics of Growth: An Update', *Brookings Papers on Economic Activity* 2: 113–206.

Carpenter, S. B. and Jensen, R. T. (2002) 'Household Participation in Formal and Informal Savings Mechanisms, Evidence from Pakistan', *Review of Development Economics* 6(3): 314–328.

Frankel, J. A. (2010) 'Mauritius: African Success Story', NBER Working Papers 16569, Cambridge, MA: National Bureau of Economic Research.

Higgins, M. and Williamson, J. G. (1996) 'Asian Demography and Foreign Capital Dependence', NBER Working Paper No. 5560, Cambridge, MA: National Bureau of Economic Research.

Higgins, M. and Williamson, J. G. (1997) 'Age Structure Dynamics in Asia and Dependence on Foreign Capital', *Population and Development Review* 23(2): 261–293.

Loayza, N., Hebbel, K. S. and Serven, L. (2000) 'Saving in Developing Countries: An Overview', *World Bank Economic Review* 14(3): 393–414.

Lucas, Robert Jr (1993) 'Making a Miracle', *Econometrica* 61(2): 251–272.

McMillan, M. and Rodrik, D. (2011) 'Globalization, Structural Change, and Economic Growth', in M. Bachetta and M. Jansen (eds) *Making Globalization Socially Sustainable*, Geneva: International Labor Organization and World Trade Organization.

Mason, A. (2001) *Population Change and Economic Development in East Asia*, Stanford, CA: Stanford University Press.

Mason, A. (2003) 'Population Change And Economic Development: What Have We Learned from the East Asia Experience?', *Applied Population and Policy* 1(1): 3–14.

Meade, J. E. (1961) 'Mauritius: A Case Study in Malthusian Economics', *Economic Journal* 71(283): 521–534.

Meade, J. E.et al. (1961) *The Economics and Social Structure of Mauritius: Report to the Government of Mauritius*, London: Methuen.

Rojid, S. and Seetanah, B. (2011) 'Analysing the Sources of Economic Growth in Africa Using Growth Accounting and a Panel VAR Approach', *Journal of Developing Areas* 44(2): 367–390.

Romer, P. (1993) 'Two Strategies for Economic Development: Using Ideas and Producing Ideas', in *Proceedings of the World Bank Annual Conference on Development Economics*, Washington, DC: World Bank.

Sachs, J. D. and Warner, A. M. (1995) 'Economic Reform and the Process of Global Integration', *Brookings Papers on Economic Activity* 1: 1–118.

Sannassee, R. V., Seetanah, B. and Lamport, M. J. (2014) 'Export Diversification and Economic Growth: The Case of Mauritius', inM. Jansen, M. S. Jallab and M. Smeets (eds) *Connecting to Global Markets – Challenges and Opportunities: Case Studies Presented by WTO Chair-Holders*, Geneva: World Trade Organization, pp. 11–23. Available at www.wto.org/english/res_e/booksp_e/cmark_full_e.pdf.

Senhadji, A. (2000) 'Sources of Economic Growth: An Extensive Growth Accounting. Exercise', *IMF Staff Papers* 47(1): 129–157.

Shaw, Edward S. (1973) *Financial Deepening in Economic Development*, New York: Oxford University Press.

Sobhee, K. S., Tandrayen-Ragoobur, V., Kasseeah, H. and Thoplan, R. (2016) *An In-depth Analysis of Rising Household Indebtedness in an Upper-Middle-Income Economy: The Case of Mauritius*, New York: Nova Publishers.

Statistics Mauritius (2015) *Economic and Social Indicators*, Port Louis: Ministry of Finance and Economic Development. Available at http://statsmauritius.govmu.org/English/Pages/default.aspx.

Statistics Mauritius (2017) *Household Budget Survey 2017*, Port Louis: Ministry of Finance and Economic Development.

Statistics Mauritius (2018) *Digest National Accounts of Mauritius*, Port Louis: Ministry of Finance and Economic Development.

Stiglitz, J. (2011) 'The Mauritius Miracle', *Project Syndicate*.

Subramanian, A. (2001) 'Mauritius: A Case Study', *Finance and Development* 38(4): 22–25.

Subramanian, A. and Roy, D. (2001) 'Who Can Explain the Mauritian Miracle: Meade, Romer, Sachs, or Rodrik?', IMF Working Paper 01/116, Washington, DC: International Monetary Fund.

Svirydzenka, K. and Petri, M. (2014) 'Mauritius: The Drivers of Growth – Can the Past be Extended?' IMF Working Paper No. 14/134, Washington, DC: International Monetary Fund. Available at www.imf.org/external/pubs/ft/wp/2014/wp14134.pdf.

Tandrayen-Ragoobur, V. and Kasseeah, H. (2017) 'Is Gender an Impediment to Firm Performance? Evidence from Small Firms in Mauritius', *International Journal of Entrepreneurial Behavior & Research* 23(6): 952–976. Available at https://doi.org/10.1108/IJEBR-11-2016-0385.

World Bank (2018) *World Development Indicators, 2018*, Washington, DC: World Bank. doi:10.1596/978-1-4648-0683-4.

Zafar, A. (2011) *Mauritius: An Economic Success Story*, Washington, DC: World Bank. Available at http://siteresources.worldbank.org/AFRICAEXT/Resources/Mauritius_success.pdf (accessed 11 September 2018).

3 Why are institutions key determinants in the development of emerging economies?

The case of Mauritius

L. A. Darga

Introduction

It is widely recognized that the spectrum, adequacy and effectiveness of its different categories of institutions has been critical to the successful economic, social and human development of post-independence Mauritius over the past 50 years. How and why institutions come into being in any society, and under what circumstances, will determine how social forces are unleased and mobilized to create wealth, how that wealth is used, who will have the opportunity and assets to participate in capital accumulation for the nation, what redistributive policies there will be, how conflicts of interest will be managed, and how human and social development is achieved.

The Mauritian state was never an autonomous one in the Weberian sense. It was embedded in society but had a certain level of and capacity for autonomy that has allowed it to be able to balance the interests of different social forces in the superior interest of development of the country even if at times it had to give space to rent-seeking interests.

In this chapter, it is explained how appropriate institutions have been and the extent to which they have been critical in enabling Mauritius to make the transition from a very poor country with a vulnerable monocrop economic base at independence, to sustaining its economic development to become an emerging middle-income economy 50 years later. It is argued that economic, social and human development cannot be achieved without strong, balanced political governance which unleash the social forces necessary for the creation of wealth, namely an indigenous entrepreneurial class, and the formation of human capital to fuel this development drive. It is also argued that the way in which institutions evolve is not just about the will and determination of individual leaders, of the ruling political elite, but is the result of specific conditions and, more importantly, of the interaction of different social forces.

In a settler colonial society country with a multi-origin, multi-ethnic, multi-religious population which for a very long period has been organized in a ranked class system, institutions are essential for the orderly interaction of people and for their trusting relations with the state, their mobilization for engaging in wealth creation and the distribution of that wealth.

The concept of the developmental state is based on the institutionalist argument that states with strong institutional capacities and high levels of autonomy from various sections of society can achieve their economic development goals. Mauritius is not the only African country to have inherited a democratic political system with some good institutional capacity at independence but it is one of the few to have created, developed, maintained and cultivated new institutions that are able to serve its developmental needs (Darga, 1998)

Institutional endowment and the sustainability of fundamental institutions

Mauritius, like most British colonies, inherited the three fundamental pillars of governance: a legislature, an executive and a judiciary whose roles, powers and independence are clearly enshrined in the country's Constitution. Newly independent Mauritius also inherited an informal but powerful 'quasi-institution', namely an independent media which could never be thwarted even when the ruling powers have from time to time wanted to and tried to.

Some observers explain the sustainability of these governance institutions by the fact that since the first post-independence prime minister whose beliefs were rooted in Fabian ideology,[1] Mauritius has had leaders who are democratic at heart. This view can be easily contradicted by the mere fact that the same leaders have ruled their parties in the most autocratic manner and have ensured that the main political parties of Mauritius have never been and are still not democratic in their internal manner of functioning.

A more relevant explanation rests with the interplay of social forces and can be traced back to the colonial period. As a settler colonial society, during the period of French rule (1715–1810) Mauritius witnessed the emergence of a settler bourgeoisie which, through land concessions that were obtained or taken by force and the use of slave labour, successfully created and accumulated wealth so that it become a force to be reckoned with even when the British took over the country in 1810 and had to make concessions such as accepting the Roman Catholic church as the dominant religious body, the French language to be almost at par with English, and the continuing use of French laws for civil matters (Darga, 1998). One of the most powerful expressions of the power of the settler bourgeoisie was the establishment of the private Mauritius Commercial Bank in 1832 which was owned exclusively by the sugar planters. To this day it remains the main bank of the Republic of Mauritius. Another private sector institution that was established as far back as 1850 is the Mauritius Chamber of Commerce and Industry.[2]

Following the increase in the island's volume of trade during the first decades of British administration, the Mauritian business community felt the need for a more formal framework to foster the interests of the trading community and to settle disputes and conflicts arising from trade-related activities. The private sector institutions therefore regrouped themselves as early as 1850, more than a century before Mauritius gained independence from the British.

In 1855 the private sector created the SWAN Insurance company. Thus, the private sector had endowed itself with a banking arm, an insurance provider and an institutional capacity for the collective representation of its interests.

As labour unrest in the sugar plantations began to accelerate, a political party emerged with a middle-class leadership and strong working-class base, the Labour party. As the influence of the Labour party grew in momentum, the British in their typical strategy saw the opportunity of supporting the emergence of a countervailing bourgeoisie to be the future state bourgeoisie (Darga, 1998). As it became more and more evident that Mauritius was moving towards independence, the settler bourgeoise, which by then had become a nationalistic bourgeoisie in its own right, opposed independence fearing that the state bourgeoisie to be would be against its interests and this prompted the creation of a political party, the Parti Mauricien (later known as the Parti Mauricien Social Democrate) to oppose the Labour party. The competition between the two parties became intense and was based on ethnicity. The end result was that the election for independence gave an outcome of 56 per cent for and 44 per cent against and was totally polarized in ethnic terms. The new state bourgeoisie had political power but over a country divided almost in the middle and no control over economic power. The settler bourgeoisie controlled fully the economic base of the country but political power was not theirs. Economic and political power were not in the same hands. Both sides decided that it was in their best interests to find a modus vivendi to work alongside one another rather than taking a path towards mutual destruction.

This modus vivendi as well as the forceful militancy of the working class in the immediate post-independence years created the conditions for the sustainability of the fundamental governance pillars, as well as ensuring alternance in the ruling parties to govern the country. It also ensured the maintenance of a professional independent civil service tasked with implementing law enforcement institutions, namely the police. This chapter will explain how, over the past few decades, these institutions have been eroded and weakened.

Post-independence creation of new institutions

Mauritius has never been a de jure or de facto one-party state, except for a short period from 1969 to 1976 when general elections which were scheduled to take place in 1972 were postponed sine die. However, the then ruling political party had to give in to pressure from social forces, namely the working class and the small-scale sugar cane planters who comprised part of the petty bourgeoisie.

It is important to understand that although the plantation bourgeoisie was the most powerful economic force and a critical driver of wealth creation for the country, it was not the only one and did not have an absolute monopoly. Mauritius had a very early agrarian reform forced by the impact of exogenous factors, namely international market conditions (Darga, 2011). The crash of sugar prices in the London market in the 1840s, and the need to finance increased milling efficiency in the 1870s, forced the sale of a certain number of plantations, albeit the marginal ones to be sold by the plantation bourgeoisie. These small parcels of land were bought by labourers from their savings, thereby creating a class of small-scale planters which at one time contributed up to 35 per cent of total sugar production. In a situation where the small-scale planters were producing the sugar cane but the plantation controlled the value chain for the production of sugar, the state had to create institutions that would mediate between the two interest groups and ensure a relatively fair distribution of gains.

The small-scale planter category of the quasi-petty bourgeoisie became another productive force contributing to economic development. Through the investment of their own labour in the small plantations that they purchased, the small-scale planters accumulated more capital, which was used on the one hand to build up human capital through the high level of education they financed for their children, and on the other hand was channelled into savings. Domestic savings have accounted for the bulk of domestic capital formation to a great extent, and stood at 18 per cent of gross domestic product at the time of independence (Moreno *et al.*, 2014.).

Another emerging economic force was the trading community. This group determined that they needed to invest the capital accumulated from trading into import substitution industries. They canvassed for support for their initiatives that would create jobs and expand the economy, and lobbied the government to establish the Development Bank of Mauritius to facilitate access to finance. The Development Bank became for 40 years a vital institution to fuel industrial development, provide access to finance for small and medium-sized enterprises, women entrepreneurs, small-scale farmers and livestock producers.

So has it been almost every ten years over the last fifty years with the convergence of the urge of existing private sector and emerging entrepreneurs to find new avenues to create more wealth, the need for government to see more job creation in consonance with changing profile of human resource. New economic pillars have been created and new enabling and regulatory institutions set up.

A very important factor that has driven the economic development and growth of the country has been the ongoing dialogue and partnership between the private sector and the government.[3] Although in the early days the nature of such a relationship was not an easy one, both parties resolved early on to maintain a dialogue for the sake of their own interests, to resolve contradictions and for the purpose of common endeavours. Over the years, the dialogue became institutionalized to membership on the boards of parastatals, key economic and social institutions. Mauritian delegations to negotiate bilateral, regional or multilateral economic agreements have always comprised representatives from both the state and the private sectors. Interestingly, empirical work by Rojid *et al.* (2010) investigated the role of an

effective State Business Relationship (SBR) in promoting economic performance in the case of Mauritius during the period 1975–2005. Results from
their analysis revealed that the SBR has had a positive and significant effect
on economic growth in the island in the long term. In fact, the impact
remained positive even after the inclusion of a measure of institutional quality
(degree of executive constraint), implying strong support that effective SBR
remains an important ingredient for economic growth in Mauritius. Moreover, an indirect effect of the SBR on national output levels via the investment
channel and trade openness was observed. Rojid *et al*. (ibid.) undertook a
survey among business associations as well as with 40 large companies in the
country. The findings validated the fact that the decisions made by these
associations were usually taken on a democratic and consensus basis and that
good SBR was essential to the progress of Mauritius.

Following the 2008 global financial crisis, which threatened closure for
enterprises as a result of the impact on the export markets, Mauritius was the
first country to introduce a Stimulus Package (Darga, 2011). The purpose of
this was not to salvage the country's banking sector, but to bring together the
banks, a state investment institution and enterprises in crisis to work out
rescue packages. No formal institution was set up. The Minister of Finance
simply put together an ad hoc team co-chaired by the public and private
sectors called the Mechanism for Transitional Support to Private Sector
(MTSP).[4] Through dialogue and gentle arm twisting, the MTSP managed to
persuade all parties to accept some streamlining and restructuring, thereby
saving thousands of jobs (see also Morisset *et al*., 2010).

The smooth articulation of labour/capital relations has also been critical in
sustaining development strategies. Since the 1930s the labour force has been
strongly organized and militant, and has staged fierce actions to obtain what
it considers a fair deal. This confrontational relationship continued up to the
mid-1970s, when both capital and labour were still seeking an equilibrium in
their relationship in the new context of industrial development. In a multi-
party democracy, the government had to find the proper articulation of such a
relationship, which would neither jeopardize its electoral base nor its development strategy (Darga, 1998, 2011). This was done by setting up appropriate labour relations and wage-setting institutions for the proper and
acceptable mediation of industrial relations. Local capital on the other hand
learned how to develop confidence-building relations with labour, while the
latter espoused the consensus of the need for development. Although the
trade unions have remained active, the economy has seldom been subjected to
work disruption since the mid-1980s.

Following independence, political competition became firmly entrenched and
institutions were established to manage and regulate electoral processes, thus
ensuring that ruling parties could not win by cheating even if some might at
times have sought to do just that, competition for winning votes came through
promises or actual state dispensation to a very broad spectrum of the electorate.
Thus, as early as the first post-independence national assembly elections, the

ruling party announced that free secondary education would be available to all children. Successive governments and electoral competition have witnessed the broadening and deepening of the most comprehensive welfare state in Africa. Benefits include 88 per cent home ownership, universal non-contributory pensions for all elderly people aged sixty years and above, free education up to tertiary level, free health care, and free bus fares for students and elderly people. In so doing, Mauritius also built its human resource and human development that further fuelled its capital accumulation capacity. Mauritius managed to become a middle-income economy by the early 2000s.

It is universally acknowledged that the country is caught in the middle-income trap and is struggling to extricate itself from it (*The Economist*, 2015). Not surprisingly, Afrobarometer Surveys[5] carried out in 2014 and 2017 showed a relative decline in the trust of the Mauritian population in many of the national institutions including a few pillar ones such as the judiciary, the National Assembly and the Mauritius Revenue Authority as well as some watchdog institutions. All stakeholders except the government of the day share the same view based on abundant empirical evidence that implementing and regulatory institutions have become weaker, thus failing in their capacity to make development strategic decisions become reality and creating a trust deficit in the strength of the regulatory ones. Over the past 15 years, a rise in cronyism, rent seeking and clientelism have weakened the institutions and this has further created space for such destructive practices. Thus, Mauritius is now caught in a vicious circle which although it has now pulled down the country, is impacting negatively and preventing it from further pulling itself up to a high-income country level the population is expecting it to.

Conclusion

Institutions will always be the nexus of contending social forces. Strong pillar institutions such as the legislature or the judiciary will, if they have been well grounded right from their inception, will stand the test of time in as much as they have the trust of the citizenry and are accepted as being fair, balanced and necessary for advancing the overall well-being of a nation (Rojid *et al.*, 2010). Mauritius has managed to retain such pillar institutions. Many others will, however, require reform over time so as to more adequately meet the challenges and aspirations of the time and also because of the unavoidable tension between social forces seeking to capture institutions for their interest. This chapter has attempted to delineate how Mauritius has addressed this challenge since independence, and how it must now address the challenge in the context of a stronger emerging middle class, greater youth aspirations and the imperative to foster its economic development in order to break free from the middle-income trap. The question is who will engineer the necessary reforms and the upgrading of the weakened institutions. The majority of Mauritians believe that a simple changing of the guard as to which of the established political forces will be the ruling one will not bring about the required institutional reforms since they all pursue the same modus operandi. The country will reboot its road to becoming a higher-income country only if the political equilibrium changes in a way that gives more power to those who want to push through the requisite reforms.

Notes

1 See Cole (1961).
2 This was originally known as the Chamber of Commerce. The institution became the Mauritius Chamber of Commerce and Industry in 1965.
3 The primary private institution for state-business relations in Mauritius is the Joint Economic Council (JEC, established in 1970, merged with the Mauritius Employers Federation and now named Business Mauritius). The JEC met with the prime minister on a regular basis and participated in budget proposals and policy advocacy. The JEC was funded entirely by its members, including the Mauritius Chamber of Commerce and Industry, the Mauritius Chamber of Agriculture, the Mauritius Employers' Federation, the Mauritius Sugar Producers' Association, the Mauritius Exports Association, the Mauritius Bankers' Association, the Mauritius Insurers' Association, the Association des Hôteliers et Restaurateurs de l'île Maurice, and the Association of Mauritian Manufacturers. The JEC's main goal was to ensure a stable macroeconomic environment, foster greater fiscal discipline, restore financial health, and integrate all sectors of the economy in order to reduce distortions and improve efficiency of investment. Since October 2015 Business Mauritius, which was created as result of a merger of two business associations, namely the Mauritius Employers Federation and the Joint Economic Council, has acted as the coordinating body and the voice of local business, regularly engaging with government officials and local authorities while also contributing to policy formulation and providing a role. See www.businessmauritius.org/.
4 The Mechanism for Transitional Support programme (MTSP), co-funded by the government, the commercial banks and the firms themselves, was set up as part of a broader stimulus package to help the manufacturing sector. The firms that were temporarily in distress and seeking additional financing, participated with equity of 20 per cent with commercial banks assisting with loans of 40 per cent, at concessionary interest rates, not exceeding the savings rate, while the remaining 40 per cent was contributed by the government. Interestingly, the committee set up to screen applicants for the MTSP was co-chaired by representatives from the public and private sectors.
5 www.afrobarometer.org/.

References

Acemoglu, D. and Robinson, J. (2010) 'The Role of Institutions in Growth and Development', *Review of Economics and Institutions* 1(2): 1–30.
Bheenick, R. and Shapiro, M. (1989) 'Mauritius: A Case Study of the Export Processing Zone', *EDI Development Policy Case Studies 1*, Washington, DC:World Bank.
Cole, M. (1961) *The Story of Fabian Socialism*, Stanford, CA: Stanford University Press.
Darga, L. A. (1998) 'Mauritius: Governance Challenges in Sustained Democracy in a Plural Society'. Available at http://unpan1.un.org/intradoc/groups/public/docum ents/cafrad/unpan008595.pdf.

Darga, L. A. (2011) 'The Mauritius Success Story: Why Is This Island Nation an African Political and Economic Success?', in Moeletsi Mbeki (ed.) *Advocates for Change: How to Overcome Africa's Challenges*, Johannesburg: Picador Africa.

Dinan, P. (1979) *Dix Ans d'Economie Mauricienne, 1968–1977*, Port Louis: Editions IPC.

Frankel, J. A. (2010) 'Mauritius: African Success Story', NBER Working Papers 16569, Cambridge, MA: National Bureau of Economic Research.

Greenaway, D. and Milner, C. (1989) 'Nominal and Effective Tariffs in a Small Industrializing Economy: The Case of Mauritius', *Applied Economics*, 21(8): 995–1009.

Gulhati, R. and Nallari, R. (1990) *Successful Stabilization and Recovery in Mauritius*, EDI Development Policy Case Series, Washington, DC: World Bank.

International Monetary Fund (IMF) (2008) 'Mauritius: Selected Issues', Mauritius Article IV Consultation Staff Report, Washington, DC: IMF.

Lall, S. and Wignaraja, G. (1998) *Mauritius: Dynamizing Export Competitiveness*, London:Commonwealth Secretariat.

Meade, J. E. *et al.* (1961) *The Economics and Social Structure of Mauritius: Report to the Government of Mauritius*, London: Methuen.

Moreno, R., Tandrayen-Ragoobur, V., Seetanah, B. and Sannassee, R. V. (2014) 'Demographic Transition and Savings Behaviour in Mauritius', in M. Arouri, S. Babouker andD. K.Nhuyen (eds) *Emerging Markets and the Global Economy: A Handbook*, Amsterdam: Elsevier.

Morisset, O., Bastos, R. and Rojid, S. (2010) 'Mauritius' Response to the Economic Crisis, World Bank note, Africa Region, Washington, DC: World Bank.

Ng Ping Cheun, E. (2018) *Fifty Economic Steps: The Economy of Mauritius from 1968 to 2017*, Port Louis:PluriConseil.

Rojid, S., Seetanah, B. and Shalini, R. (2010) 'Are State Business Relations Important to Economic Growth? Evidence from Mauritius', Discussion Paper 36, London: IPPG.

Subramanian, A. (2009) 'The Mauritian Success Story and Its Lessons', Research Paper No. 2009/36, Helsinki: UNU-WIDER.

Subramanian, A. and Roy, D. (2003) 'Who Can Explain the Mauritian Miracle: Meade, Romer, Sachs, or Rodrik?', in D. Rodrik (ed.) *In Search of Prosperity: Analytic Narratives on Economic Growth*, Princeton, NJ: Princeton University Press.

The Economist (2015) 'Stuck in a Middle-Income Trap', *The Economist*. Available at http://country.eiu.com/article.aspx?articleid=213440405&Country=Mauritius&topic=Economy&subtopic=Forecast&subsubtopic=Policy+trends.

4 The expansion of export-oriented enterprises and development in Mauritius

S. Fauzel, R. V. Sannassee and B. Seetanah

Introduction

Mauritius is regarded as one of the most successful economies in Africa with one of the highest levels of per capita gross domestic product (GDP) in the region. The main underlying reason for its success may be explained by the trade-led development which was supported by exports of textiles, sugar and tourism. From a tacitly monocrop economy, the island is now a well-diversified economy registering non-negligible growth rates. Furthermore, in recent years it has been able to attract massive inflows of foreign capital due to its skilled workforce, political and social stability, a good business environment and an adequate infrastructure. Moreover, the country has some undeniable location advantages as well as an efficient tax regime and various double taxation agreements with several countries. These, together with the ever increasing interest being shown by foreign investors from Europe and East Asia, offer an excellent opportunity for the government to market the country as a platform for reinvestment in the region (Sannassee *et al.*, 2014).

In order to diversify the economy, the Mauritian government has introduced various incentives to encourage both local and foreign investors to manufacture goods for the export market. The government's main objectives are to promote high rates of investment, create employment, diversify the economy, and boost economic growth and development in the country. While we can observe that the theoretical and empirical literature has focused on export-led growth, there are, however, only a few studies on the link between manufactured exports and more particularly between the export-oriented enterprises (EOEs) and economic development. Bearing this in mind and also given the importance of the EOEs to the Mauritian economy, the aim of this chapter is to investigate the interplay between the EOEs and economic development in Mauritius during the period 1987–2015.

The remaining parts of the chapter are structured as follows: section two provides some stylized facts on the expansion of EOEs in Mauritius. Section three discusses briefly the empirical literature and sections four and five present the methodology and the results obtained from the analysis undertaken on Mauritius. Finally, section six attempts to draw some conclusions.

Expansion of export-oriented enterprises in Mauritius

When Mauritius gained its independence in 1968, the economy was still heavily dependent on the sugar sector (which represented approximately 95 per cent of total exports) and it was very vulnerable to market and weather vagaries. This sector was the largest contributor to national output and also the largest employer. In 1967 sugar accounted for about one-third of the gross national product at factor cost. Thus, exports of sugar accounted for nearly 92 per cent of total export earnings (Yeung, 1998).

Mauritius was confronted by a number of economic problems in the 1960s. These included a high unemployment rate and a low growth rate. The Mauritian government felt the urge to act very rapidly after independence. Hence, the main action taken was the passing of legislation embodied in the Export Processing Zone (EPZ) Act No.51 of 1970, which led to the establishment of an EPZ. Generally, this chapter refers to EOEs[1] is used instead of EPZs.

In the 1970s the government of Mauritius introduced a number of incentives to encourage domestic and foreign investors to manufacture goods for the export market. Moreover, the co-existence of an import substitution strategy and an export-oriented strategy, as a two-pronged approach, met with considerable success over three decades of diversifying the economy, promoting an industrial culture, generating exports, creating employment and driving economic growth. The rapid build-up of the manufacturing sector in Mauritius was initially predominantly based on the manufacture and export of textiles to Europe, the United States, and the Eastern and Southern African countries where Mauritius enjoys free market access.[2]

The following incentives were introduced by the government of Mauritius in the 1970s:

1 no payment of import duties on productive machinery, equipment and spare parts;
2 complete exemption from payment of import and excise duties on raw materials and components except spirits, motor cars and petroleum products;
3 exemption from payment of income tax on dividends and profits for the first ten years of operation and favourable corporate tax rate;
4 availability of factory buildings and fully serviced land at reasonable or subsidised rates;
5 subsidised electricity or water rates;
6 favourable labour laws.

Additional incentives to encourage foreign investment included:

1 guarantees against nationalization;
2 free repatriation of capital (except capital appreciation), profits and dividends;

3   availability of permanent residence and work permits for foreign technicians and managers.(Yeung, 1998)

Another advantage for investors was the island's strategic location between Africa and Asia.

In terms of labour supply, Mauritius had an adequate labour force willing to work for low wages. Furthermore, it was observed that there was a significant number of female workers who were contributing to the success of the industries in the EPZ. Former housewives were being recruited on a large scale to work in the EPZ. Foreign workers, mainly from the People's Republic of China, were also employed in this sector.

Overall, the EOEs have been very successful in creating jobs, fostering export diversification and increasing the level of inward foreign direct investment in the country. In the late 1980s and 1990s the EOEs were the main source of employment, accounting for approximately one-third of total employment. (Vercillo, 2010). These development successes were a result of economic stabilization and various structural adjustment programmes that were initiated with the assistance of the World Bank and the International Monetary Fund. These programmes incorporated successive devaluations of the local currency and in 1983 the adoption of a flexible exchange rate. By 1986 the gross value of exports from the EOEs amounted to almost 55 per cent of total exports, while the traditional export commodities, sugar and molasses, were responsible for only 40 per cent of the total value (Rogerson, 1993). In the 1980s the clothing sector accounted for over half of exports from Mauritius, which was ranked as the third largest exporter of woollen goods in that decade (Ramtohul, 2008). Furthermore, in the 1990s the textile and clothing sectors employed 87 per cent of the EOE workforce.

The EOEs recorded high growth, overtaking sugar, which was the main export-earning sector, and ultimately employed more workers than the sugar industry. Remarkably, in 1986 Mauritius recorded its first trade surplus in 12 years.

The Africa Growth and Opportunity Act (AGOA) was approved by the US Congress in May 2000, and played a large part in the economic development of Mauritius. The purpose of this legislation was to assist the economies of sub-Saharan Africa and to improve economic relations between the United States and the region.

Between 200 and 2017 Mauritius exported around 40 per cent of its domestic exports annually to the United States . Additional support has been successfully achieved through the SADC Protocol with the dismantling of tariffs between Southern African Development Community (SADC) member countries and the Common Market for Eastern and Southern Africa (COMESA) free trade area.

Hence, we can argue that over the years, the manufacturing sector, including the EPZ/EOE industry, has played an important role in transforming the economy and in lifting Mauritius to the rank of a middle-income country. In

2015 the manufacturing sector accounted for approximately 16 per cent of GDP, and employment level was estimated to be about 112,000 (representing 20 per cent of the total workforce). Therefore, this sector can still be regarded as a major pillar that has helped Mauritius in its endeavour to achieve structural transformation. Furthermore, this sector has helped in spreading the use of technology and in sparking innovation throughout the economy and it has boosted overall productivity.

EPZ/EOE exports

Table 4.1 shows EPZ/EOE exports in Mauritius from 2000 to 2017. It can be observed that total exports increased by approximately 39.4 per cent during this period.

The new industrial paradigm

The new manufacturing framework which now comprises of high-technology manufacturing has been possible mainly due to design innovation, the availability of skilled labour and a friendly investment and regulatory climate. The new industrial paradigm comprises of a wide range of activities spanning from fashion, textiles and garments, and food processing to high-end jewellery and watches, electronic components and instrumentation, original equipment for the aerospace industry, telecommunications and medical devices and pharmaceuticals.

Table 4.1 EPZ/EOE exports in Mauritius from 2000 to 2017

	2000	2005	2010	2015	2016	2017
Total exports	30,961	28,954	41,622	48,687	44,422	43,145
Food and live animals	1,190	3,613	9,108	10,980	11,626	12,350
Crude materials, inedible, except fuels	83	96	297	176	302	143
Chemicals and related products	76	123	486	373	341	349
Manufactured goods classified chiefly by material	3,064	3,191	4,632	7,675	5,729	5,732
Machinery and transport equipment	149	200	264	507	280	222
Miscellaneous manufactured articles	26,390	21,710	26,749	28,633	25,691	23,610
Other sections	9	21	86	343	453	739

Source: Statistics Mauritius (2017).[3]
Note: All figures are in Rs million.

A brief review of the literature

Developing countries typically establish EPZs and free trade zones in order to boost economic development. This practice has been observed in nearly all of the Asian countries. Indeed, the expansion of the EPZs can confer many advantages on a country. These include employment creation, the inflow of foreign currencies, an expansion in national revenues as well as an increase in exports (Rondinelli, 1987). Other benefits include managerial and technological advantages resulting from foreign investors entering the economy in order to invest in these sectors.

However, as discussed by Rondinelli (1987), the expansion of EPZs is not entirely beneficial to the economy. For instance, there might also be some adverse effects associated with these industrial enclaves. These can be in terms of high construction and maintenance costs, employment of low-wage and unskilled female labour, offer an unstable employment base, generate little domestic added value, develop few labour or managerial skills, transfer little modern technology or know-how and have weak linkages to domestic manufacturers. Moreover, large EPZs may stimulate undesirable in-migration from rural areas, and result in greater dependence on foreign-owned firms that tend to relocate or cut back on production when wages, costs or international trends change. Referring to the literature and analysing case studies for specific countries, it is observed that the EPZs may be even more successful if they are implemented as part of an overall trade-oriented reform programme aimed at opening up the whole country rather than treating them as enclaves. This was the case for the Mauritian EPZ in the quest to pursue economic reforms. Export-oriented strategies are very important for developing countries because they are highly dependent on foreign countries for their inputs and the technology needed for their production (Kinunda-Rutashobya, 2003).

Referring to previous theoretical and empirical literature, most studies have concentrated on the relationship between export and economic growth while there are relatively few studies geared towards analysing the impact of manufactured exports on economic growth and development. For instance, we have observed that a large number of empirical studies have investigated the export-led growth hypothesis (see, for example, Kravis 1970 and Michaely 1977).

However, other studies analysing the causality effect between export growth and economic growth have recorded mixed results. For instance, a unidirectional causality from economic growth to exports in the case of Egypt was found by Dodaro (1993) and bidirectional causality in the case of Israel was uncovered. However, this study revealed a positive causality from exports to growth in seven out of a sample of 87 economies. Moreover, there was no evidence of causality between growth and exports in the cases of Algeria, Jordan, Morocco, Sudan or Tunisia.

Other studies, such as that by Nushiwat (2008), investigated the direction of causation between exports and economic growth by applying Granger's causality test to the time series data for six countries (Brazil, India, Indonesia,

South Korea, Mexico and Thailand) during the period 1981–2005 and found that the direction of causality was inferred only in the cases of India and Thailand. A more recent study by Ozturk and Acaravci (2010) analysed the relationship between export growth and economic growth in Turkey by employing quarterly data from 1989 to 2006 and used the Toda and Yamamoto procedure for testing for Granger non-causality in the augmented vector autoregression (VAR) methodology. The empirical results supported the export-led growth hypothesis for Turkey and the Granger causal flow was unidirectional flowing from real exports to real GDP.

In general, studies dealing with the export-led growth and development causality concerning manufactured exports or even those that deal specifically with EOEs are rather scant. Hence, this chapter focuses on the important question regarding whether exports by EOEs have led to economic development in Mauritius. In this study, instead of using output and focusing on economic growth, the human development index is used as a proxy for economic development. In fact, it is the arithmetic mean of the income index, the longevity index and the education index.

Methodology

For the purposes of this study, time series data were used for the period 1987–2015. This section explains the econometric model that was employed and defines the variables before going on to build a dynamic model to investigate the potential links among the variables of interest.

Economic development has mostly been measured merely by economic growth or economic performance. In fact, economists and researchers have been preoccupied with material production and thus the debate rests on whether economic growth is synonymous with economic development. When the concept of economic growth is examined, only the aspect of production is taken into consideration. Although economic growth is a necessary condition for economic development, it is not sufficient on its own. Other factors are needed to classify an economy as experiencing true economic development. Hence, with the introduction of the human development index (HDI) and the publication of the first *Human Development Report*, the economic development perspective underwent a fundamental change. In this case, development is not just about economic performance, but most importantly is about people and their well-being. This is explained by the fact that people are the ultimate objective of development. Economic growth is not an end in itself; it is a means to enhancing people's lives. Therefore, the benefits of growth must be translated into the lives of people (Jahan, 2002). With this in mind, this chapter uses the HDI as a proxy for economic development.

In order to construct the econometric model, reference was made to a number of earlier studies focusing on this issue, such as those by Gohou and Soumaré (2009) and Fauzel *et al.* (2015), using the HDI as a proxy for welfare. The model is specified below:

$$HDI = f(X, GOVTEX, UNEM, DEBT) \tag{1}$$

The variables utilized in the econometric model are defined as follows:

HDI: an indicator of development. The HDI is made up of three components, notably an income component, an educational component and a health/longevity component which is directly measured by life expectancy. A country's HDI is, therefore, the arithmetic mean of its three indexes: HDI = 1/3 (income index + longevity index + education index).

X: an indicator for the volume of exports by EOEs.

GOVTEX: represents government expenditure. Normally, the higher the government expenditure (investment by the government) in a country the more it will contribute to boosting economic development. Hence, a positive sign for this variable is expected.

UNEM: represents the percentage of people unemployed in the country. Unemployment is a major problem that will negatively influence development. It is seen as a social evil.

DEBT: the variable government debt is also included as another independent variable. For instance, the more indebted an economy is, more resources will be spent on the repayment of debts rather than investing in the economy and social programmes. Hence, it is expected that government debt will negatively influence development and welfare of the population.

Data for the model were extracted from Statistics Mauritius and United Nations Development Programme reports.

The econometric specification can be written as follows:

$$\ln HDI_t = \beta_0 + \beta_1 \ln X_t + \beta_2 \ln GOVTEX_t +$$

$$\beta_3 \ln UNEM_t + \beta_4 \ln DEBT_t + \mu_t \tag{2}$$

Here t denotes the time dimension and the variables are expressed logarithmically for ease of interpretation (i.e. in percentage terms).

Before proceeding with the estimation of the model, it is important to investigate the univariate properties of all the individual data series. The presence of unit roots is first tested, and once the order of integration has been determined, the possibility of a long-term relationship among the variables of interest is investigated.

Unit root tests

Indeed, applying regression to time series data may generate spurious results (Granger and Newbold, 1974; Phillips, 1986) given the possibility of non-stationary data. As such, undertaking a check as to the stationarity of data is a prerequisite for applying the cointegration test. As a result, the Augmented Dickey-Fuller (ADF) test (Dickey and Fuller, 1979) and the Phillips-Perron test (Phillips and Perron, 1988) were applied. The results show that the variables are stationary at first difference.

The Johansen cointegration test

The Johansen maximum likelihood approach was subsequently used to test the presence of cointegration in a vector error correction model (VECM) in both specifications. Trace statistics and maximal eigenvalue confirmed the presence of cointegration and we thus concluded that a long-term relationship exists in the above specification.

According to our analysis, a VAR model would be the most appropriate to test the presence of cointegration in a VECM. Hence, in this investigation a VAR approach was used to explain the relationship between EOEs and economic development. Such an approach does not impose a priori restrictions on the dynamic relations among the different variables. It resembles simultaneous equation modelling, whereby several endogenous variables are considered together.

Findings

Having recognized the presence of cointegration, and therefore a long-term equilibrium relationship among the variables, the next step was to specify and estimate a VECM including the error correction term to investigate the dynamic nature of the model. The VECM specification forces the long-term behaviour of the endogenous variables to converge on their cointegrated relationships, which accommodate short-term dynamics. In this study, the VECM was estimated using an optimum lag length of 1. Table 4.2 and Table 4.3 illustrate the results of the model.

Table 4.2 The short-term estimates

Error correction	D(LHDI)	D(LX)	D(LDEBT)	D(LGEX)	D(LUNEM)
CointEq1	−0.019248**	−0.493110	2.555439	−0.744395*	2.429828*
D(LHDI(−1))	0.893825	12.98376	−57.11592	5.851990	−8.167213
D(LX(−1))	0.002254**	0.141175	0.242694	−0.171307	−0.090065
D(LDEBT(−1))	−0.001000***	0.068298**	−0.108288	0.002310	0.009704*
D(LGEX(−1))	0.006837***	−0.014969	−0.955443	0.078957	−0.138584
D(LUNEM(−1))	0.000446	0.095926	−0.951600	0.053485	0.152767
C	0.000787***	−0.046923**	0.505865	−0.023820**	0.079703**
R-squared	0.99	0.37	0.24	0.38	0.74

Note: * significant at 10 per cent, ** significant at 5 per cent, *** significant at 1 per cent

Table 4.3 Pairwise Granger causality tests

Null hypothesis	F-Statistic	Probability
LX does not Granger cause LHDI	3.95334	0.0328
LHDI does not Granger cause LX	1.34508	0.2795

Note: * Indicates the significance at 10 per cent, ** the significance at 5 per cent and *** the significance at 1 per cent.

Empirical results

$$\ln HDI_t = 0.2621 + 0.082^{***}\ln X_t + 0.030^{**} \ln GOVTEX_t +$$

$$0.111 \ln UNEM_t - 0.483^* \ln DEBT_t \qquad (3)$$

The equation above displays the long-term results between development (the HDI), the main variable of interest X, (exports by EOEs), and the other control variables. Looking at the results, it is noted that the expansion of EOEs in Mauritius has been favourable to the country's development. Indeed, according to this study, a 10 per cent growth in EOEs has led to a 0.82 per cent increase in the economic development of Mauritius. Similar results were found by Nushiwat (2008) and Ozturk and Acaravci (2010).

It is true that successive governments have implemented various strategies to boost the export performance of the manufacturing sector in Mauritius. Since the 1970s the manufacturing sector has played a crucial role in changing the structural pattern of the economy. The economy has also benefited from this transformation in terms of an increase in GDP and a greater enrolment of female workers. Hence, along with an increase in income, the economy registered an increase in standards of living and a reduction in poverty levels.

Furthermore, the results show that government expenditure has positively contributed to the development of the country. For instance, a 10 per cent increase in government expenditure has led to a 0.30 per cent increase in development. This result can be explained by the fact that the Mauritian government spends massively on public and merit goods. Moreover, in order to ensure adequate access to free education, cost-free transport is provided for students up to tertiary level. The government also subsidizes the cost of examination fees at secondary level which may partly account for the upsurge in educational attainment in Mauritius. The government has invested heavily in the health sector. There are several public hospitals in the country as well as health centres that provide free health services. These facilities have helped to increase life expectancy in the country.

A closer examination of the results shows that the level of government debt has a negative impact on the country's level of development . Similar results were found by Pegkas (2018). This result is explained by the fact that a highly indebted country will have to spend more on servicing the debt. Such resources could have been used to invest in expanding the economy. Finally, while unemployment hampers development levels, the present study could not find any significant evidence of this relationship. This result is in contrast with Al-Habees *et al.* (2012).

The short-term results

Given the presence of cointegration, we subsequently estimated a VECM including the error correction term which should allow for an investigation into the dynamic nature of the model. The VECM specification forces the long-term behaviour of the endogenous variables to converge towards their cointegrated relationships, which accommodates short-term dynamics. In this study, the VECM was estimated using an optimum lag length of 1. The empirical results of the short-term estimates of the VECM are displayed in Table 4.2.

Table 4.2 is a composite table, whereby each column can be viewed and analysed as an independent function, i.e. each column in the table corresponds to an equation in the VECM. The variable named in the first cell of each column is viewed as the dependent variable. The estimated coefficient of the explanatory variables is reported in the cells. Our focus will be on the first column.

Analysing the short-term results and the regression equation with the HDI as the dependent variable, it may be argued that the expansion of the EOE sector is an important contributor to development, although the coefficient is relatively small compared to the long-term results. In addition, but similarly to the findings uncovered for the long-term equation, government spending is also positive and significant. Finally, the level of debt has a negative impact on development in the short-term.

Furthermore, and as discussed previously, the VAR/VECM framework allows us to gauge more interesting insights on endogeneity issues and also allows us to detect any potential indirect effects. While our results show that expansion of the EOEs improves economic development, the results reported in Table 4.2 do not show that the development level in the country has any impact on the EOEs. Thus, the results demonstrate that there is a unidirectional relationship between the EOEs and the country's development level. This is further confirmed by the Granger causality tests reported in Table 4.3.

From the above table, we can observe that there is a unidirectional causality flowing from exports by EOEs to economic development. This implies that while the EOE sector boosts development the reverse does not apply here. Similar results were found by Ozturk and Acaravci (2010).

Given the above, the overall results tend to support the existence of a positive and significant relationship between the EOE sector and development levels, both in the short and long term.

Conclusion

The study presented in this chapter provided an overview of the evolution of the Mauritian economy over time. Particular emphasis has been laid on the EOEs and the link to economic development. Moreover, an empirical investigation was undertaken to analyse the impact of exports by the EOEs on economic development in the country. Importantly, the HDI has been used as a proxy for economic development instead of GDP as this index is not limited to economic growth only, but rather takes into consideration other aspects necessary for development such as education and health. For the purpose of this study, a VECM framework was applied.

Results from the empirical investigation have shown that indeed EOEs have been a key determinant of development in Mauritius both in the short and long term. Other major findings were also reported, including the positive impact that government expenditure has on the developmental level of the economy while high levels of debt are perceived to hamper that development. Referring to the Granger causality test, a unidirectional relationship flowing from exports by the EOEs to development was observed.

The EOEs have significantly contributed to the transformation and development of the Mauritian economy. In the 1980s this sector took off, with most of the enterprises engaged in textile production. It should be noted that the Mauritian government has devised various policies which have helped to transform the structural base of the country. Appropriate policies were set up which ultimately helped in the diversification of the economy and resulting in the development of the EOEs in the country. Today, Mauritius has a relatively well-diversified economy which is believed to be conducive to growth. We can therefore conclude that the expansion of the EOEs has helped the country to diversify and prosper. This sector remains an instrumental ingredient for the future development of Mauritius.

In order to boost the sector yet further, Enterprise Mauritius is, in fact, operating a Speed to Market Scheme with a view to increasing exports and improving product delivery times. Meanwhile, the government has set up an Exchange Rate Support Scheme (ERSS) to support the export market through the provision of beneficial exchange rates for the EOEs.

Notes

1 EOEs are enterprises that previously operated with an EPZ certificate as well as those manufacturing goods for exports and holding a registration certificate issued by the Board of Investment.
2 www.investmauritius.com.
3 http://statsmauritius.govmu.org.

References

Al-Habees, M. A. and Rumman, M. A. (2012) 'The Relationship between Unemployment and Economic Growth in Jordan and Some Arab Countries', *World Applied Sciences Journal* 18(5): 673–680.

Dickey, D. A. and W. A. Fuller (1979) 'Distribution of the Estimation for Autoregressive Time Series with Unit Root', *Econometrica* 49(4): 1057–1072.

Dodaro, S. (1993) 'Exports and Growth: A Reconsideration of Causality', *Journal of Developing Areas* 27(2): 227–244.

Fauzel, S., Seetanah, B. and Sannassee, R. V. (2015) 'Foreign Direct Investment and Welfare Nexus in Sub-Saharan Africa', *Journal of Developing Areas* 49(4): 271–283.

Gohou, G. and Soumaré, I. (2009) 'Impact of FDI on Poverty Reduction in Africa: Are There Regional Differences', in *African Economic Conference*, paper presented at the African Economic Conference on Fostering Development in an Era of Financial and Economic Crises, 11–13 November, United Nations Conference Centre, Addis Ababa.

Granger, C. and Newbold, P. (1974) 'Spurious Regressions in Econometrics', *Journal of Econometrics* 2(2): 111–120.

Jahan, S. (2002) 'Measuring Living Standard and Poverty: Human Development Index as an Alternate Measure', *University of Massachusetts Political Economy Research Institute. Available at* www.peri.umass.edu/fileadmin/pdf/gls_conf/glw_jahan.pdf.

Kinunda-Rutashobya, L. (2003) 'Exploring the Potentialities of Export Processing Free Zones (EPZs) for Economic Development in Africa: Lessons from Mauritius', *Management Decision* 41(3): 226–232.

Kravis, I. B. (1970) 'Trade as a Handmaiden of Growth: Similarities between the Nineteenth and Twentieth Centuries', *Economic Journal* 80(320): 850–872.

Michaely, M. (1977) 'Exports and Growth: An Empirical Investigation', *Journal of Development Economics* 4(1): 49–53.

Nushiwat, M. (2008) 'Exports and Economic Growth: A Re-Examination of the Causality Relation in Six Countries, 1981–2005', *Applied Econometrics and International Development* 8(2).

Ozturk, I. and Acaravci, A. (2010) 'Testing the Export-Led Growth Hypothesis: Empirical Evidence from Turkey', *Journal of Developing Areas* 44(1): 245–254.

Pegkas, P. (2018) 'The Effect of Government Debt and Other Determinants on Economic Growth: The Greek Experience', *Economies* 6(1): 10.

Phillips, P. C. B. (1986) 'Understanding Spurious Regression in Econometrics', *Journal of Econometrics* 33(3): 311–340.

Phillips, P. C. and Perron, P. (1988) 'Testing for a Unit Root in Time Series Regression', *Biometrika* 75(2): 335–346.

Ramtohul, R. (2008) 'Trade Liberalization and the Feminization of Poverty: The Mauritian Scenario', *Agenda* 78: 55.

Rogerson, C. M. (1993) 'Export-Processing Industrialisation in Mauritius: The Lessons of Success', *Development Southern Africa* 10(May): 177.

Rondinelli, D. A. (1987) *Development Administration and US Foreign Aid Policy*, Boulder, CO: Lynne Rienner Publishers.

Sannassee, R. V., Seetanah, B. and Lamport, M. J. (2014) 'Export Diversification and Economic Growth: The Case of Mauritius', in M. Jansen, M. S.. Jallab and M.. Smeets (eds) *Connecting to Global Markets – Challenges and Opportunities: Case*

Studies Presented by WTO Chair-Holders, Geneva: World Trade Organization, pp. 11–23. Available at www.wto.org/english/res_e/booksp_e/cmark_full_e.pdf.

Vercillo, S. (2010) *EPZs and Lack of 'Decent Work': The Feminisation of Poverty within Mauritius*, Word Press.

Yeung, L. K. L. (1998) *The Economic Development of Mauritius since Independence*, Sydney: University of New South Wales, School of Economics.

5 Financial development and economic growth in Mauritius

J. Matadeen and S. Fauzel

Introduction

Mauritius is often regarded as an economy which has been able to develop at a fast rate compared to other countries in Africa. It has been able to transform itself from a low-income economy into an upper-middle-income economy. The government is actively devising policies to make the economy become a high-income economy by 2025. The main factors contributing to the success story of the island rest on strong institutions as well as a stable social and political environment resulting in the appropriate business environment for investment. Moreover, the country has made effective use of trade preferences with Europe and India which has contributed towards its strong economic development.

When the country gained its independence, the economy was completely dependent on the sugar sector. This small island agrarian economy was highly vulnerable. However, over time the economy started to diversify its activities into other sectors. More specifically, the economy was restructured to incorporate the export processing zone, thereby providing employment for former housewives. The economy further diversified into tourism, financial services and information and communication technology. The small island economy is now classified as successful and rapidly growing , with a rising standard of living, and a poverty rate of less than 1 per cent of the population.

The financial sector is a strong pillar of the Mauritian economy and is believed to have been an important ingredient in the country's economic growth. The contribution of financial and insurance activities to the gross domestic product (GDP) of Mauritius increased from 11.9 per cent in 2015 to 12 per cent in 2017, according to Statistics Mauritius (2017).[1] The country's domestic financial system is well developed. Moreover, the offshore sector is expanding. However, the country still needs to further diversify its financial sector particularly within the banking system. For instance, there is a need to strengthen the level of banking supervision, fostering the development of alternatives to bank lending in order to reduce portfolio concentrations, and increase competition. Moreover, sound international risk diversification needs to be encouraged. This can be done by strengthening provisioning levels so as to enhance the resilience of the system to a downturn in economic activity, and by reducing the government's implicit contingent liability in the banking system.[2]

This chapter examines the financial development and economic growth in Mauritius. Section 2 provides an overview of the country's financial development and economic growth followed by a review of literature on the topic in section 3. Section 4 presents an econometric estimation of the link between financial development and economic development in Mauritius from 1988 to 2016. Finally, the conclusions are presented in section 5.

Financial development in Mauritius

The financial sector comprises of both the banking and non-banking financial institutions and is an important pillar that has helped the Mauritian economy to prosper.

The banking sector's balance sheet has grown broadly in line with GDP, while banks' foreign assets have increased faster than domestic assets since 2014. There has been a massive increase in foreign assets held by subsidiaries of foreign-owned banks and by that of domestically owned banks. The growth in foreign assets held largely by domestically owned banks is explained by ventures with local banks in India and frontier markets in Africa with their associated growth in credit and market risk (Financial Stability Report, 2015).[3]

With regard to the domestic banking sector, it can be observed that there is a high degree of market concentration whereby the four largest banks hold 56.5 per cent of total banking assets. A Lorenz curve is used to depict the market concentration and it can be seen that there is a more unequal distribution of the bank's assets. However, smaller banks have been aggressively advertising their services to attract customers and this may eventually reduce the concentration ratio over time.

A number of non-banking financial institutions have been set up in the country. These are important in encouraging saving, stimulating investments and providing financial support to other productive economic sectors. As at 31 May 2016 there were eight Non-Bank Deposit Taking Institutions in Mauritius.[4] The Bank of Mauritius is the regulatory body for the banking sector, while the Financial Services Commission regulates the non-banking financial institutions.

The Stock Exchange of Mauritius (SEM) was established in 1989 as a private limited company before becoming a public company in 2008. The main objective of the SEM is the operation and promotion of an efficient and regulated securities market in Mauritius. Initially, the SEM operated within the Official Market with only five listed companies at that time and a market capitalization of nearly US $92 million in 1989. The size of the market has grown from a market capitalization-to-GDP ratio of less than 4 per cent in 1989 to a current market capitalization-to-GDP ratio exceeding 100 per cent in an economy that has witnessed annual average growth of 5 per cent over the past 25 years. Moreover, the SEM established a Central Depository System in 1997, operated by its subsidiary, the Central Depository & Settlement Co., in order to provide centralized depository, clearing and settlement services. In June 2001 the SEM also became the first exchange in Africa to move to a fully automated and electronic stock market infrastructure.[5]

The SEM is actually well positioned and is an attractive capital raising and listing platform for both local and international issuers. Furthermore, it is the only exchange in Africa and one of the few exchanges in the world to possess since 2011 a multi-currency listing and trading technology platform, which is also open for dual-currency trading and can list, trade and settle equity and debt products in US dollars, euros, pounds sterling, and the South African rand as well as the local currency, the Mauritius rupee. International investors have become key participants in the SEM's markets. Local investors account for about 55 per cent of all daily trading activities, and foreign investors account for the remaining 45 per cent. Some 75 per cent of that local volume is generated by institutions such as mutual funds, pension funds and insurance companies (see Stock Exchange of Mauritius).

Mauritius has also a relatively well-developed offshore sector. This has been possible mainly because of the following:

- an extensive network of Mauritian double tax treaties;
- cost-efficient administration;
- confidentiality;
- the authorities' commitment to maintaining the reputation of Mauritius as a very important international finance centre;
- Mauritius has been praised by the United States for setting a good example to other African countries;
- Mauritius is member of various regional blocs that favour free trade;
- excellent telecommunications facilities;
- good courier services;
- there is a wide range of international and local banks;
- the presence of large pool of professionals;
- flexible company law, securities and trust legislations;
- business friendly and healthy regulation by the Mauritius Financial Services Commission;
- good corporate governance code based on international norms;
- low and reasonable tax rates for corporate and individuals at 15 per cent;
- occupation and residence permits are granted to expatriates within three days, and business licences and permits normally within 15 days;
- Mauritius has a stock exchange known as the Stock Exchange of Mauritius. There are more than 30 domestic listed companies and more than 50 other companies trading on the Development and Enterprise market with modern norms of trading. The exchange is open to global business companies and funds seeking a primary or secondary listing;
- Mauritius is a member of the International Court of Justice and the International Centre for Settlements of Investment Disputes;
- Mauritius has concluded a number of Investment Promotion and Protection Agreements.

Source: www.premier.mu.

Financial development and economic growth

Between 1993 and 2016 GDP grew at an average annual rate of 4.46 per cent
in Mauritius (Figure 5.1) compared with an average annual rate of 4.21 per
cent in sub-Saharan Africa. Economic growth decreased sharply following the
financial crisis in 2008, and the economic recovery of the country has been
constantly threatened by the uncertain global economic climate. As such, the
growth rate over the past few years has fluctuated at a sluggish rate of 3.5 per
cent annually. On the other hand, financial intermediation continues to play a
key role in the development of the economy of the island. To capitalize on its
benefits, the government is tenaciously ensuring the development of the
financial hub in Mauritius, and continues to take new measures to attract
capital from all over the world. Indeed, financial development witnessed an
upward trend from 1993–2016 (Figure 5.1). Development in banking and the
stock market, as captured by the domestic credit to private sector and market
capitalization ratio, respectively, has been on the rise despite the numerous
challenges faced along the way.

According to Statistics Mauritius (2017), the contribution of financial
and insurance activities to GDP in Mauritius increased slightly from 11.9
per cent in 2015 to 12 per cent in 2017. Although this increase is small, it
is nonetheless reassuring as it suggests that insurance activities are still
able to trigger economic growth in the island, despite the recent challenges
faced by the financial sector (for example the revised Double Taxation
Avoidance Agreement between Mauritius and India, the expected decline
in tourist arrivals due to the United Kingdom's decision to leave the

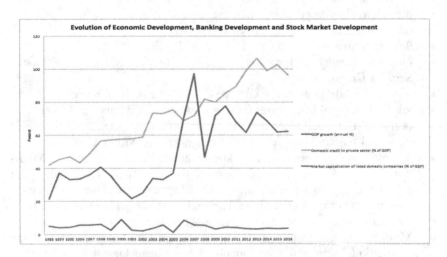

Figure 5.1 Evolution of economic development, banking development and stock
market development in Mauritius from 1993–2016
Source: World Development Indicators, World Bank (2017).

European Union (referred to as Brexit), the reduced demand for exports from the main markets of the country, the weaker pound in the UK, and a decrease in the number of tourist arrivals from France and the UK). Indeed, both the government and private operators are trying their best to counter the expected slowdown in demand for financial services in Mauritius. In fact, the 'financial and insurance activities' category is the third biggest driver of economic growth in the country (Figure 5.2). It tags closely behind the 'manufacturing' category and the 'wholesale and retail trade' category, which account for 13.4 per cent and 12.1 per cent of the island's GDP, respectively.

Figure 5.3 provides a breakdown of the contribution to GDP of each component of financial and insurance activities in Mauritius from 2015 to 2017. As can be seen, monetary intermediation is the main driver of financial and insurance activities in Mauritius. Indeed, in 2017 its contribution amounted to 7 per cent of GDP growth in the island, compared to only 6.7 per cent in 2015. The second biggest contributor was insurance, reinsurance and pensions, which accounted for 3.1 per cent of GDP growth in 2017. On the other hand, financial leasing and other credit granting activities made only a slight contribution to GDP, and have been stagnant at 0.7 per cent for the past three years.

Literature review

The importance of financial development on economic growth has long been recognized in the literature (Goldsmith, 1969; Shaw, 1973; McKinnon, 1973).

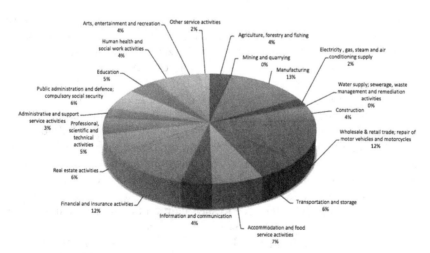

Figure 5.2 Contribution of different industry groups to GDP in 2017
Source: Statistics Mauritius (2017).

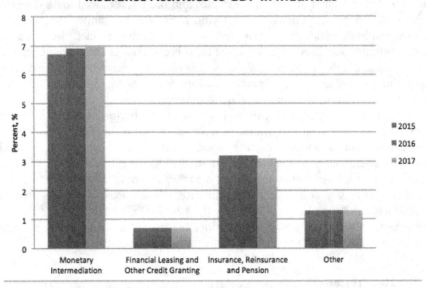

Figure 5.3 Contribution of the financial and insurance activities to GDP in Mauritius
Source: Statistics Mauritius (2017).

This can be attributed to the fact that financial development is able to reduce costs in areas such as information, transactions and monitoring costs, thereby enhancing economic development. Historically, research has focused solely on the role that the banking sector plays in economic growth (King and Levine, 1993a, 1993b; Demetriades and Hussein, 1996; Levine *et al.*, 2000; Rousseau and Sylla, 2003; Christopoulos and Tsionas, 2004). However, the focus has shifted recently on to the role that stock markets have to play on economic growth as well (Levine and Zervos, 1998; Rajan and Zingales, 1998; Rousseau and Wachtel, 2000; Beck and Levine, 2004; Ngare *et al.*, 2014). The existing theoretical literature highlights various channels through which stock market development has a positive impact on economic growth. Indeed, with enhanced liquidity, better risk diversification, improved savings mobilization, exceptional information aggregation and dissemination, and superior corporate control, stock market development can help to stimulate economic growth (Pagano, 1993; Levine 1997; Dow and Gorton, 1997; Levine, 2004). More recent studies have attempted to shed light on the simultaneous effect of banking development and stock market development on growth rather than their separate impacts (Shen and Lee, 2006; Naceur and Ghazouani, 2007; Hou and Cheng, 2010; Anyamele, 2010; Demirhan *et al.*, 2011; Pradhan *et al.*, 2014). On balance, despite some conflicting results among different countries, there is mostly strong evidence in favour of a positive relationship between financial development and economic growth.

As discussed earlier, financial services are one of the main pillars of the Mauritian economy. It is therefore important to investigate the empirical relationship that might exist between financial development and economic growth in the island in order to make the relevant policy decisions. Unfortunately, little analysis of the relationship between financial development and economic growth in Mauritius has been carried out, and, among the few studies that exist, most of them focus only on the banking component of the financial sector. Seetanah (2008) analysed the dynamic link between financial development and economic performance in Mauritius during the period 1952–2004 through the use of an autoregressive distributed lag framework. The study captured financial development through two proxies, namely the ratio of liquid liabilities to the country's GDP and the value of credit offered by financial intermediaries to the private sector divided by GDP. The results indicated that financial development does indeed promote economic growth in Mauritius both in the short and the long term. Meanwhile, Nowbutsing and Odit (2009) conducted a study on Mauritius that placed particular emphasis on the stock market component of the financial sector. The researchers used an error correction model to examine the impact that stock market development had on the economic growth of Mauritius during the period 1989–2006. Two different proxies were used to capture stock market development, namely stock market size (as measured by market capitalization over GDP) and stock market liquidity (as measured by volume of share traded over GDP). Their results indicated that stock market development has a positive effect on economic growth in Mauritius both in the short and the long term. On the other hand, Matadeen and Seetanah (2015) employed a dynamic vector error correction model (VECM) to scrutinize the impact of stock market and banking development on the economic growth of Mauritius during the period 1988–2011. Their results indicated that stock market development helps to promote economic growth in the island only in the long term rather than in the short term. Meanwhile, banking development was seen to have a positive impact on economic growth both in the short and the long term. Moreover, stock market development is also seen to indirectly stimulate economic growth through banking development, thereby suggesting that banking development and stock market development complement each other.

Furthermore, other studies have analysed the link between financial development and economic growth in a sample of countries which includes Mauritius. For instance, Ghirmay (2004) investigated the causal link between financial development and economic growth in 13 sub-Saharan African countries, including Mauritius, across a time span of 30 years. Interestingly, Ghirmay (ibid.) also detected the presence of a long-term causal effect of economic growth on financial development in Mauritius and eight other sub-Saharan African countries. In the same vein, Seetanah *et al.* (2009) tested the link between financial development and economic growth in a sample of 20 island economies, including Mauritius. They used both static and dynamic panel data techniques during the period 1980–2002. The study captured financial development through two proxies, namely the ratio of liquid liabilities to the country's GDP and the value of credit offered by financial intermediaries to the private sector divided by GDP. Their results show that financial development contributes positively to economic growth in the islands. Seetanah (2008) previously also validated a positive association in the financial development-growth relationship for the case of Mauritius using a dynamic time series approach. Adding to the literature, Ibrahim and Alagidede (2017) investigated whether the impact of finance on economic growth depended on the initial levels of countries' income per capita, human capital and financial development. Their results were captivating because they demonstrated that economic growth is sensitive to financial development beyond a certain threshold level of per capita income, human capital and finance.

Econometric estimation of the link between financial development and economic development in Mauritius

In order to investigate the link between stock market development and economic development in the island, the chapter uses annual time series data for the period 1988–2016 (data were extracted from the World Bank's World Development Indicators database).[6] This particular time span was chosen due to the fact that the stock market of Mauritius started its operations in 1989. Since this chapter focuses on the impact of financial development on the economic growth of the island, the basic specification of the model used in the chapter is adapted from previous similar studies such as Seetanah *et al.* (2009) and Matadeen and Seetanah (2015):

$$Y = f(\mathrm{SMD}, \mathrm{BD}, \mathrm{DI}, \mathrm{FDI}) \qquad (1)$$

For the purpose of this study, the dependent variable Y captures economic growth, which is measured by GDP. SMD denotes stock market development, which is captured through three different indicators (Levine and Zervos, 1998; Rajan and Zingales, 1998; Matadeen and Seetanah, 2015), namely market capitalization ratio (MCR), turnover ratio (TR) and total value traded share ratio (TVTSR). While MCR (value of listed shares in the stock exchange expressed as a percentage of GDP) captures the size of the stock market, TR (value of traded shares expressed as a percentage of total market capitalization) and TVTSR (value of shares traded expressed as a percentage of GDP) capture the liquidity of the stock market. On the other hand, to capture banking development (BD) in the country, the indicator domestic credit to private sector (DCTPS) is used in a similar manner to the studies of Levine and Zervos (1998) and Beck and Levine (2004). DCTPS is in fact the value of credit offered by financial intermediaries to the private sector expressed as a percentage of GDP. Following Naceur and Ghazouani (2007), two measures of investment are included as control variables, namely domestic investment (DI) and foreign direct investment (FDI). DI is captured through the country's gross fixed capital formation (GFCF) expressed as a percentage of GDP and FDI is measured by FDI divided by GDP.

The model in this study is a double logarithm linear one and takes the following form:

$$y_{it} = \beta_0 + \beta_1 smd_t + \beta_2 bd_t + \beta_3 di_t + \beta_4 fdi_t + \varepsilon_t \tag{2}$$

where t denotes the time dimension. Henceforth, any small letters denote the natural logarithm of the variables.

The study employs the dynamic vector autoregressive model (VAR). However, before proceeding with the estimation of the model to investigate the statistical relationship between financial development and economic growth, a few preliminary tests are essential. First, it is important to determine whether the time series under investigation is stationary. To do so, the study resorts to augmented Dickey-Fuller (ADF) unit root tests. The results of the ADF tests indicate that the unit root tests reject stationarity in favour of a unit root for all the variables. This implies that the variables are integrated of order 1, i.e. they are non-stationary in levels but achieve stationarity after being differenced once. Having determined that all the variables are integrated of order 1, it is crucial to determine if a long-term equilibrium relationship exists among the underlying variables. In other words, although non-stationary variables may deviate from each other in the short term, economic forces may act in response to the deviations from equilibrium, thus bringing back their association in the long term. The results of a Johansen cointegration test indicate the presence of a cointegrating relationship among the variables. Thus, having established the presence of a long-term relationship, the study opts for a VECM, and proceeds with its estimation.

The VECM is an econometric model which caters for the dynamic nature of the data under consideration. In addition to treating all the variables as endogenous and accommodating for the non-stationary features of the data in order to offer a convenient way to parameterize and specify any cointegration present, it also allows for the detection of any indirect effects which might be present among the variables. Interestingly, the VECM specification forces the long-term behaviour of the endogenous variables to converge to their cointegrated relationships, while simultaneously accommodating for the short-term dynamics as well. Moreover, given the possibility of endogeneity and causality issues, the VECM also proves to be particularly helpful in scrutinizing the link between stock market development and economic growth. The pth order VECM is specified as follows:

$$\Delta y_t = \Pi y_{t-1} + \Gamma_1 \Delta y_{t-1} + \ldots + \Gamma_{p-1} \Delta y_{t-p+1} + u_t \tag{3}$$

where y_t is a vector comprising five variables used in the model as defined above (GDP, SMD, BD, DI, FDI), and t denotes the time dimension, and u_t is a standard white noise process. Π is defined as the product of two matrices, α and β, mathematically represented as $\Pi = \alpha\beta$, where β corresponds to the cointegrating vectors (or long-term parameters) defining the equilibrium relation, while α gives the amount of each cointegrating vector known as the adjustment parameters which quantify the speed at which deviation from equilibrium is corrected.

Three different models are estimated for the purpose of this study, whereby each model considers a different proxy of stock market development:

$$\text{Model 1}: Y_{it} = \beta_0 + \beta_1 mcr_t + \beta_2 dctps_t + \beta_3 gfcf_t + \beta_4 fdi_t + \varepsilon_t$$

$$\text{Model 2}: Y_{it} = \beta_0 + \beta_1 tr_t + \beta_2 dctps_t + \beta_3 gfcf_t + \beta_4 fdi_t + \varepsilon_t$$

$$\text{Model 3}: Y_{it} = \beta_0 + \beta_1 tvtsr_t + \beta_2 dctps_t + \beta_3 gfcf_t + \beta_4 fdi_t + \varepsilon_t$$

The long-term results of the VECM are reported in Table 5.1.

Interestingly, the results indicate that in the long term, all the variables except GFCF appear to play a significant role in promoting economic growth in Mauritius. Of importance to this chapter, it can clearly be seen that financial development, as captured by both stock market development and banking development, is crucial for stimulating growth in the island. Indeed, all the three proxies of stock market development (MCR, TR and TVTSR) have a

Table 5.1 The long-term results of the VECM[7]

Variables	Model 1		Model 2		Model 3	
	Coefficients	T statistic	Coefficients	T statistic	Coefficients	T statistic
GDP	1		1		1	
MCR	0.508632***	[7.19195]				
TR			3.827151***	[6.14973]		
TVTSR					0.77842***	[7.59352]
DCTPS	2.590212***	[7.59675]	0.92549**	[2.23850]	0.49554*	[1.71642]
GFCF	0.192955	[1.44114]	−0.89758	[−0.58170]	1.393239	[1.63827]
FDI	0.081239***	[3.17139]	0.28298*	[1.86506]	0.069812*	[1.73484]
C	−17.68509		−24.9121		−25.7169	

Note: *, **, *** indicate that the coefficients are significant at 10 per cent, 5 per cent and 1 per cent, respectively.

positive and significant impact on economic growth. Model 1 shows that stock market capitalization triggers a 0.51 per cent increase in economic growth, while model 2 and model 3 show that the TR ratio and the TVTSR ratio trigger a 3.8 per cent and a 0.8 per cent rise in economic growth, respectively. This positive impact is in keeping with previous studies such as those by Levine and Zervos (1998), Nowbutsing and Odit (2009), and Matadeen and Seetanah (2015). As for banking development, it is also seen to have a significantly beneficial impact on the economic development of the country as indicated by the positive and significant coefficients of DCTPS in each model. The result is in keeping with studies by Seetanah *et al.* (2009) and Hou and Cheng (2010). On the other hand, of the two proxies of investment, only FDI gives a positive and significant boost to the Mauritian economy.

The study emphasizes the importance of a well-developed financial system in the island for the stimulation of a much needed boost in economic growth. However, it is worth noting that despite all the ongoing efforts to transform Mauritius into an international financial centre in Africa, the country still faces several challenges. Indeed, Mauritius must begin implementing international standards and regulations, and adjust to new regulations such as the Foreign Account Tax Compliance Act which requires foreign financial institutions and non-financial foreign entities to report on the foreign assets held by US account holders or be subject to withholding on withholdable payments; the Multilateral Base Erosion and Profit Shifting Convention which affects 23 tax treaties and prevents multinational corporations from engaging in base erosion and profit shifting strategies; the Common Reporting Standard which forces financial institutions to report annually to the Mauritius Revenue Authority on financial accounts held by non-residents who seek to deal with Mauritian treaty partners; the endorsement of the recommendations of the Financial Action Task Force of the Eastern and Southern African Anti Money Laundering Group to combat money laundering and terrorist financing, and it must adjust to changes such as the Double Taxation Treaty with India. As such, Mauritius will constantly have to innovate and remodel in order to overcome the ever changing constraints and challenges inherent within the financial sector. Moreover, the skills required by the financial services sector of Mauritius must be upgraded and Mauritius must try to move up the value chain and develop new products and services that will attract new financial players.

Conclusion

Through the above analysis, it can be concluded that Mauritius has a well-established and well-developed financial sector. The financial sector is a strong pillar of the economy and has helped the country to achieve both economic and social development. Moreover, it has a strong banking regulator, the Bank of Mauritius. While financial development is crucial for economic growth, certain weaknesses have been identified, however. For instance, the dominant role of a number of financial institutions in the banking sector can undermine competition and innovation. Moreover, too many small-scale players in the sector may become a source of systemic risk. Also, an inadequate supply of skilled manpower with international experience may explain the lack of innovation in the provision of financial services (Global finance, Mauritius).

An econometric investigation into the link between financial development shows that both banking development and stock market development are crucial for stimulating growth in the island. Indeed, all three proxies of stock market development (MCR, TR and TVRSR) have positive and significant coefficients. Interestingly, it is also seen that the impact of banking development on GDP is higher than that of market capitalization but lower than that of the two liquidity proxies of stock market development.

In terms of policies, Mauritius need to further develop its policies in order to strengthen banking supervision. It needs to encourage the development of alternatives to bank lending to reduce portfolio concentrations and increase competition. Furthermore, the country should promote international risk diversification in order to protect it from adverse economic conditions. The fact that both stock market development and banking development have promoted economic development in the long term hints that banks and equity are complementary financing tools, each playing a different role in the economy of the island. As such, the Mauritian finance sector should not focus on just one of them, but rather should take action to continue to promote both of these sectors. The SEM is one of the leading and most developed exchanges in Africa. Nevertheless, it is crucial to continue this development strategy to ensure that the exchange continues to encourage private led and sustainable growth in the island. With regard to the banking sector in Mauritius, the focus should now be directed towards further promoting the development of investment banks. Investment banks will be able to provide strong financial analysis and underwriting services, facilitate mergers and other corporate reorganizations, and even act as brokers or financial advisers to institutional investors. Such developments in the banking sector are more likely to be able to complement stock market development, which will eventually stimulate economic growth.

Notes

1 http://statsmauritius.govmu.org/English/StatsbySubj/Pages/default.aspx.
2 https://openknowledge.worldbank.org/handle/10986/14340.
3 www.bom.mu/publications-and-statistics/publications/financial-stability-report.
4 See Bank of Mauritius. Available at www.bom.mu/sites/default/files/pdf/Research_and_Publications/Monthly_Statistical_Bulletin/May16/list_of_financial_institutions_may_2016.pdf.
5 See Stock Exchange of Mauritius. Available at www.stockexchangeofmauritius.com/sem-at-a-glance.
6 https://databank.worldbank.org/source/world-development-indicators.
7 The short-term results have not been reported but are available upon request.

References

Anyamele, O. D. (2010) 'The Role of Stock Market in Sub-Saharan African Economies', *International Journal of Business, Accounting, & Finance* 4(2): 129–143.

Beck, T. and Levine, R. (2004) 'Stock Markets, Banks, and Growth: Panel Evidence', *Journal of Banking & Finance* 28(3): 423–442.

Christopoulos, D. K. and Tsionas, E. G. (2004) 'Financial Development and Economic Growth: Evidence from Panel Unit Root and Cointegration Tests', *Journal of Development Economics* 73: 55–74.

Demetriades, O. and Hussein, A. (1996) 'Does Financial Development Cause Economic Growth? Time Series Evidence from 16 Countries', *Journal of Development Economics* 51: 387–411.

Demirhan, E., Aydemir, O. and Inkaya, A. (2011) 'The Direction of Causality between Financial Development and Economic Growth: Evidence from Turkey', *International Journal of Management* 28(1): 3.

Dow, J. and Gorton, G. (1997) 'Stock Market Efficiency and Economic Efficiency: Is there a Connection?' *Journal of Finance* 52: 1087–1129.

Ghirmay, T. (2004) 'Financial Development and Economic Growth in Sub-Saharan African Countries: Evidence from Time Series Analysis', *African Development Review* 16(3): 415–432.

Goldsmith, R. (1969) *Financial Structure and Development*, New Haven, CT: Yale University Press.

Hou, H. and Cheng, S. Y. (2010) 'The Roles of Stock Market in the Finance-Growth Nexus: Time Series Cointegration and Causality Evidence from Taiwan', *Applied Financial Economics* 20(12): 975–981.

Ibrahim, M. and Alagidede, P. (2017) 'Nonlinearities in Financial Development–Economic Growth Nexus: Evidence from Sub-Saharan Africa', *Research in International Business and Finance.*

King, G. and Levine, R. (1993a) 'Finance, Entrepreneurship, and Growth: Theory and Evidence', *Journal of Monetary Economics* 32: 513–542

King, G. and Levine, R. (1993b) 'Finance and Growth: Schumpeter Might Be Right', *Quarterly Journal of Economics* 108: 717–738.

Levine, R. and Zervos, S. (1998) 'Stock Markets, Banks and Economic Growth', *American Economic Review* 88: 539–558.

Levine, R. (1997) 'Financial Development and Economic Growth: Views and Agenda', *Journal of Economic Literature, American Economic Association* 35(2): 688–726.

Levine, R. (2004) 'Finance and Growth: Theory and Evidence', in Philippe Aghion and Steven Durlauf (eds) *Handbook of Economic Growth*, 1st edn, vol. 1, Amsterdam: Elsevier, pp. 865–934.

Levine, R., Loayza, N. and Beck, T. (2000) 'Financial Intermediation and Growth: Causality and Causes', *Journal of Monetary Economics* 46: 31–77.

McKinnon, R. (1973) *Money and Capital in Economic Development*, Washington, DC: Brookings Institution.

Matadeen, J. and Seetanah, B. (2015) 'Stock Market Development and Economic Growth: Evidence from Mauritius', *Journal of Developing Areas* 49(6): 25–36.

Naceur, S. B. and Ghazouani, S. (2007) 'Stock Markets, Banks, and Economic Growth: Empirical Evidence from the MENA Region', *Research in International Business and Finance* 21(2): 297–315.

Ngare, E., Nyamongo, E. M. and Misati, R. N. (2014) 'Stock Market Development and Economic Growth in Africa', *Journal of Economics and Business* 74: 24–39.

Nowbutsing, B. M. and Odit, M. P. (2009) 'Stock Market Development and Economic Growth: The Case of Mauritius', *International Business & Economics Research Journal* 8(2): 77–88.

Pagano, M. (1993) 'Financial Markets and Growth: An Overview', *European Economic Review* 37(2–3): 613–622.

Pradhan, R. P., Arvin, M. B., Hall, J. H. and Bahmani, S. (2014) Causal Nexus between Economic Growth, Banking Sector Development, Stock Market Development, and other Macroeconomic Variables: The Case of ASEAN Countries', *Review of Financial Economics* 23(4): 155–173.

Rajan, R. and Zingales, L. (1998) 'Financial Development and Growth', *American Economic Review.*

Rousseau, L. and Wachtel, P. (2000) 'Equity Market and Growth: Cross-Country Evidence on Timing and Outcomes, 1980–1995', *Journal of Banking and Finance* 24: 1933–1957.

Rousseau, P. L. and Sylla, R. (2003) 'Financial Systems, Economic Growth, and Globalization', in *Globalization in Historical Perspective*, Chicago, IL: University of Chicago Press, pp. 373–416.

Seetanah, B. (2008) 'Financial Development and Economic Growth: An ARDL Approach for the Case of the Small Island State of Mauritius', *Applied Economics Letters*, 15(10): 809–813.

Seetanah, B., Ramessur, S. T. and Rojid, S. (2009) 'Financial Development and Economic Growth: New Evidence from a Sample of Island Economies', *Journal of Economic Studies* 36(2): 124–134.

Shaw, E. (1973) *Financial Deepening in Economic Development*, New York: Oxford University Press.

Shen, C. and Lee, C. (2006) 'Same Financial Development, yet Different Economic Growth – Why?', *Journal of Money, Credit & Banking* 38(7): 1907–1944.

Online references

Bank of Mauritius. Available at www.bom.mu/sites/default/files/fsr-feb-2015-full_0.pdf.

Premier Financial Services. Available at www.premier.mu/MRUoffshore/mruoffshore.php.

Statistics Mauritius. Available at http://statsmauritius.govmu.org/English/StatsbySubj/Pages/default.aspx.

Stock Exchange of Mauritius. Available at www.stockexchangeofmauritius.com/sem-at-a-glance.

World Development Indicators, World Bank. Available at https://databank.worldbank.org/source/world-development-indicators.

6 Impact of the tourism sector on economic growth in Mauritius

P. Dinan, B. Seetanah and K. D. Padachi

Introduction

Travel and tourism are two of the world's largest economic sectors, creating jobs, driving exports, generating revenue for governments and bringing prosperity around the world (Lea, 1988; Sinclair, 1998; Song and Liu, 2017). According to the World Travel and Tourism Council (2018), the economic impact of the travel and tourism sector was expected to account for 10.4 per cent of global gross domestic product (GDP) and over 300 million jobs, or almost 10 per cent of total employment in 2017. In fact, the so-called tourism-led growth hypothesis postulates that international tourism is considered to be a potential strategic ingredient for economic growth (see Sinclair and Stabler, 2002). Moreover, spending by tourists (which can be regarded as an alternative form of exports) contributes to a country's balance of payments through foreign exchange earnings and proceeds generated from the expansion of tourism, representing a sizeable source of income for a recipient economy (Balaguer and Cantavella-Jordá, 2002). Earnings from tourism are believed to be used subsequently to finance imported capital goods in order to produce goods and services, thus leading to economic growth (McKinnon, 1964). Other economic benefits that can be derived from tourism-related activities include tax revenue, job creation (the industry is labour intensive) and foreign direct investment (Archer, 1995; Durbarry, 2002; Uysal and Gitelson, 1994). Indeed, theoretical analysis tends to confirm that tourism expansion should make a positive contribution to economic growth (Balaguer and Cantavella-Jordá, 2002; Dritsakis, 2004; Kim *et al.*, 2006; Noriko and Motosugu, 2007 and more recently Tang and Tan, 2015 and Paramati *et al.*, 2017). At the regional level, Proença and Soukiazis (2005) examined the impact of tourism while Shan and Wilson (2001) studied the causality between tourism and trade and confirmed positive relationships. However, it is also noteworthy that a number of empirical studies were unable to establish a link between tourism development and economic growth (see Chen and Devereux, 1999; Oh, 2005, Lee, 2006, Singh *et al.*, 2010; Palamalai and Kalaivani, 2016) while others even reported that tourism can have a negative impact on economic growth (see Capo *et al.*, 2007; Grullon, 2013; Mishra *et al.*, 2016).

Like many other small island economies, Mauritius is no exception in having a heavy dependence on the tourism industry. Indeed, the tourism sector in Mauritius is believed to have played an instrumental role in its economic development and remains one of the main pillars of the economy. The development of this industry was part of the diversification strategy which Mauritius adopted in the 1960s in order to halt its reliance on the monocrop cane sugar economy. The sector has registered decent progress. The direct contribution of the tourism sector to GDP stood at around 7.5 per cent of total GDP in 2017 and was forecast to rise by 4.6 per cent annually during the period 2018–2028; it reached a contribution of more than 8 per cent in 2018 (WTTC, 2018). The total contribution of the sector was estimated to be around 24 per cent of GDP in 2017 and was expected to reach over 26 per cent in the next ten years. It is noteworthy that the sector has directly supported 41,500 jobs, representing around 7.2 per cent of total employment (this was predicted to rise to 8.5 per cent by 2028) and contributed approximately 36 per cent of total exports in 2017 (ibid.).

The aim of this chapter is two-fold. First, it presents the historical facts and figures relative to the development of tourism in Mauritius and second, using past empirical evidence, it examines the impact that the development of tourism has had on the Mauritian economy.

The rest of the chapter is organized as follows. Section two shows how the tourism sector has evolved in Mauritius and looks at the contribution that the sector has made to Mauritius' economic progress. In section three, we consider some of the available empirical evidence relating to the tourism-growth nexus, and make particular reference to a number of studies that specifically relate to Mauritius. The final section summarizes the results and attempts to draw some conclusions.

The evolution of the Mauritian tourism sector

The early days

The early days refer to a period extending from the 1950s to the 1970s. In 1952 a large residential villa was converted into a domestic hotel, named the Park Hotel, particularly for providing overnight accommodation and catering services to aircrews. This was followed in 1961 by the opening of a 15-room hotel close to the airport. It is interesting to observe that the hotel industry first developed in response to the requirements of civil aviation which was also in its infancy.

The first modern hotels were constructed in the late 1960s; two on the south-west coast, one on the north-west coast, and one in Rodrigues Island, a dependency of Mauritius. The process of tourism development and hotel building was supported jointly by the government and the private sector. It is of significance that the Prime Minister, Sir Seewoosagur Ramgoolam, gave his full support to the pioneering efforts of a visionary businessman, Amédée Maingard, who was closely involved in the launch of Air Mauritius, the national airline, and in the country's nascent hotel industry.

A Development Plan to expand the tourism sector was subsequently drawn up in 1971 in close collaboration with the private sector. The 1971–1975 Plan recognized the critical role of the private sector in the development of the industry while highlighting the contribution of the public sector in the provision of basic infrastructural services and marketing of the destination (Government of Mauritius, 1971). The Plan formulated policy guidelines aimed at facilitating the development of the industry and also at ensuring that the benefits accrued to the economy as a whole.

In fact, the development of the tourism industry was part of the diversification strategy which Mauritius adopted in the 1960s in order to halt the country's reliance on the monocrop cane sugar economy. Fiscal incentives were devised, with the result that initially investment in hotels was sourced mainly from local capitalists.

Facts and figures

Table 6.1 and Table 6.2 outline the progress made by the tourism industry in Mauritius.

Table 6.1 Gathering speed

	1977	1985	1989	Average growth rate p.a. (%)
Number of hotels	37	55	67	5.0
Number of rooms	1,881	2,630	3,605	5.6
Number of beds	3,688	5,387	7,374	5.9
Average number of beds per hotel	100	98	110	0.8
Number of tourists (000)	92.6	148.9	263.4	10.1

Table 6.2 Scaling up

	1995	2005	2010	2016	Average growth p.a. (%)
Number of hotels	95	99	102	114	0.8
Number of rooms	5,977	10,497	11,456	13,547	4.5
Number of bed places	12,359	21,072	24,698	29,139	4.5
Average number of bed places per hotel	130	213	242	258	3.4
Number of tourists (000)	422.5	761.1	934.8	1,275.2	5.5

How has the process matured?

As the diversification strategy was strengthened and deepened over the years, Mauritius placed particular emphasis on the service sector, with tourism leading the way, but also included global financial business and information and communication technology (ICT). In that favourable environment, local and foreign investment in larger hotels was boosted, particularly as there was a deliberate marketing strategy targeting middle- and upper-income tourists.

This is how Mauritius rapidly developed to the point that it now ranks in 49th position in the world in terms of competitiveness (World Economic Forum, 2018).

Tourism and the transformation of the economy

Although the first steps towards establishing a hotel industry in Mauritius date back to the 1950s and 1960s, as already observed, the strategy aiming at the diversification of the economy away from cane sugar initially paid little attention to tourism. During the 1960s and 1970s the emphasis was on import substitution coupled with export promotion, mainly through the establishment of light manufacturing enterprises in the export processing zone (EPZ), and thanks to the duty-free entry of foreign raw materials for transformation by relatively cheap labour.

However, the diversification strategy was radically modified in the 1980s, when it was realised that import substitution and export promotion were mutually exclusive. A choice had to be made, and export promotion became the hallmark of the diversification strategy. This meant promoting not only the EPZ, but also the tourism industry for the export of services. During this period the EPZ was thrust into the limelight, while the tourism industry lagged behind in its wake.

In other words, tourism is one of the main agents responsible for the transformation of the Mauritian economy, but it is not the only one. This does not, however, belittle its contribution to economic growth in the island. The following factors testify to that contribution:

1   In the 1970s the industry recorded gross earnings of just US $6 million; in 2018, it was estimated that earnings would amount to some $1,800 million. Such figures epitomize the continuous growth of the tourism sector over a span of 50 years.
2   There were only approximately 1,500 jobs in the sector in 1970; in 2017 direct employment stood at 31,000 jobs, i.e. about 5.3 per cent of total employment in Mauritius. In that year, hotels accounted for 78 per cent of employment in the tourism industry, restaurants 10 per cent and travel and tourism 12 per cent. Given the nature of the tourism industry with its collateral effects on other sectors, it is interesting to note that taken together direct and indirect employment in 2017 totalled 131,000 jobs, i.e. about 22.6 per cent of total employment.

3   Tourism accounted for 1.4 per cent of GDP in 1970; the comparative
     figure for 2017 was 8.5 per cent and the estimate for 2018 was 8.3 per
     cent. It is noteworthy that, during that 50-year span, the GDP of Maur-
     itius had been multiplied 66 times over, up from US $180 million in 1970
     to an estimated $14,000 million in 2018.
4   In effect, the tourism industry leads the pack in respect of contribu-
     tion to GDP. Comparative ratios for 2018 were 5.8 per cent for
     global business, 5.6 per cent for ICT, and 4.8 per cent for the EPZ.
     This was not the case in the 1980s when the EPZ manufacturing
     sector lead the way. The rising contribution of the tourism sector
     reflects its capacity to be sustainable over time, though one would be
     wrong to assume that this can go on forever, without proper safe-
     guards for the natural and institutional environments. This point is
     further developed later.
5   Earnings from tourism have also been beneficial to the current account
     balance of Mauritius.Source: Statistics Mauritius (2017)

From the above figures, there are indications that, had the annual earnings
from tourism been absent, the year-in year-out deficit on the current account
of the balance of payments of Mauritius would have been larger still.

Qualitative effects

The tourism industry is contributing to the economy of Mauritius not only
quantitatively but also qualitatively from the point of view of infrastructure.
The majority of the 111-plus hotels are at a world-class level, and as most of
them are located by the seaside, the sites they occupy are well looked after
and the beaches well preserved.

Given the need to welcome some 1.2 million tourists per year, since 2013
Mauritius has boasted a modern airport, and there are plans for its modernization and for increasing its capacity. Moreover, modern shopping malls are
being developed in various parts of the island.

It is also observed that the classic tourist model has evolved in Mauritius,
giving rise to the Integrated Resort Scheme (IRS), whereby foreign visitors
can extend the duration of their visit by renting residential buildings which

Table 6.3 Current account balance

Year	Balance of visible trade	Tourist earnings	Balance on current account
2000	−14,046	14,234	−899
2005	−30,063	25,704	−9,570
2010	−65,332	33,457	−25,371
2016	−43,698	58,000	−18,293

Source: Statistics Mauritius (2017).

are fully serviced. Furthermore, hotel rooms provide suitable accommodation for business visitors, particularly cross-border investors.

Clearly the existence of a well-developed tourist industry in Mauritius enhances the image of the country abroad and, in the process, enhances investor confidence for the benefit of the cross-border financial services industry. In that sense, one can consider that tourism is a driver of growth for the economy of Mauritius as a whole.

Contribution to the fight against poverty

Economic success is never an end in itself. It is assessed by its contribution to the fight against inequality in a given country. Since tourism has, as shown above, contributed significantly to the transformation of the local economy for the better, it is appropriate and important to assess to what extent it has, if at all, improved the social landscape. The first indicator shows a negative evolution, with the Gini coefficient (a standard indicator of national income distribution) at 0.400 in 2016, having gradually deteriorated from 0.379 in 1991–1992. The gradual spread of inequality in Mauritius cannot be ascribed to the tourism industry alone, but it is likely that it has contributed to the process.

As shown in Table 6.4, the percentage of persons living in relative poverty has increased from 8.2 per cent in 1996/1997 to 10.3 per cent in 2017.

Relative property is defined as half of the median household income per adult equivalent. However, when poverty indicators are worked out in comparison with a fixed historical threshold, namely the 1996/1997 poverty line, it is observed that the percentage of poor persons declined from 8.2 per cent in 1996/1997 to 5.3 per cent in 2012.

A similar exercise was carried out by Statistics Mauritius in order to compare the number of poor persons between the last two Household Budget Surveys, which were carried out in 2012 and 2017, respectively. Using the 2012 figures as a threshold poverty line instead of the previous one (1996/1997), the results were

Table 6.4 Relative poverty in Mauritius

	1996/1997	2001/2002	2006/2007	2012	2017
Relative poverty line (rupees)	2,004	2,804	3,821	5,652	7,497
Households in relative poverty					
Number	23,800	23,700	26,100	33,600	36,100
Proportion (%)	8.7	7.7	7.9	9.4	9.4
Persons living in relative poverty					
Number	92,700	93,800	105,200	122,700	140,500
Proportion (%)	8.2	7.8	8.5	9.8	10.3

Table 6.5 Number of poor people in Mauritius

	1996/1997	2001/2002	2006/2007	2012
Relative poverty line (rupees)	2,004	2,665	3,572	4,750
Number of households	23,800	19,600	20,700	18,000
Proportion of all households (%)	8.7	6.4	6.2	5.0
Estimated number of poor persons	92,700	76,500	83,100	67,000
Percentage of poor persons	8.2	6.4	6.7	5.3

as follows: between 2012 and 2017 the relative poverty line increased from Rs 5,652 to Rs 6,404, but the number of households below that line decreased from 33,600 to 20,900, equivalent to 9.4 per cent and 5.5 per cent of the respective number of total households. Consequently, the estimated number of poor persons dropped from 122,700 (9.8 per cent) to 79,300 (6.3 per cent).

As can be observed, the indicators relative to the reduction of income inequality constitute a mixed bag. Inequality is widening, but poverty is receding. Also, it is comforting to note that the percentage of the population of Mauritius living below the poverty level, defined by the World Bank at US $2 per day, was below 2 per cent in 2012, compared to 2.9 per cent in 1996/ 1997. Such percentages bear no comparison with those of countries such as South Africa (2.6 per cent) and Madagascar (9.5 per cent).

In effect, given its characteristics as a labour-intensive industry, tourism has not only been an important factor in helping Mauritius to reach the level of an upper-middle-income country, it has also contributed to job creation, par- ticularly in poor rural areas, thanks to the presence of hotels and tourists. Moreover, it has boosted economic activities such as retail trade, and services in the respective fields of restaurants, car hire and taxis.

Supportive environment

As mentioned above, the future sustainability of the tourism sector calls for the observance of a number of essential conditions. Undoubtedly, the

Table 6.6 Number of poor people in Mauritius

	2012	2017
Relative poverty line (rupees)	5,652	6,404
Number of households	33,600	20,900
Proportion of all households (%)	9.4	5.5
Estimated number of poor persons	122,700	79,300
Percentage of poor persons	9.8	6.3

natural environment of Mauritius has been an important factor in the development of tourism. Not many tourist destinations can boast of sand, sun and sea all the year round, suitability for sports on land and water, and a subtropical climate. The island is attractive to holidaymakers in search of exoticism, far away from busy urban centres. In addition, malaria was eradicated from Mauritius in the middle of the 20th century and the country is free from endemic communicable diseases. Such natural characteristics need to be preserved at all costs and care must be taken to nurture and protect the natural environment.

Human attitudes

While natural beauty is an essential component, the friendly and welcoming behaviour of the population at large towards tourists is of paramount importance. Generally, the tourism industry of Mauritius scores well in that respect. Whether in the hotel where they are accommodated or on the streets, tourists are generally warmly welcomed by the local population, which displays a variety of cultures with Asian, Creole and European characteristics. Staff are well trained thanks to training facilities available at hospitality and hotel management schools, and communication is facilitated by the widespread use of two international languages, English and French. It also helps that visitors from some 116 countries are exempt from visa requirements, while those from another 64 countries can be granted a visa on arrival.

Political environment

The tourism industry is highly sensitive to risks which may arise from social disturbances in the country. This is why a supportive political environment is essential and it is gratifying to note that this prevails in Mauritius.

Democratic principles have been observed since independence in 1968. General elections are held every five years and the separation of powers (executive, legislative and judiciary) provides considerable assurance to investors. That part of the written and spoken press which is privately held is vibrant, public institutions are in place to regulate and to market tourism, while the ownership of hotels restaurants, transport and recreational services is private. The air access policy has also been extended in the last few years and the official strategy is to further diversify the tourism market, particularly with respect to Asian countries.

Related empirical literature

Empirical work analysing the relationship between tourism development and economic progress has flourished over the past few decades. This includes pioneering work by Balaguer and Cantavella-Jordá (2002) who found a long-term positive relationship between tourism and economic growth for the case of Spain. Dritsakis (2004) assessed the effect of tourism on the economic growth of Greece using the Granger causality test and also confirmed a strong causal relationship between tourism earnings and economic growth. Dritsakis also reported a causal effect of economic growth on tourism receipts, supporting both tourism-led economic development and economic-driven tourism growth (ibid.). Tosun (1999), and later Gunduz and Hatemi-J (2005), confirmed empirical support for the tourism-led growth hypothesis for the case of Turkey. Similar results were validated by Kim *et al.* (2006) and Brida *et al.* (2008) for the cases of Taiwan and Mexico, respectively, using a cointegration approach. These authors also reported the bicausal nature of the hypothesized link, namely that tourism and economic development tend to reinforce each other. Using the convergence approach based on Barro and Sala-i-Martin's (1992) analysis at the regional level, Proença and Soukiazis (2005) concluded that tourism can be considered as an alternative solution for enhancing regional growth in Portugal. In the case of Spain and Italy, Cortes-Jiminez and Pulina (2006) empirically concluded that both domestic and international tourism have had a significant and positive effect on regional economic performance.

Studies based on examples from other countries also reported positive effects of tourism development on economic growth. In Africa, for instance, Cunado and Perez de Garcia (2006 observed evidence of conditional convergence towards the African regional average and even the US average for some countries. Brau *et al.* (2003), while comparing the relative economic performance of a sample of 'tourism countries' interestingly reported that the economies of these countries grew relatively faster than all the other subgroups. Martin *et al.* (2004) analysed the relationship in the Latin American context for the period 1985–1998. The authors observed that the tourism sector was growth-conducive for medium- or low-income countries but that this was not always the case for developed countries.

It is noteworthy that some pieces of research were unable to establish that tourism makes a significant contribution to economic growth. Lee (2008), for instance, using the bounds test developed by Pesaran *et al.* (2001) could not find any cointegrating (or long-term) relationship between tourism and economic growth but instead found support for the growth-led tourism hypothesis for the case of Singapore. Oh (2005) also denied the existence of the tourism-led growth hypothesis for the case of South Korea after making use of cointegration analysis during the period 1975–2001. Based on panel data analysis, Sequeira and Campos (2005) accounted for endogenous relationships in the tourism-growth nexus and concluded that tourism alone cannot explain the relatively higher growth rates of the sample of countries under study. Other researchers who could not validate the tourism-led growth hypothesis include Capo *et al.* (2007) for the Balearics and the Canary Islands, Katırcıoğlu (2009a) for the case of Turkey, Singh *et al.* (2010) for the case of three Caribbean countries (the Bahamas, Barbados and Jamaica), Grullon (2013) for the case of the Dominican Republic, and more recently Palamalai and Kalaivani (2016) for the case of Asia-Pacific countries and Mishra *et al.* (2016) for the case of India.

Mauritian studies

There have been several studies on the determinants of tourism development (see Khadaroo and Seetanah, 2007; Sannassee and Seetanah, 2015; Seetanah *et al.*, 2015) and on its impact on the local community (Nunkoo and Ramkissoon, 2011, 2012). Interestingly, three empirical works related to the assessment of the tourism-growth nexus in Mauritius can be identified from the research literature and are briefly discussed here.

The first study was undertaken by Durbarry (2004) and focused on tourism as an important element of Mauritius' economic success. The author used data for the period 1970–1999 in a cointegration approach and employed a production function to test the link between tourism and growth, disaggregating exports into the primary, secondary and tertiary sectors. Using a dynamic time series, it was found that the tourism sector has had a considerable impact on the Mauritian economy during the three decades under study. More specifically, it was found that a 1 per cent increase in tourism would increase the GDP of the island by 0.8 per cent.

A subsequent study by Seetanah (2011) used the panel data of 19 island economies, including Mauritius, for the period 1990–2007 to assess the economic impact of tourism. Using a conventional augmented Solow growth model and dynamic panel data analysis, Seetanah reported that tourism had a significant positive effect on growth. Granger causality analysis revealed the existence of a bi-causal relationship between tourism and growth. In addition, when compared to sample sets of developing and developed countries, the economic benefits of tourism for the case of island economies were reported to be relatively higher (a 1 per cent increase in tourism arrivals was associated with a 0.12 to 0.14 per cent increase in the output levels of the islands under study in the short term).

More recently, Solarin (2018) studied the impact of tourism on the Mauritian economy during the period 1980–2011. Solarin used data from ten major tourist origin countries and, employing causality techniques, he validated the positive economic effect that tourism has on Mauritius. However, the disaggregate analysis revealed that this was not the case for all the markets under study. In fact, it was established that the tourism-led growth hypothesis held true for those countries that accounted for the largest share of tourism flows to the island.

A brief summary of the empirical studies on Mauritius tends to confirm that tourism has been beneficial to the island's successful economic growth and that this trend appears likely to continue.

The challenges ahead

Looking ahead, one can see that the main challenge to the continued progress of the tourism industry in Mauritius is the maintenance of the supportive factors described above, such as the preservation of the natural and institutional environment, the continuous provision of training to personnel and staff, as well as a favourable air access policy. In addition, reduced dependence on Europe and enhancement of the safety and security of tourists are also essential elements for the development of tourism in the island.

There are indications that the public authorities are willing and prepared to pursue policies in support of the requirements listed above. There is one challenge, however, where Mauritius has yet to organize itself: this is with reference to the diversification of tourism. Sun, sand and sea are undoubtedly a popular and highly successful mix, but Mauritius is not unique in displaying such characteristics and offering such advantages. There is a need to enhance the product by encouraging tourists to discover what else Mauritius has to offer in terms of cultural and religious diversity. It goes without saying that the successful promotion of inland tourism depends on an active official policy of renovating town centres, sprucing up public buildings and halls, and opening museums worth visiting.

Conclusion

It is clear that tourism has contributed significantly to the transformation of the Mauritian economy, along with other economic sectors. The mix of supportive public policies and of private sector financing and management has been highly beneficial. However, success would not have been achieved if the labour force carrying out the numerous activities linked to tourism had not performed their professional duties with singular competence, and if the population at large had not adopted a welcoming and friendly attitude towards the visitors to the country.

All these positive factors must continue to operate in the future. It is up to the population of Mauritius to ensure the continuity and sustainability of the tourism industry, a major pillar of the economy and a mirror of the positive and welcoming behaviour of its culturally and ethnically diverse population.

References

Archer, B. (1995) 'Importance of Tourism for the Economy of Bermuda', *Annals of Tourism Research* 22(4): 918–930.

Balaguer, J. and Cantavella-Jordá, M. (2002) 'Tourism as a Long-Run Economic Growth Factor: The Spanish Case', *Applied Economics* 34: 877–884.

Barro, R. J. and Sala-i-Martin, X. (1992) 'Convergence', *Journal of Political Economy* 100(2): 223–251. DOI: 10.1086/261816.

Brau, R., Lanza, A. and Pigliaru, F. (2003) 'How Fast Are the Tourism Countries Growing? The Cross-Country Evidence ', working paper no. 03–9, Cagliari: Centro di Ricerche Economiche Nord Sud (CRENoS). Available at www.crenos.it/work ing/pdf/03-09.pdf.

Brida, J. G., Carrera, E. S. and Risso, W. A. (2008) 'Tourism's Impact on Long-Run Mexican Economic Growth', *Economics Bulletin*, 3(21): 1–8.

Capo, J., Font, A. and Nadal, J. (2007) 'Dutch Disease in Tourism Economies: Evidence from the Balearics and the Canary Islands', *Journal of Sustainable Tourism* 15(6): 615–627.

Chen, L. L. and Devereux, J. (1999) 'Tourism and Welfare in Sub-Saharan Africa: A Theoretical Analysis', *Journal of African Economies* 8: 209–227.

Cortes-Jimenez, I. and Pulina, M. (2016) *A Further Step into the ELGH and TLGH for Spain and Italy, 2006.* Available at www.feem.it/NR/rdonlyres/C6F679FC-64E0-4 CA5-AB1E-943B04B9A241/2375/11808.pdf.

Cunado, J. and Perez de Garcia, F. (2006) 'Real Convergence in Africa in the Second-Half of the 20th Century', *Journal of Economics and Business* 58(2006): 153–167.

Dritsakis, N. (2004) 'Tourism as a Long-Run Economic Growth Factor: An Empirical Investigation for Greece Using Causality Analysis', *Tourism Economics* 10(3): 305–316.

Durbarry, R. (2002) 'The Economic Contribution of Tourism in Mauritius', *Annals of Tourism Research* 29(3): 862–865.

Durbarry, R. (2004) 'Tourism and Economic Growth: The Case of Mauritius', *Tourism Economics* 10(3): 389–401.

Government of Mauritius (1971) *Mauritius Economic Review, 1971–75*, Port Louis: Government Press.

Grullon, S. (2013) 'Is the Tourism-Led Growth Hypothesis Valid for the Dominican Republic: Results from the Bounds Test for Cointegration and Granger Causality Tests', *European Journal of Business and Management* 5(25): 1–8. Available atwww.semanticscholar.org/paper/Is-the-Tourism-Led-Growth-Hypothesis-Valid-for-the-Grull%C3%B3n/4037a92323e0084da0f740e2e97df6e203136e2b..

Gunduz, L. and Hatemi-J, A. (2005) 'Is the Tourism-Led Growth Hypothesis Valid for Turkey?', *Applied Economics Letters* 12: 499–504.

Katırcıoğlu, S. (2009) 'Revisiting the Tourism-Led Growth Hypothesis for Turkey Using the Bounds Test and Johansen Approach for Cointegration', *Tourism Management* 30(1): 17–20.

Khadaroo, A. J. and Seetanah, B. (2007) 'Transport Infrastructure and Tourism Development', *Annals of Tourism Research* 34(4): 1021–1032.

Kim, H. J., Chen, M. and Jan, S. (2006) 'Tourism Expansion and Economic Development: The Case of Taiwan', *Tourism Management* 27: 925–933.

Khan, H., Seng, C. F. and Cheong, W. K. (1990) 'The Social Impact of Tourism on Singapore', *Service Industries Journal* 10(3): 541–548.

Lea, J. (1988) *Tourism and Development in the Third World*, New York:Routledge.

Lee, C. G. (2008) 'Tourism and Economic Growth: The Case of Singapore, Regional and Sectoral Economic Studies', *Euro-American Association of Economic Development* 8(1): 89–98.

Louca, C. (2006) 'Income and Expenditure in the Tourism Industry: Time Series Evidence from Cyprus', *Tourism Economics* 12(4): 603–617.

McKinnon, R. (1964) 'Foreign Exchange Constraints in Economic Development and Efficient Aid Allocation, *Economic Journal* 74: 388–409.

Martin, J., Morales, N. and Scarpa, R. (2004) 'Tourism and Economic Growth in Latin American Countries: A Panel Data Approach', *Nota de Lavoro* 26. Available at http://ssrn.com/abstract=504482.

Mishra, P. K., Rout, H. B. and Sanghamitra (2016) 'Tourism in Odisha: An Engine of Long-Run Growth', *Journal of Tourism Management Research* 3(2): 74–84. Available at https://doi.org/10.18488/journal.31/2016.3.2/31.2.74.84.

Noriko, I. and Mototsugu, F. (2007) 'Impacts of Tourism and fiscal expenditure to Remote Islands: The Case of the Amami Islands in Japan', *Applied Economics Letters* 14: 661–666.

Nunkoo, R. and Ramkissoon, H. (2011) 'Developing a Community Support Model for Tourism', *Annals of Tourism Research* 38(3): 964–988.

Nunkoo, R. and Ramkissoon, H. (2012) 'Power, Trust, Social Exchange and Community Support', *Annals of Tourism Research* 39(2): 997–1023.

Oh, C. (2005) 'The Contribution of Tourism Development to Economic Growth in the Korean Economy', *Tourism Management* 26(1): 39–44.

Owen, E. (1987) *The Future of Freedom in the Developing World*, Oxford: Pergamon Press.

Palamalai, S. and Kalaivani, M. (2016) 'Tourism Expansion and Economic Growth in Asia Pacific Nations: A Panel Causality Approach', *IUP Journal of Applied Economics* 15(2) 53–84.

Paramati, S. R., Alam, M. S. and Chen, C. F. (2017) 'The Effects of Tourism on Economic Growth and CO2 Emissions: A Comparison between Developed and Developing Economies', *Journal of Travel Research* 56(6): 712–724.

Pesaran, M. H., Shin, Y. and Smith, R. J. (2001) 'Bounds Testing Approaches to the Analysis of Level Relationships', *Journal of Applied Econometrics* 16: 289–326.

Proença, Sara and Soukiazis, Elias (2005) 'Tourism as an Alternative Source of Regional Growth in Portugal: A Panel Data Analysis at NUTS II and III Levels', *Portuguese Economic Journal* 6(2).

Sannassee, R. V. and Seetanah, B. (2015) 'The Influence of Trust on Repeat Tourism: The Mauritian Case Study', *Journal of Hospitality Marketing & Management* 24(7): 770–789.

Seetanah, B. (2011) 'Assessing the Dynamic Economic Impact of Tourism for Island Economies', *Annals of Tourism Research* 38(1): 291–308.

Seetanah, B., Sannassee, R. V. and Rojid, S. (2015) 'The Impact of Relative Prices on Tourism Demand for Mauritius: An Empirical Analysis', *Development Southern Africa* 32(3): 363–376.

Sequeira, T. N. and Campos, C. (2005) 'International Tourism and Economic Growth: A Panel Data Approach', working paper, 141, Milan: Fondazione Eni Enrico Mattei.

Shan, J. and Wilson, K. (2001) 'Causality between Trade and Tourism: Empirical Evidence from China', *Applied Economics Letters* 8: 279–283.

Sinclair, T. (1998) 'Tourism and Economic Development: A Survey', *Journal of Development Studies* 34(5): 1–51.

Sinclair, T. and Stabler, M. (2002) *The Economics of Tourism*, London:Routledge.

Singh, D. R., Wright, A. S., Hayle, C. and Craigwell, R. (2010) 'Is the Tourism-Led Growth Thesis Valid? The Case of the Bahamas, Barbados, and Jamaica', *Tourism Analysis* 15(4): 435–445. DOI: doi:10.3727/108354210X12864727453223.

Solarin, S. A. (2018) 'Does Tourism-Led Growth Hypothesis Exist in Mauritius? Evidence from Dissaggregated Tourism Markets', *Current Issues in Tourism* 21(9): 964–969.

Song, H. and Liu, H. (2017) 'Predicting Tourist Demand Using Big Data', in Z. Xiang and D. Fresenmaier (eds) *Analytics in Smart Tourism Design,* Cham: Springer International, pp. 13–29.

Statistics Mauritius (2017) *Economic and Social Indicators*, Port Louis: Government of Mauritius. Available at http://statsmauritius.govmu.org/English/Pages/default.aspx.

Tang, C. F. and Tan, E. C. (2015) 'Does Tourism Effectively Stimulate Malaysia's Economic Growth?', *Tourism Management* 46: 158–163.

Tosun, C. (1999) 'An Analysis of Contributions International Inbound Tourism to the Turkish Economy', *Tourism Economics* 5: 212–217.

Uysal, M. and Gitelson, R. (1994) 'Assessment of Economic Impacts: Festivals and Special Events', Journal of Festival Management and Event Tourism 2(1): 3–10.

World Economic Forum (2018) *The Global Competitiveness Report 2018*, Cologny-Geneva: World Economic Forum.

World Travel and Tourism Council (WTTC) (2017) *Travel and Tourism Economic Impact 2017*, London: WTTC.

7   Harnessing FDI for growth in Mauritius

S. Gunessee and B. Sooreea-Bheemul

Introduction

The Mauritian economic miracle has been fuelled by a number of factors, chiefly foreign direct investment (FDI). Indeed, from an agrarian inward-looking small island with little foreign capital and consequently a poor economic performance, Mauritius opened up by liberalizing both trade and investment. Following the establishment of the export processing zone (EPZ) in the 1970s the influx of foreign capital has helped the country to harness strong economic growth (Subramanian and Roy, 2001; Subramanian, 2009). Although Mauritius has historically been the recipient of a relatively small inflow of FDI, this foreign capital – especially the initial influx – has undeniably contributed to Mauritian economic development in the 1980s and thereafter (Moran, 2006; UNCTAD, 2001, 2017).

Key to this success story was the institutional business environment and policy framework put in place which allowed FDI to flourish alongside the domestic private sector (Frankel, 2010; Wignaraja *et al.*, 2004). This domestic-foreign combination became an important engine of early growth (Ancharaz, 2003a). With changing times, the policy and institutional setting had to adapt to allow FDI to continue its inroad into the Mauritian economy, beyond clothing and textiles and into the financial and tourism sectors in the 1990s – albeit with domestic investment being far more significant (OECD, 2014; UNCTAD, 2001).[1] Further diversification and structural transformation of the Mauritian economy has seen the surge of inward FDI into the economy in information and communications technology (ICT), health, higher education and real estate in the 2000s and beyond (UNCTAD, 2017; Zafar, 2011).

Furthermore, another recent trend has been the notion of 'opening up to go out' with Mauritius developing an Africa strategy with various initiatives for Mauritian investors to branch out into Africa (MABC, 2013; OECD, 2014). As an emerging market economy this outward FDI (OFDI) is expected to play an even more important role in the next phase of Mauritian growth (Gunessee, 2017).

This chapter tracks Mauritius' economic progress and the island's relationship with FDI and FDI policies. We narrate and document the role that

FDI has played since independence up to the present day, and review the way in which the FDI policy framework has evolved to keep pace with developments. The chapter then raises the question of whether the influx of FDI promoted economic growth and development, highlighting its sectoral composition and geographical origin/destination.

This chapter argues that looking at inward FDI is just one facet and that taking a broader view of OFDI is just as important. This is because successful FDI outflows from Mauritius, balanced with a steady flow of inward FDI, should be conducive to further Mauritian economic development.

Section two outlines the role of inward FDI for the Mauritian economy, tracing its origins to initial economic development and its continued (or reduced) role over time. This is followed by a discussion of the notion of 'opening up to go out' and thus we highlight the role of outward FDI. Then, section four expounds on the challenges for FDI, as the Mauritian economy looks for new opportunities to sustain economic growth and embarks on the path towards a high-income economy. The chapter finishes with some concluding remarks.

Opening up with inward FDI

Chronological review

With an economy that was highly dependent on the sugar industry and was rife with unemployment given the limited scope of the import substitution-led industrial sector, the Mauritian economy was seen to have a grim future in the 1960s. Indeed, with high population growth and a lack of job opportunities there was a need for 'productive' capital, that is, there was a need to equip this surplus labour that could only be financed by domestic or foreign investment (Meade, 1961; Meade *et al.*, 1961; Titmuss and Abel-Smith, 1961).

As such, the need for productive foreign capital had already been foreseen in pre-independence Mauritius by the oft-cited *Meade Report*. Unfortunately, the inward-looking domestic investment-centred import substitution strategy of the 1960s and early 1970s facing a small market could not fully exploit economies of scale (Bheenick and Schapiro, 1989; Greenaway and Gooroochurn, 2001). Furthermore, being relatively more capital-intensive the import substitution firms could hardly deal with the surplus labour problem.

The situation required an *outward-looking strategy* unconstrained by scale that was more labour-intensive. The answer was provided by an export-led industrialization achieved through the creation of the export processing zone (EPZ) in the 1970s.[2] The idea was to encourage foreign investors through favourable fiscal incentives. Thus, opening up to the world to allow an influx of FDI was seen as essential (Durbarry, 2001; Wignaraja *et al.*, 2004).

However, this outward-looking strategy through the EPZ did not succeed immediately for a number of reasons, as an initial take-off phase in the early to mid-1970s was followed by period of stagnation in the late 1970s and early 1980s, which heralded a false dawn for export-led industrialization and growth (see Durbarry, 2001). This changed in the early to mid-1980s. First, the economy adopted structural adjustment policies advocated by the International Monetary Fund and the World Bank with the goal of supporting export-led growth (Greenaway and Gooroochurn, 2001). Second, some of the incentives to promote the export sector were revised with firms operating under the EPZ being able to enjoy 100 per cent corporate tax exemption for the first ten years and a five-year dividend tax exemption (Durbarry, 2001; Sacerdoti *et al.*, 2005). Third, the Mauritius Export Development and Investment Authority (MEDIA) was set up in 1984 with the key objective to promote exports and investment promotion activities (Mistry and Treebhoohun, 2009; Wignaraja *et al.*, 2004). For example, the latter launched an international campaign in South-East Asia and Europe to attract foreign investors (Durbarry, 2001).

These policies succeeded as the 1980s saw the largest inflow of FDI into the EPZ with an upward trend that lasted until 1989. The largest source of this FDI was from Hong Kong and France (Durbarry, 2001; Hein, 1996). The Hong Kong investors fuelled the remarkable growth of the clothing and textiles (C&T) industry (Mistry and Treebhoohun, 2009).[3] The success of the C&T industry was also due to Mauritius taking full advantage of the Multi-Fibre Agreement, which limited the entry of the larger South-East Asian garment producers into the European and US markets, by attracting FDI into the C&T industry (Sobhee, 2009). The importance of the C&T industry during this development phase cannot be underestimated. By the end of the century, its contribution to employment and gross domestic product (GDP) stood at roughly 25 per cent and 10 per cent, respectively (Wignaraja *et al.*, 2004).

The EPZ fuelled the export-led growth in the 1980s but the C&T industry accounted for the bulk of it, and therefore such expansion was unlikely to be sustainable. In fact, rising wages and resulting reduced competitiveness meant that Mauritius became less attractive as a destination for foreign investors who opted for more competitive destinations in Vietnam and Bangladesh (Sobhee, 2009). In the African region, Madagascar and Mozambique proved to be more attractive, with domestic investors also reshuffling part of their production facilities to these neighbouring low-cost economies (Durbarry, 2001; Sobhee, 2009).

This slowdown prompted a diversification strategy within the C&T industry, within the EPZ, and across sectors.[4] First, there was an attempt to upgrade from low-end towards medium- to high-end garments (Wignaraja *et al.*, 2004)[5]. Second, the industrial base of the EPZ saw the emergence of non-textile-based production with industrial products such as cut flowers, jewellery, watches and sports equipment (Durbarry, 2001; Moran, 2006).[6] Third, under the diversification programme new pillars were added to the economy through a shift to the tourism and financial sectors. This took the shape of a gradual structural transformation from being manufacturing-oriented to one in which sectors were more evenly balanced (OECD, 2014; Sacerdoti *et al.*, 2005).

The contribution of FDI in this endeavour remained surprisingly small yet stable and *salient*, with domestic investment playing a more prominent role

(Ancharaz, 2003b; Wignaraja *et al.*, 2004). A key message that emerges from an overview of the pre-millennium development period is one where high investment levels have been sustained through more noticeable domestic investment, though with initial outlays of foreign capital to develop a particular sector (Subramanian and Roy, 2001).

Loosely connected to the EPZ is the freeport sector. As a commercial free zone established in 1992 the Mauritius freeport has enabled the island economy to position itself as a regional trading hub (OECD, 2014; Sacerdoti *et al.*, 2005). It is seen as a logistics and distribution platform in the region that offers facilities such as warehousing, cold storage, sorting, grading, processing, freight forwarding and bulk breaking (Jeetah, 2017). These duty-free facilities have led to investment from several foreign operators in the Mauritius freeport, and in recent years the key aim has been to facilitate exports to Africa.[7]

The story of the tourism sector is similar to that of the EPZ; i.e. an initial influx of FDI with a later domestic-foreign combination to sustain sectoral growth. A contributing factor of this state of affairs in tourism had to do with the restrictive FDI policies in the early years, as wholly owned foreign ownership was permitted only for hotels with more than 100 rooms (UNCTAD, 2001). This changed in later years and foreign investment now also includes villas and restaurants. By 2010, of the 104 registered hotels on the island, 26 were foreign-owned (Srivastava, 2012).

Nevertheless, the role of FDI in the tourism sector has been crucial. For instance, it is undeniable that the South African Sun Resorts Group played a key pioneering role in the sector and has been an important contributor to employment; its substantial investment in the 1980s resulted in the establishment of some of the most well-known high-end hotel brands on the island (UNCTAD, 2001). This contributed enormously to growth because the Mauritian tourism development strategy was mostly about targeting the upscale market segment (Sacerdoti *et al.*, 2005). In recent years, this goal of targeting upmarket high-end tourism with diversification within the industry, while maintaining sustainable tourism development, has meant a constraint on new investment and few new hotels being set up.[8] However, the upscale tourism target coupled with diversified cultural, business and medical tourism has seen global brands such as the Sheraton opening for business in Mauritius (Vangerow-Kühn, 2011).

From the late 1980s and 1990s the financial sector became an important source of growth alongside the manufacturing sector. Several pieces of legislation were passed to facilitate the establishment of the Stock Exchange of Mauritius in 1989, and the Mauritius Offshore Business Activities Authority (MOBAA) in 1992, the latter with the aim of establishing an offshore financial centre (OFC), through the liberalization of interest rates and foreign exchange controls (OECD, 2014; Vangerow-Kühn, 2011).

However, OFC activities and the financial sector took time to develop, given the reluctance of foreign banks and financial service corporations to establish operations. This was despite the fact that offshore banks could only have non-residents as majority owners in the early years post-independence (Sacerdoti *et al.*, 2005). This changed in the mid-1990s. The opening of the Indian economy to foreign investors and the advantages posed by the 1985 ratified double tax agreement (DTA) with India enabled Mauritius to act as a channel for investment into India. As a treaty jurisdiction it started routing investments of high-net-worth individuals and institutional investors from the United States and the European Union into emerging economies such as India and China (Mistry and Treebhoohun, 2009).

Recently there have been attempts to diversify the financial sector and to remove the reliance on the DTA with India through the signing of several DTAs. As such, the Global Business Sector is now geared towards further developing the Africa Gateway (OECD, 2014; UNCTAD, 2006). Over time Mauritius developed a robust financial system which proved resilient during the 2008 global financial crisis (Willem te Velde *et al.*, 2010). Unsurprisingly, a number of global banks have established operations on the island with Barclays and HSBC being pioneers, although the local banks – the Mauritius Commercial Bank (MCB) and the State Bank of Mauritius – continue to dominate the scene. Reform via the 2004 Banking Act and adherence to the 2008 Basel II Accord locally have fostered greater stability and transparency and thereby the internationalization of the Mauritian banking industry, making it more conducive for foreign investment as a result (Bhantooa, 2012).

The last decade or so has seen further transformation of the Mauritian economy with the resurgence of FDI. This is because, while reinvested earnings from the sugar and textile industries had a key role in fuelling high levels of domestic investment in the pre-millennium development phase, the disappearance in the 2000s of such sugar and textile profits has led to an increasing reliance on inward FDI to finance investment (Subramanian and Roy, 2001; Svirydzenka and Petri, 2017).

The sectors which have benefited from this re-channelling comprise ICT, higher education, health and real estate with varying degrees of success. Progress in the ICT sector and higher education was geared to contribute to the so-called knowledge hub (Isaacs, 2007; TEC, 2018a). The former has helped to improve the service sector in Mauritius, in particular providing employment opportunities to the younger generation (Mistry and Treebhoohun, 2009; Sacerdoti *et al.*, 2005). The foundations of the ICT sector were laid in the late 1990s following the publication of a White Paper and the National ICT Strategic Plan which promulgated ICT as another pillar of the Mauritian economy with the stated aim of developing Mauritius into a cyber-island (Chan-Meetoo, 2007; Jeetah, 2017).

Initially, Business Process Outsourcing (BPO) companies from Europe, the United States and Asia opened their back office processes. The availability of a bilingual and adequately trained workforce with relatively competitive salary expectations made it attractive for these global companies to invest in the Mauritian ICT sector (Sacerdoti *et al.*, 2005; Vangerow-Kühn, 2011). These companies included Accenture, Huawei, Orange Business Services and

Infosys. When it comes to the foreign-local divide, the BPO segment of the sector is dominated by foreign operators, while the IT segment is serviced by local players – among them small enterprises. By 2018 around 700 ICT-BPO enterprises were in operations employing around 22,000 professionals, making it an important contributor to Mauritian growth (UNCTAD, 2017).[9]

While in its infancy the ICT sector was widely regarded as being entirely made up of call centres, the sector has evolved so that the Ebene Cyber City – where most of this expansion has taken place – has become a cornerstone of the island economy (Vangerow-Kühn, 2011). Indeed, the sector has diversified into sub-sectors such as banking, insurance, financial services, telecoms, human resource recruitment and development, IT application development, and maintenance support (UNCTAD, 2017). A category that has seen rapid growth in the IT sector is media, entertainment, and animation services. This is epitomized by the interesting cases of Diadeis, the French publishing and digitization company, and Identical Pictures Ltd, set up by a German film-maker – which has taken full advantage of a film rebate scheme (Mistry and Treebhoohun, 2009; Habermeyer, 2018).

In the case of the higher education sector, the last 15 years has seen greater involvement from the private sector including foreign establishments such as Middlesex University (UK) and Curtin University (Australia), although not all of these initiatives have met with success (TEC, 2018b). Some universities have either closed down, such as Aberystwyth University (UK), or have come under scrutiny, like some of the branches of Indian universities. Overall, an expansion of private sector involvement with several joint ventures with foreign institutions is expected, albeit with more careful pruning. The aim of this endeavour is to build a knowledge hub (TEC, 2018a; Vangerow-Kühn, 2011).

FDI in the health sector has been rather timid but is somewhat in line with the government initiative to develop Mauritius into a 'medical hub', partly connected with its initiative to develop 'medical tourism' (BOI, 2017c; Rawat, 2012). Examples include foreign investment by major Indian hospital chains such as Apollo Hospitals Enterprise and Fortis Healthcare in joint ventures with local Mauritian companies to set up the Apollo Bramwell Hospital, now Welkin Hospital, and Fortis Clinique Darne, respectively (Vangerow-Kühn, 2011).

A sector which has enjoyed considerable success in attracting FDI is real estate (BOI, 2017a). Although the seed of its development was planted in 2005 with the Integrated Resort Scheme, it took a while for the sector to develop and further initiatives like the Real Estate Development Scheme have proved to be helpful. While the Integrated Resort Scheme was targeted at the high end of the property market and at foreigners only, allowing them to obtain Mauritian residency for a minimum investment of US $500,000, the Real Estate Development Scheme was opened up to Mauritians as well and had no minimum bounds, although residency was not an automatic consequence (Jeeha, 2012). One such company is Anahita Mauritius which continues to offer luxury real estate development options such as allowing non-citizens to buy freehold property in Mauritius.[10]

FDI policy evolution

It is hard to imagine FDI operating in a vacuum. As such, several factors have helped to harness FDI. A key factor is the FDI-related policies that trace their origins to the early days of the EPZ and thus the EPZ Act of 1970. This regulatory framework has of course evolved to keep pace with economic development, at times harnessing FDI to fuel such development.

Following the establishment of the EPZ in 1970, a package of fiscal and financial incentives was developed to attract export-oriented FDI, particularly in the C&T industry. It comprised numerous incentives including tax holidays on corporate profits, tax-free dividends for five years, free repatriation of profits and dividends, duty-free imports of inputs and loans offered at preferential rates (Durbarry, 2001).

In 1983 a revised investment scheme was introduced for export-oriented FDI[11] and included graduating income tax relief (dependent on operational years), duty-free imports of inputs, partial tax exemption on reinvested earnings, loans at preferential rates, and freight rebates (Durbarry, 2001). This was accomplished in part by the Companies Act 1984, which became effective from March 1985 (UNCTAD, 2006). The institutional support to guide this new phase of expansion was provided by the establishment of the Mauritius Export Development and Investment Authority in 1984, following the enactment of the MEDIA Act of 1983 (Mistry and Treebhoohun, 2009; Wignaraja *et al.*, 2004).

The Industrial Expansion Act of 1993 was an attempt to sustain the EPZ and to pre-empt its slowdown through the provision of tax incentives to manufacturing firms catering for the local market. The Export Processing Zone Development Authority (EPZDA) was tasked with improving the competitiveness of EPZ enterprises, and offered training, consultancy and various information services (Wignaraja *et al.*, 2004). Although some incentives were provided, eventually the EPZ scheme was discontinued in 2006 (OECD, 2014). In order to understand the net effect of the EPZ on the Mauritian economy, Rojid et al. (2009) conducted a formal cost-benefit analysis and found that the sector was successful in creating jobs and raising foreign exchange, yet the overall cost of the incentives given with respect to domestic borrowing and subsidized electricity usage outweighed the benefits.

In an attempt to further diversify the economy, the government provided incentives to attract FDI beyond manufacturing, especially in the tourism sector. This included similar incentive schemes offered to manufacturing firms (OECD, 2014). Yet inflows of foreign capital in the sector were somewhat small because of restrictive initial policies, as highlighted above. For instance, full ownership was allowed for larger hotels, while foreign equity participation was permitted up to 49 per cent in smaller establishments (Srivastava, 2012; UNCTAD, 2001). Although significant changes took place in later years with FDI now being permitted in restaurant businesses for example (Srivastava, 2012), some limitations for FDI still subsist. For instance, FDI for diving centres is restricted to 30 per cent (OECD, 2014).

The Mauritius Tourism Promotion Authority (MTPA) Act of 1996 established an agency which not only helped to promote Mauritius as a tourist destination but also encouraged investment in the island. The MTPA is still operational, although with re-focused functions. It has come to play a significant role given the governmental attention and support it receives (OECD, 2014).

In the 1990s a number of financial incentives such as the complete liberalization of foreign exchange, the abolishment of bank credit ceilings to priority sectors and the injection of bank liquidity helped to improve the macroeconomic environment of Mauritius. The country's legal and regulatory framework was reinforced through the enactment of both the Mauritian Offshore Business Activities Act and the Offshore Trust Act in 1992, and the International Companies Act in 1994 (UNCTAD, 2006). The adoption of these acts facilitated the creation of offshore entities for international business and investment activities by non-residents and ushered in the creation of the financial sector (Mistry and Treebhoohun, 2009).

The financial sector, and in particular the global business sub-sector, has prospered and benefited greatly from regional cooperative agreements and bilateral tax and investment treaties (Seetanah, 2013; UNCTAD, 2006). Indeed, as highlighted above, the DTA with India was and remains a cornerstone of the Mauritian global business sector till its recent re-negotiation in 2017. Regional cooperation in the form of the Southern African Development Community (SADC) has also helped to promote Mauritius as a tourist destination.

In 2000 the MEDIA was replaced by the Board of Investment (BOI), which was set up via the Investment Promotion Act to serve as a one-stop agency to promote, facilitate and improve the investment climate in Mauritius. Its goal was to upgrade and intensify the diversification drive (UNCTAD, 2001).

Several schemes were introduced with a view to expanding and attracting FDI into new, high-value areas such as the Integrated Resort Scheme (2002), the Information Communication Technology Scheme (2002), and the Freeport Act (2004). The Business Facilitation Act was introduced in 2006 in order to greatly simplify business procedures, as a result of which 26 laws were amended. The Freeport Act (2004) provided the legal means to integrate the Mauritius Freeport Authority within the BOI (OECD, 2014; Seetanah, 2013; UNCTAD, 2017).

The real estate sector was identified as a key sector for diversification purposes, and it has clearly received an appropriate share of policies enacted with a view to attracting FDI. It was hoped that the Integrated Resort Scheme (2005) and the Real Estate Development Scheme (2008) would herald the development of the sector. Through the former, there was an influx of FDI, but the latter – which was supposed to allow small freeholder landowners to become property developers – failed to deliver (OECD, 2014). Real estate promoters were reluctant to commit as several off-plan projects failed to attract developers given the near impossibility of resales and the restrictive legislative framework with high transfer costs. Consequently, these policies led to the deepening of the unequal distribution of resources as only a very few, poor-quality unskilled jobs were created. In addition, the Integrated Resort Scheme led to environmental degradation, deprivation of access to the beach by locals and loss of income by local fishermen (Tandrayen-Ragoobur and Kasseeah, 2018).

By 2015 the sector had made some progress. First, the Integrated Resort Scheme and Real Estate Scheme were replaced by the Property Development Scheme (BOI, 2015a). This facilitated the development of a mixture of residences for sale to non-citizens, citizens and members of the Mauritian diaspora. In 2016 and 2017 gross FDI inflows into real estate accounted for 72.8 per cent and 50.3 per cent of total FDI, respectively (UNCTAD, 2017; BOM, 2018). The real estate sector remains the highest recipient of FDI inflows and can be said to be contributing to the prominence gained by the construction and tourism industries as the market shifts towards more high-class leisure and commercial facilities. The Smart City Scheme, introduced in 2015, presented a plethora of fiscal and non-fiscal incentives to attract global investors in projects developing smart sustainable homes packed with technological innovations to attract retired non-residents and foreign skilled workers. Nevertheless, the price of land and completed dwellings has increased significantly though these factors do vary from areas to area (Brooks *et al.*, 2017). Environmental concerns about property development, especially of prime sea-facing land, need to be addressed.

As Mauritius faced an increasingly competitive environment, the government adopted a strategic approach and introduced a wide variety of initiatives such as the Film Rebate Scheme (2013), the Smart City Scheme (2015), the Mauritian Diaspora Scheme (2015) and the Bio Farming Promotion Scheme (2017). Investment opportunities are being provided in financial technology, the digital sector and the ocean economy (BOI, 2017b; Jeetah, 2017).

The most recent investment policy development on the island has been the establishment of the Economic Development Board, which has assumed the functions of the BOI, Enterprise Mauritius and the Financial Services Promotion Agency.

If one were to summarize or evaluate the FDI policy framework for Mauritius, it is undeniable that the evolution of FDI policies in Mauritius has reflected the ongoing changes in the developmental objectives set by the government and the challenges that the economy has been facing over the last five decades. The small, capital-scarce economy has experienced a constant need to diversify into new industries and markets. Its size and the need for capital has necessitated a broad development strategy espousing an outward-looking strategy.[12] This in turn has meant that FDI policies designed to attract foreign capital have kept pace with the Mauritian outward-looking development strategy, thus playing an instrumental role in this process. For example, the 1970 EPZ Act was repealed and replaced by the EPZ Act of 1990, while the 1990s saw the creation of the EPZDA which, it was hoped, would allow the industrial sector to remain competitive.

It should also be noted that several other policies and factors have contributed to the influx of FDI, although it is beyond the scope of this chapter to elaborate on them all here (see Mistry and Treebhoohun, 2009; Wignaraja *et al.*, 2004). This can be seen as a second facet of the notion that 'FDI does not operate in a vacuum'.

FDI's importance for growth

What do the facts say about FDI? Figure 7.1 comprises two graphs, which depict FDI inflows (see section 3 for details on OFDI). Graph B shows inward FDI to have been virtually non-existent – a consequence of the predominant import

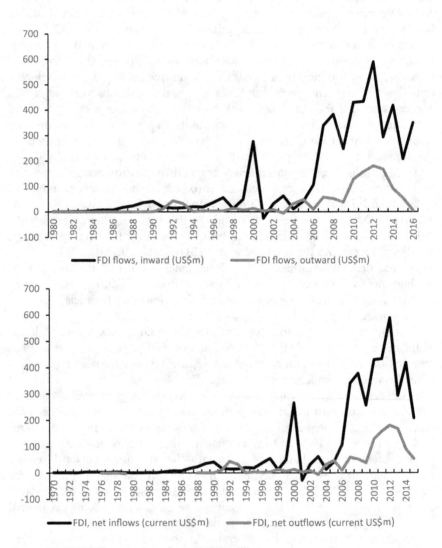

Figure 7.1 FDI inflows and outflows, US $ millions
Source: Graph A, UNCTAD; Graph B, World Development Indicators, World Bank.

substitution strategy of the time and the slow take-off of the EPZ, as mentioned above. It was not until the post-1985 period – coinciding with the take-off of the EPZ – that FDI inflows increased, although these remained modest owing to the fact that indigenous firms began to make their mark. There were small levels of investment in the 1990s but these a peaked with a one-off investment in 2000, namely the acquisition of a 40 per cent stake in Mauritius Telecom by France Telecom for US \$26 million (OECD, 2014; UNCTAD, 2001).

The 2000s witnessed some investment growth coinciding with the consolidated efforts of the government to foster investment through the BOI and the Business Facilitation Act of 2004 as well as the Integrated Resort Scheme that launched the real estate sector. However, since 2008 investment levels have fluctuated with substantial one-off and short-term investments having been made, but these could hardly sustain long-term support (see Sooreea-Bheemul and Sooreea, 2012), and this activity peaked in 2012.

An examination of the sectoral composition and geographical origin of inward FDI (see Table 7.1) reveals some interesting facts. Inward FDI had a strong presence in the service sector. Tourism (accommodation and food service activities) and the tradeable sector (wholesale and retail trade) benefited the most in the early 1990s, while the financial sector (financial and insurance activities) assumed a more important role in the late 1990s. In the 2000s, while manufacturing and the primary sectors remained modest in their contribution to overall FDI, the service sector saw the significant rise of the real estate sector alongside the financial sector and the tourism sector. The latter registered some stable levels of direct investment. Investment in real estate was fuelled by the Integrated Resort Scheme and post-2010 real estate has overtaken the tourism and financial sectors as the sector of prominence for FDI inflows.

The geographical origin of these investments is also shown in Graph B in Table 7.1. The 1990s were dominated by investment from the developing world, with Hong Kong in early part of the period and South Africa in the late 1990s, although there was some non-negligible investment by France in the early 1990s. Investment post-2000 came chiefly from the developed world and this has remained the case in recent years. This has been engineered by investment from France, which provides the largest source of FDI. Meanwhile, investment from South African is stable and has grown, and there has been significant investment from the People's Republic of China, India and the United Arab Emirates (UAE); together these four countries have accounted for the bulk of African and Asian FDI in recent years.

Evidence on what determines FDI in Mauritius. Ancharaz (2003b) empirically investigated the determinants of export-oriented FDI in Mauritius during the period 1971–1998, using a simple ordinary least squares (OLS) estimation. He found that the trade liberalization of the 1980s played a positive significant role, as did the real exchange rate – thus implying that a depreciating currency would have boosted export competitiveness. Domestic capital stock is also positively related to FDI, while rising wages acted as a deterrent.

Table 7.1 Sectoral composition and geographical origin of FDI inflows (Rs million)

	1990–1994	1995–1999	2000–2004	2005–2009	2010–2014	2015–2016
Grand total	1,767	3,682	12,943	41,755	79,478	29,915
Graph A: Sectors						
Agriculture, forestry and fishing	n.a.	n.a.	498	510	1,179	4
Manufacturing	n.a.	n.a.	620	1,349	4,340	1,303
Accommodation and food service activities	509	227	333	12,322	10,416	2,138
Financial and insurance activities	54	1,509	2,620	14,056	15,493	5,185
Real estate activities	n.a.	n.a.	475	13,882	28,512	18,429
Wholesale and retail trade	736	623	813	1,141	3,393	356
Graph B: Regions/countries						
Developed countries	529	872	9,961	27,554	45,555	16,995
France	231	149	8,121	5,625	17,205	8,596
United Kingdom	90	541	472	10,739	12,747	2,317
Switzerland	79	20	327	3,075	1,990	1,183
Luxemburg	17	66	29	746	1,893	998
United States	48	0	589	4,358	2,701	407
Developing countries	927	2,752	2775	14,,154	33,763	12,895
South Africa	14	1,538	1,979	2,487	13,197	3,970
India	122	325	294	3,680	4,866	422
China	35	0	51	471	5,594	3,013
UAE	0	213	74	2,636	2,172	1,181
Hong Kong	166	19	13	63	n.a.	n.a.

Source: Bank of Mauritius (1995, 2015, 2017).

Note: The table presents data over a five-year period, except for 2015 and 2016. Sectoral categorization has changed over the period, although we use loosely connected sectors with more recent labelling.

Subsequent evidence on what drives the influx of FDI in the island economy reveals the role of trade openness, domestic investment, real exchange rates, wages and the quality of labour, with market size being either insignificant or exhibiting smaller size effect (Beghum et al., 2011; Seetanah and Rojid, 2011). Evidence produced by Kisto (2017), which uses data from the period 1975–2015, estimates a vector error correction model (VECM). She finds that inflation and exchange rate are the only determinants of FDI. Inflation is seen as reflecting the higher profit margins which attract foreign investors, while the latter factor echoes the finding of Ancharaz (2003b) on the role of a depreciating currency.

While the above econometric evidence provides an understanding of the host country factors that mattered for FDI, still they are 'quantitative' in nature and so we cannot neglect 'qualitative' factors. It is undeniable that fiscal incentives and FDI-related policies along with broader institutional support have played a central role; whether in the EPZ, the tourism, financial and real estate sectors. Similarly, it is well documented that FDI in the EPZ sector was driven by low labour costs, domestic political uncertainty for Hong Kong investors, and beneficial trade agreements (Nath and Madhoo, 2004).

What does the evidence say about the role of FDI in Mauritian growth? Durbarry (2001), Ancharaz (2003b), and Nath and Madhoo (2004) all provide factual evidence and explanations for the FDI export-led industrialization and growth. Depicting the macroeconomic effects of the EPZ, Durbarry places it at 13 per cent of GDP in the 1990s compared to 2.6 per cent of GDP in 1976, so FDI played a key initial role in the sector.

Shifting attention to the econometric evidence, the long-term FDI-growth relationship is supported by Blin and Ouattara (2009)'s autoregressive distributed lag (ARDL) bounds cointegration estimation for the period 1975–2000. Sooreea-Bheemul and Sooreea (2012) confirm this evidence, but with the added qualification that it is FDI stock and not FDI inflows that have fuelled economic growth. Furthermore, Damoense-Azevedo (2013) provides interesting evidence that FDI affected growth through financial sector development.

Linked to this is the evidence provided in a number of works on the way in which FDI is linked to productivity spillovers in the manufacturing sector (an important source of growth), poverty reduction channelled via employment (as a by-product of growth), and financial market development (Fauzel *et al.*, 2015; Fauzel *et al.*, 2016; Fauzel, 2016).

Rationalization of why the FDI-growth link is significant despite the fact – as argued earlier – that FDI inflows have remained relatively small can be found when thinking about the channels through which FDI affects growth. Generally speaking, there are direct and indirect effects. The direct effect is the impact of FDI as foreign capital stock accumulation which is a major source of capital and henceforth a crucial component of growth. Instead, the indirect effect is channelled through two sources, exports and domestic investment. The first is export-led growth fostered through export spillovers. The second emerges thanks to knowledge or technology spillovers, often captured as productivity spillovers on domestic establishments contributing to capital formation (see Sooreea-Bheemul and Sooreea, 2012).

In the Mauritian context, with small FDI inflows, the direct impact would have been modest. Export-oriented FDI-led growth was of greatest importance in the formative years, but of greater significance in later years are technology spillovers and idea generation driven by domestic firms. Indeed, while foreign firms led the period of export-driven industrialization in the

1980s, this has changed because currently local firms lead the way in driving exports (UNCTAD, 2001). Domestic firms have learnt from foreign firms by copying and imitating them (Sooreea-Bheemul and Sooreea, 2012). It is noteworthy that several owners of indigenous firms in the EPZ had worked for neighbouring foreign firms (Moran, 2011).

Another source of horizontal spillovers are skills transfer. FDI appears to have enhanced the skills of local personnel through training and local players have entered into new market niches. This has been particularly evident in the services sectors such as tourism and finance. An example in tourism is the introduction of marketing know-how and modern reservation systems (UNCTAD, 2001).

When it comes to vertical spillovers indications suggest limited backward linkages, due to reliance on importing and thus a lack of supply chain integration. Nevertheless, linkages within the local economy have been observed (UNCTAD, 2001). Evidence shows that Mauritius compares favourably to other developing economies in the area of subcontracting. In the case of the EPZ, this partly relates to the initial zone set-up being unconstrained geographically; i.e. both foreign and local firms could choose to locate their operations wherever suited them best. Later the 1993 Industrial Expansion Act attempted to support local firms (Moran, 2011).

Support for spillovers in the Mauritian context is not surprising. As highlighted by the work of Fauzel et al. (2015), FDI had a positive impact on total factor productivity and labour productivity in the manufacturing sector, according to their estimates taken during the period 1980–2010. This is further supported by anecdotal evidence in several sectors: domestic firms sourcing the dyeing of fabric, and embroidery and sewing in the C&T industry; two Mauritian banks setting up in the offshore sector; the EPZ generating demand for services across a whole array of non-manufacturing activities which include packaging, consultancy and transport.

One explanation of how FDI could have fostered Mauritian growth can be drawn from the work of Paul Romer (Moran, 2006). This goes beyond envisioning FDI merely as a source of capital. FDI is a transmission mechanism for ideas and innovation, which consist of new and more sophisticated activities (ibid., 2011). More specifically, these could be marketing techniques, advanced production processes, and quality control procedures, that FDI provides to the local economy (ibid., 2006). Although the notion of spillovers as expounded above reverberates with the success stories in the tourism and financial sectors, the case of the C&T industry is less clear.

There are two sides to this. On the one hand, one could contend that Hong Kong-based businessmen helped to jumpstart the C&T industry by introducing the idea of C&T manufacturing (Frankel, 2010). As such,

> [w]hat foreigners brought were new ideas about managing clothing production and navigating the complex import quota system of the developed world ... What the foreigners added was the orchestration of the production

and marketing process that purely indigenous firms were initially incapable of achieving on their own.

(Moran, 2006: 19)

In short, FDI altered the production frontier of the country.

Yet a second line of thinking contends differently. Subramanian and Roy (2001) and Subramanian (2009) contest Romer's viewpoint. Their thinking is grounded on the notion that the presence of foreign companies in the EPZ had remained relatively small, even in the early years. However, Frankel (2010) suggests that 'idea of ideas' can be copied and learnt, as local firms did, but this does not take anything away from foreign firms as 'first movers'. A more thoughtful argument is that the idea of C&T production is somewhat obvious and it was favourable conditions such as the preferential treatment of Mauritian exports that helped (Subramanian, 2009).[13]

Still, critics argue that Mauritius faced other unfavourable conditions – such as its remote geographical location – and that other low-income economies also had similar favourable opportunities. For them, the key was that the island economy made the most of those favourable conditions, harnessing FDI to serve its purposes (Lin, 2012; UNCTAD, 2001). Moreover, the Romer argument does not dispute that C&T production may seem trivial, and in fact points to the fact that the production technology, such as weaving and sewing equipment, was readily obtainable on the global market. Instead, it emphasizes the 'softer' side – the technical ability required to steer through the global quota system or the necessary marketing expertise (Moran, 2006). Therefore, the debate remains open.

Opening up to go out

From a Mauritian perspective, a natural next step in its development and for export-oriented Mauritian firms is to 'go out' via foreign direct investment as a natural extension of its exporting activities. Page and Willem te Velde (2004) highlight some of the reasons for *outward investment from Mauritius.*

The first reason is a possible efficiency-seeking motive to reduce production costs given that higher factor costs reduced the competitiveness of Mauritian apparel and textiles. Nath and Madhoo (2004) argue that rising costs in the late 1980s and early 1990s led to a diversification strategy that gave impetus to FDI from Mauritius to foreign neighbouring countries. This led to the relocation of EPZ firms' plants to Madagascar and Mozambique, where production costs were relatively lower.

The second reason is driven by the need for a bigger market and an opportunity to expand in the light of a small-sized economy seeking to go beyond traditional export channels and exploit economies of scale (Page and Willem te Velde, 2004). Given the small local market, direct investment by Mauritian multinational companies is about exploiting their competencies gained over the years by moving abroad in search of new markets (Gunessee, 2017).

The third reason is connected to the idea of positioning the island as a gateway or platform to investing in third jurisdictions, such as a gateway to Africa. From this perspective, DTAs and bilateral investment treaties (BITs) play a significant role. Thus, the conclusion of a number of DTAs and the simplification of the corporate tax system strategically enhanced the attractiveness of Mauritius as a low-tax platform acting as a conduit for FDI to 'third countries' such as South Africa and India (OECD, 2014). Undoubtedly, the offshore/global business sector benefited greatly as a result of the DTA with India because Mauritius became a preferred means through which to channel investment to India (OECD, 2001). After the elaboration of its New Africa Strategy in 2012, Mauritius actively sought DTAs and BITs with several African countries to ensure not only a favourable tax regime but investor protection (OECD, 2014).

Figure 7.1 depicts FDI flows during the period 1970–2016. Graph A (1980–2016) and Graph B (1970–2015) show that OFDI from Mauritius was non-existent until the early 1990s. The spike in investment that occurred in 1992 coincided with the DTA with India becoming an important instrument through which to channel FDI for the first time as the offshore sector took off. However, it was not until the 2000s that OFDI became important, coinciding with the changing attitudes of Mauritian businesses and the Mauritian government. There was a surge in OFDI between 2010 and 2013 but it then plummeted.

The financial sector was a key purveyor of outbound investment in the early 1990s, along with a one-off hotel-related investment. In the 2000s, while finance and insurance activities have remained a central source of outward investment, other industries took a more prominent role including manufacturing and accommodation and food service activities (hotel and restaurant business) and some non-negligible investment in the primary sector. Recent investment from manufacturing, primary sector and hotel-related services have shown stable levels, with finance and insurance activities exhibiting a surge from 2010 onwards.

Prior to 2002 the geographical decomposition saw some one-off and short-term investments in Réunion and India, although at still quite modest levels. In the 2000s much of the investment has been to the developing world, in particular to Madagascar, Mozambique, Seychelles and the Maldives. It is interesting to note that OFDI to India and South Africa appear small. This is due to the fact that the detailed geographical data is sourced from the Bank of Mauritius which factors out the global business sector (cf. Figure 7.1).

UNCTAD's 2001 *Investment Policy Review* for Mauritius provides a number of examples of Mauritian companies that have ventured abroad with some degree of success. One leading Mauritian company, the MCB, has established a strong presence in the Indian Ocean and also ventured abroad through its acquisition of the Banque Française Commerciale Océan Indien in 1992. In C&T, Floreal Knitwear was first to venture into Madagascar in 1990, followed by the Compagnie Mauricienne de Textile.

In tourism, several well-known hotel establishments have sought to exploit their core competencies in hotel management in Seychelles and the Maldives, including the less successful Moroccan venture by New Mauritius Hotels (Beachcomber) through its Royal Palm brand and recent venture in France in the form of Beachcomber French Riviera. Instead, in telecommunications, *Emtel* – a subsidiary of the Currimjee Group – has invested in Seychelles and Madagascar.

As a way to promote the New Africa Strategy a Mauritius Africa Fund valued at Rs 500 million was set up to support projects in the African continent, and an African Centre for Excellence, under the aegis of the BOI, is providing networking and business intelligence services. A recent initiative, following the 2015–2016 National Budget, to foster investment opportunities in Africa is the launch of special economic zones in African countries that so far include Ghana, Côte d'Ivoire and Senegal (BOI, 2017b).

Gunessee (2017) studies what determines outbound FDI from Mauritius into Africa. He finds certain 'dynamism' in FDI location, with previous or current investment acting as 'information' for subsequent investment. A larger market is also found to be crucial, although potential market opportunities are not as significant. The study confirms the role of the incentive effect of DTAs, while regional economic cooperation in the form of the SADC is salient.

A few policy implications are outlined in his work, but the most relevant is from a development perspective, noting the absence of concrete evidence on the OFDI-growth link. It is argued that it is difficult for Mauritius to achieve high-income economy status without balanced inward-outward FDI. This is explained using the Investment Development Path (IDP) lens (see Dunning and Narula, 2000). Using the IDP, we can view an economy's growth or development trajectory in stages where first it receives little inward FDI and almost zero outward FDI as they are at a low-income stage. As it progresses and the economic structure within the economy changes it becomes the recipient of growing inward FDI but still engages in little OFDI. As part of further restructuring, the next development stage sees dominant inward FDI, though now with rising OFDI. It is during the subsequent stage that inward FDI is outstripped by outward FDI levels, with a final stage of balanced investment. At 2019, Mauritius is probably at the third stage, with growing OFDI that is still modest compared to inward FDI.

What next?

In this section, we enumerate the key challenges (and opportunities) for Mauritius in terms of FDI. These challenges include structural vulnerabilities and transformation; a coherent FDI policy framework; and other 'supporting' factors.

Structural vulnerabilities and transformation

In its continued attempt to attract FDI the Mauritian economy is constrained by a small market that necessitates frequent policy changes, the loss of cost competitiveness due to rising wages that are not matched by productivity increases, a lack of skills and infrastructure to facilitate a move towards higher value-added activities, a predominance of short-termism among current investors with the inability to attract sustained long-term investment (partly due to the aforementioned policy changes), and a lack of quality and high-end investment. Despite these challenges, Mauritius still aspires to become a high-income economy by 2030. As such, there are structural difficulties and a need for structural transformation (OECD, 2014; Sooreea-Bheemul and Sooreea, 2012).

Thus, significant efforts have been made to address these shortcomings in recent years with attempts to expand specific sectors and sub-sectors coupled with the adoption of a vertical diversification strategy towards higher value-added segments to increase the productivity of foreign and local firms. For example, the idea of a 'seafood hub' in the 2000s seems to have metamorphosed into a broader initiative for the development of an ocean economy (BOI, 2017b). Within real estate, ideas have evolved and the concept of smart cities has been explored (BOI, 2015b). Following on from the idea of a knowledge hub and smart cities, the digital economy initiative is now in vogue (ibid., 2017b). In addition, certain niche areas in the traditional sectors are being pursued, such as seed production and bio-farming in the agro-industry (ibid., 2016). The ICT-BPO sector is seeking investment in cloud services, mobile applications and big data services (Jeetah, 2017). Health care is branching out into clinical trials and is making further inroads into medical tourism which can offer cosmetic surgery such as hair grafting, for example (BOI, 2017c).[14] A film rebate scheme has been proposed to develop the entertainment industry, with the film 'Serenity' (Habermeyer, 2018) being one of the largest Hollywood productions to benefit from this scheme. The film was almost entirely shot in Mauritius and was consequently a major source of income for the island (Habermeyer, 2018). However, it is still early days to say whether these endeavours will be successful and how FDI will react.

A coherent FDI policy framework

The Economic Development Board (EDB) was set up to ensure better coherence and more effective policy implementation,. Its aim was to further simplify procedures and to facilitate foreign investment in and out of Mauritius, to ensure increased participation of the local small and medium-sized enterprise (SME) sector, and the continued promotion of the financial architecture.[15] A key aspect of this change is unlike its predecessor, the BOI, the EDB is also tasked with 'strategic economic planning and economic policy formulation' (UNCTAD, 2017: 13). This should ensure a connection of FDI-related initiatives and policies with the development goals of the island nation.

A coherence between the foreign-local sectors is important as it can help to foster entrepreneurship, the latter being a by-product of FDI through a 'crowding-in' mechanism (SMEs as 'supporting' entities). Additionally, horizontal and vertical spillovers can develop through technology transfers from foreign to local establishments. As argued above, these externalities are an important source of growth. However, an important aspect of the EDB's mandate is to also promote the 'Africa Strategy', whether through SME exporting or outbound FDI by more accomplished Mauritian enterprises as they turn into multinationals.

What is lacking, according to UNCTAD's *Report on the Implementation of Policy Review*, is a 'consolidated investment code or policy statement on investment' (2017: 12). Such consolidated information would define time-bound and strategic investment goals, better alignment with other national strategy codes, and enable the coherence of an investment policy framework with these investment goals (OECD, 2014). For example, such policy information would document priority sectors and administration criteria (UNCTAD, 2017).

Other 'supporting' factors

Institutional change is required to match the anticipated structural transformation of the Mauritian economy. As documented by OECD (2014) and UNCTAD (2017), this could include strengthening and enforcing the intellectual property rights regime, instituting independent sector regulators that monitor possible monopoly practices, review trade strategies to sustain competitiveness, and expand BITs and DTAs, but with upgraded content that reinforces investor protection and maintains a cost-effective investment regime.

Two further supporting factors can be emphasized. One is the improvement of telecommunications and port infrastructure to deepen links with neighbouring countries and enhance port efficiency, respectively. The second is human resource development. This is essential to deal with skills mismatch and inadequate expertise in certain areas. This manifests itself in the following manner: development of the curriculum to meet industry needs; reaffirm quality in the higher education sector by encouraging private tertiary units and attracting top foreign universities and business schools or at least offering dual degrees with them; need for technical training through polytechnics and a curriculum adapted to meet that need.

Conclusion

In this chapter we outlined the evolution of FDI and FDI policies and their connection to Mauritius' economic progress. We offered a chronological review of inward FDI and how it has affected the country's economic development. A review of FDI policies documented how the FDI policy framework had to evolve over time in order to keep pace with the Mauritian development strategy, including the outward-looking strategy adopted to fuel this growth.

It is undeniable that FDI has played a key role, but unlike other developing economies, this has come through spillovers and externalities that fostered the emergence of the domestic private sector. For instance, while the early pioneers in the EPZ originated from overseas, some of these industries now have lower foreign participation. As such, Mauritius has been able to harness this initial FDI and favourable conditions to chart an export-oriented development path. Although subject to debate, it has been argued that these foreign companies were pioneers in the sense they brought the skills and expertise required to navigate the world market. These ideas in turn unlocked the Mauritian entrepreneurial potential as indigenous firms began to emerge.

In spite of its reduced role, FDI has continued to play a far from negligible role in the Mauritian economy, especially in later years defined by diversification in the economy where FDI made some important inroads. Such sectors as ICT, health, education, and real estate all received influxes of foreign capital. In effect, Mauritian economic development could be said to have been the balancing of domestic-foreign investment. FDI played a key foundational role in the development of most sectors, but thereafter Mauritian entrepreneurs have taken up the responsibility for continuing this development.

Finally, the Mauritian economy and the country's private sector have also started to look outwards by investing abroad; in particular, investment in Africa has been steadily increasing. Although not immediately apparent in its growth effect, outward FDI can undeniably help to foster progress as Mauritius moves onto a trajectory towards becoming a high-income economy. This road is fraught with challenges as well as opportunities and thus the salient aspect of this journey is one of harnessing the necessary levels of investment in order to foster sustainable and resilient economic development.

Notes

1 Indeed, during the 1990s FDI as a percentage of gross domestic capital formation stood at around 3 per cent in comparison to 7–9 per cent in the developing world, including Africa (UNCTAD, 2001; Sacerdoti *et al.*, 2005).

2 It is argued that the origins of the EPZ can be traced back to study trips to several countries such as Taiwan, Hong Kong and Singapore to understand the operation of free zones in these economies and the key encouraging role played by Prof. Edouard Lim Fat (Durbarry, 2001; Lim Fat, 2010). Nevertheless, it is also argued that these origins can be further linked to the establishment of the company Micro Jewels in 1965 by the Swiss-Mauritian businessman José Poncini, who exported processed jewellery long before the advent of the EPZ (Hein, 1996; Lim Fat, 2010). Interestingly, Poncini had interactions with Meade during his visits to the island in the early 1960s and further expounded on his idea of an export-oriented strategy when called upon by the establishment (Poncini, 2018). Critics argue that the 1970 EPZ Act drew on his ideas (Gujadhur, 2015). The initial take-off of the EPZ in the 1970s is also associated with the reinvested profits from the sugar industry (Durbarry, 2001).

3 It is argued that the uncertainty of Hong Kong's handover to the People's Republic of China played a role, whereby Mauritian nationality was also offered to these investors.

4 This diversification into the C&T industry became more pressing with the ending of the Multi-Fibre Agreement, although there was a short respite with the US African Growth and Opportunity Act (AGOA). In the case of the sugar industry the ending of the Sugar Protocol with the European Community in the mid-2000s also added to the need to diversify (Sacerdoti *et al.*, 2005). The centralization of production, local processing and refinery, branching out into by-products such as ethanol, electricity generation through bagasse, and a voluntary retirement scheme for workers under the aegis of the Sugar Sector Strategic Plan, has seen the industry morph into a diversified cane industry, with the few remaining players further diversifying their investment portfolios into other sectors (Desai and Tulsidas, 2011).

5 By the mid-2000s Mauritius had established a reputation for the production of 'fully fashioned knitwear' and 'pure new wool products', for which it had become respectively the second and third largest exporter in the world (Wignaraja *et al.*, 2004). In recent years there have been initiatives to branch out into synthetic fibre and technical textile products (BOI, 2017b).

6 A recent snapshot of the manufacturing sector reveals C&T occupying only around 30 per cent of sectoral output, with food processing – excluding processed sugar – being the most significant, while precious stones, high-end jewellery, watchmaking and precision engineering, although relatively small, have been identified as being growth poles in the sector (Jeetah, 2017).

7 Licences for foreign operators to operate in the Mauritian freeport are obtainable from the Economic Development Board of Mauritius. See www.efreeport.com/.

8 Constraining factors include conscious efforts towards environmental and sustainable development, with specific initiatives such as a 'green ceiling' with respect to the number of hotels and hotel rooms being available, and the general concept of 'Maurice – L'Ile Durable' (Vangerow-Kühn, 2011).

9 In 2005 the number of operators amounted to about 50; this number had increased eight-fold by 2009 (Mistry and Treebhoohun, 2009).

10 See 'Invest in Mauritius'. Available at www.anahitaproperty.com/.

11 It been argued that FDI inflows into Mauritius have been predominantly export-oriented (Ancharaz, 2003a, 2003b), although a more refined classification might be *export-platform* FDI (see Ekholm *et al.*, 2007). The distinction being made here is that the latter involves using Mauritius as a gateway or platform to export to a 'third country', while export-oriented FDI could also entail sending exports home, as exemplified by *vertical FDI*.

12 Although Mauritius adopted an outward-looking strategy it did not completely open up in the true sense of an open economy till later on. Indeed, it is well documented that the island economy chose a development path based on a 'dual track' approach which maintained a separate import substitution local sector and an export-oriented one till the 1990s (Lin, 2012; Sacerdoti *et al.*, 2005).

13 Under the Multi-Fibre Agreement Hong Kong businessmen had reached the export quota limit, and thus needed a new base. Furthermore, the World Trade Organization allowed developing countries to reduce their effective protection relatively slowly compared to their developed counterparts, further enhancing their exporting advantage (Sacerdoti *et al.*, 2005; Frankel, 2010).

14 The Centre de Chirurgie Esthétique de l'Océan Indien is a pioneering example.

15 See www.edbmauritius.org/.

References

Ancharaz, V. D. (2003a) 'The Effect of Trade Liberalization on Export-Oriented Output and FDI: A Case Study of the Mauritian EPZ, 1971–1998', *University of Mauritius Research Journal (Law, Management & Social Sciences)* 5.

Ancharaz, V. D. (2003b) *FDI and Export Performance of the Mauritian Manufacturing Sector*, Moka: University of Mauritius.

Bank of Mauritius (1995, 2010, 2017) *Bank of Mauritius Annual Report*, Port Louis: Bank of Mauritius.

Beghum, N., Sannassee, R. V., Seetanah, B. and Lamport, M. J. (2011) 'On the Determinants of Foreign Capital Flows: Evidence from an African Economy', Proceedings of the International Conference on International Trade and Investment, University of Mauritius and WTO Chairs Programme, December, Le Meridien Hotel, Balaclava.

Blin, M. and Ouattara, B. (2009) 'Foreign Direct Investment and Economic Growth in Mauritius: Evidence from Bounds Test Cointegration', *Économie Internationale* 117: 47–61.

Bhantooa, S. (2012) 'FDI and the Banking Sector: Can Basel II, a Banking Regulation in any Way Promote FDI?', presentation at the FDI in Mauritius National Conference, Domaine Les Pailles, April.

Bheenick, R. and Schapiro, M. O. (1989) 'Mauritius: A Case Study of the Export Processing Zone', *EDI Development Policy Case Studies 1*, Washington, DC: World Bank.

Board of Investment (BOI) (2015a) *Broadening the Economic Horizon: Annual Report 2015*, Port Louis: BOI.

Board of Investment (BOI) (2015b) *Smart Mauritius: Live, Invest, Work and Play*, Port Louis: BOI.

Board of Investment (BOI) (2016) *The Mauritius Agro-Industry: Moving towards Technology-Based and High Value Activities*, Port Louis: BOI.

Board of Investment (BOI) (2017a) *Mauritius Real Estate & Tourism: Live, Invest, Work and Play*, Port Louis: BOI.

Board of Investment (BOI) (2017b) *Mauritius: A Sustainable Investment*, Port Louis: BOI.

Board of Investment (BOI) (2017c) *L'Île Maurice: Les Soins de Santé*, Port Louis: BOI.

Bank of Mauritius (2018) *Gross Direct Investment Flows in Mauritius: Calendar Year 2017*, Port Louis: Bank of Mauritius.

Brooks, C., Lamport, M., Padachi, K., Sannassee, V., Seetah, K. and Seetanah, B. (2017) 'The Impact of Foreign Real Estate Investment on Land Prices: Evidence from Mauritius', *Review of Development Economics* 21(4): 131–146.

Chan-Meetoo, C. (2007) *ICT, Society and Poverty: The Vision of Mauritius as a Cyber Island from a Development Perspective*, Moka: University of Mauritius.

Damoense-Azevedo, M. Y. (2013) 'Modeling Long-Run Determinants of Economic Growth for the Mauritian Economy', *Journal of Developing Areas* 47(1): 1–21.

Desai, B. and Tulsidas, V. (2011) 'The Mauritian Sugar Industry', *AXYS Stockbroking Ltd*, September. Available at www.axys-group.com/media/8774/sugar_2011.09.12.pdf.

Dunning, J. and Narula, R. (2000) 'Industrial Development, Globalization and Multinational Enterprises: New Realities for Developing Countries', *Oxford Development Studies* 28(2): 141–167.

Durbarry, R. (2001) 'The Export Processing Zone', in R. Dabee and D. Greenaway (eds) *The Mauritian Economy: A Reader*, New York: Palgrave Macmillan.

Ekholm, K., Forslid, R. and Markusen, J. (2007) 'Export-Platform Foreign Direct Investment', *Journal of European Economic Association* 5(4): 776–795.

Greenaway, D. and Gooroochurn, N. (2001) 'Structural Adjustment and Economic Growth', in R. Dabee and D. Greenaway (eds) *The Mauritian Economy: A Reader*, New York: Palgrave Macmillan.

Fauzel, S. (2016) 'Modeling the Relationship between FDI and Financial Development in Small Island Economies: A PVAR Approach', *Theoretical Economics Letters* 6: 367–375.

Fauzel, S., Sannassee, R. V. and Seetanah, B. (2016) 'A Dynamic Investigation of Foreign Direct Investment and Poverty Reduction in Mauritius', *Theoretical Economics Letters* 6, 289–303.

Fauzel, S., Seetanah, B. and Sannassee, R. V. (2015) 'Productivity Spillovers of FDI in the Manufacturing Sector of Mauritius: Evidence from A Dynamic Framework', *Journal of Developing Areas* 49(2): 295–316.

Frankel, J. (2010) 'Mauritius: African Success Story', HKS Faculty Research Working Paper Series RWP10–036, Cambridge, MA: John F. Kennedy School of Government, Harvard University.

Gujadhur, A. (2015) 'Of Economic Development, Entrepreneurship and José Poncini', *Mauritius Times*, 27 November.

Gunessee, S. (2017) 'Going Out: Explaining Mauritian Outward Foreign Direct Investment in Africa', proceedings of the Mauritius after 50 Years of Independence: Charting the Way Forward Conference, Moka, Mauritius, June.

Habermeyer, A. (2018) *Mauritius: Preferred Shooting Destination*, 3 July, Blog.

Hein, P. (1996) *L'economie de L'Ile Maurice*, Paris: L'Harmattan.

Isaacs, S. (2007) *Survey of ICT and Education in Africa: Mauritius Country Report*, Washington, DC: World Bank.

Jeeha, P. (2012) 'Real Estate: A Major Driver of FDI Inflows', presented at the FDI in Mauritius National Conference, Domaine Les Pailles, April.

Jeetah, N. (2017) *Mauritius: Your Investment Platform*, Mauritius: Board of Investment.

Kisto, M. (2017) 'Determinants of Foreign Direct Investment in Mauritius: Evidence from Time Series Data', *International Journal of Scientific & Technology Research* 6(8): 367–377.

Lim Fat, E. (2010) *From Vision to Miracle: Memoirs of Sir Edouard Lim Fat and the Story of Mauritius Export Processing Zone (EPZ)*, Mauritius: T-Printers Co.

Lin, J. Y. (2012) *The Quest for Prosperity: How Developing Economies Can Take-Off*, Princeton, NJ: Princeton University Press.

Mauritius-Africa Business Club (2013) 'Strengthening Economic Growth of Mauritius through a Coherent, Deepened and Effective Mauritius Africa Strategy', advocacy paper, March, Port Louis: MABC. Available at www.myt.mu/Magic/MABC.pdf

Meade, J. E. (1961) 'Mauritius: A Case Study in Malthusian Economics', *Economic Journal* 71: 521–534.

Meade, J. E. (1967) 'Population Explosion, the Standard of Living and Social Conflict', *Economic Journal* 77: 233–255.

Meade, J. E. et al. (1961) *The Economics and Social Structure of Mauritius*, London: Methuen.

Mistry, P. and Treebhoohun, N. (2009) *The Export of Tradeable Services: A Commonwealth Case Study in Economic Transformation*, London: Commonwealth Secretariat.

Moran, T. (2006) *Harnessing Foreign Direct Investment for Development: Policies for Developed and Developing Countries*, Washington, DC: Center for Global Development.

Moran, T. (2011) *Foreign Direct Investment and Development: Launching a Second Generation of Policy Research*, Washington, DC: Peterson Institute for International Economics.

Nath, S. and Madhoo, Y. N. (2004) 'Explaining African Economic Growth Perfor-
mance: The Case of Mauritius', draft interim report on Mauritius case study for the
African Economic Research Consortium Project entitled 'Explaining African
Economic Growth Performance', Nairobi, Kenya.

Organisation for Economic Co-operation and Development (OECD) (2014) *OECD
Investment Policy Reviews: Mauritius 2014*, Paris: OECD.

Page, S. and Willem te Velde, D. (2004) 'Foreign Direct Investment by African Countries', paper prepared for InWent/UNCTAD meeting on FDI in Africa, 22–24
November,Addis Ababa. Available at www.odi.org.uk/resources/ download/4688.pdf.

Poncini, J. (2018) *Bâtir sur Ses Rêves*, Port Louis: Éditions Vivazi.

Rawat, V. (2012) 'Foreign Direct Investment in Health Care', paper presented at the
FDI in Mauritius National Conference, Domaine Les Pailles, April.

Rojid, S., Sannassee, R. and Fowdar, S. (2009) 'The Net Contribution of the Mauritian Export Processing Zone Using Benefit-Cost Analysis', *Journal of International
Development* 21(3): 379–392.

Sacerdoti, E., El-Masry, G., Khandelwal, P. and Yao, Y. (2005) *Mauritius: Challenges
of Sustained Growth*, Washington, DC: International Monetary Fund.

Seetanah, B. (2013) 'Inward FDI in Mauritius and Its Policy Context', *Columbia Profiles, Vale Columbia Center on Sustainable International Investment*, April. Available
at http://ccsi.columbia.edu/files/2014/03/Mauritius_IFDI_-_April_30_-_FINAL.pdf.

Seetanah, B. and Rojid, S. (2011) 'The determinants of FDI in Mauritius: A Dynamic
Time Series Investigation', *African Journal of Economic and Management Studies* 2(1):
24–41.

Sobhee, S. K. (2009) 'The Economic Success of Mauritius: Lessons and Policy Options
for Africa', *Journal of Economic Policy Reform* 12(1): 29–42.

Sooreea-Bheemul, B. and Sooreea, R. (2012) 'Mauritius as a Success Story for FDI:
What Strategy and Policy Lessons Can Emerging Markets Learn?', *Journal of
International Business Research* 11(2): 119–144.

Srivastava, M. (2012) 'An Analysis of Foreign Direct Investment in the Tourism Sector
of Mauritius', paper presented at the FDI in Mauritius National Conference,
Domaine Les Pailles, April.

Subramanian, A. (2009) 'The Mauritian Success Story and Its Lessons', UNU-
WIDER Research Paper No. 2009.36, Helsinki: UNU-WIDER.

Subramanian, A. and Roy, D. (2001) 'Who Can Explain the Mauritian Miracle?
Meade, Romer, Sachs or Rodrik', IMF Working Paper No. 01/116, Washington,
DC: International Monetary Fund.

Svirydzenka, K. and Petri, M. (2017) 'Mauritius: The Drivers of Growth: Can the
Past Be Extended?', *Journal of Banking and Financial Economics* 2(8): 54–83.

Tandrayen-Ragoobur, V. and Kasseeah, H. (2018) 'Mauritius' Economic Success
Uncovered', in R.. Ramtohul, and T. H.. Eriksen (eds) *The Mauritian Paradox:
Fifty Years of Development, Diversity and Democracy*, Réduit: University of Mauritius
Press.

Tertiary Education Commission (TEC) (2018a) *Regulatory Framework for Post-
secondary Education*, Réduit: Tertiary Education Commission.

Tertiary Education Commission (TEC) (2018b) *Private Tertiary Education Institutions
in Mauritius*, Réduit: Tertiary Education Commission. Available at www.tec.mu/p
rivate_institutions.

Titmuss, R. M. and Abel-Smith, B. (1961) *Social Policies and Population Growth in
Mauritius*, London: Methuen.

United Nations Conference on Trade and Development (UNCTAD) (2001) *Investment Policy Review: Mauritius*, Geneva: UNCTAD.

United Nations Conference on Trade and Development (UNCTAD) (2006) *Country Profile: Mauritius*, Geneva. UNCTAD.

United Nations Conference on Trade and Development (UNCTAD) (2017) *Report on the Implementation of the Investment Policy Review: Mauritius*, Geneva: UNCTAD.

Vangerow-Kühn, T. B. (2011) *From Cane to Computers: Structural Change in Mauritius – Threatened by Brain Drain*, Saarbrücken: AV Akademikerverlag.

Wignaraja, G., Lezama, M. and Joiner, D. (2004) *Small States in Transition: From Vulnerability to Competitiveness*, London: Commonwealth Secretariat.

Willem te Velde, D., Massa, I. and Calì, M. (2010) *Supporting Investment and Private Sector Development in Times of Crisis: Strategies for Small States*, London: Commonwealth Secretariat.

Zafar, A. (2011) 'Mauritius: An Economic Success Story', in P. Chuhan-Pole and M. Angwafo (eds) *Yes Africa Can*, Washington, DC: World Bank.

8 Analysing the human capital-economic growth nexus

The case of Mauritius

H. Neeliah and B. Seetanah

Introduction

The historical perspective

Since gaining its independence in 1968, Mauritius has made the transition from a low-income to an upper-middle-income country. It has relied on an export-oriented strategy, supported by preferential trade agreements. Mauritius had the capability and capacity to respond to the opportunities offered by these agreements (Subramanian, 2009). Successive governments have continually invested in the provision of free education and health services, with the objective of upholding the country's social fabric as well as contributing towards building a labour force capable of contributing to and reaping the benefits of socio-economic development. Annual gross domestic product (GDP) has averaged growth of more than 5 per cent since 1968, with Mauritius concomitantly straddling the three traditional stages of development, from the primary sector towards services.

A number of factors have contributed to this exceptional socio-economic growth (see, for example, Subramanian and Roy, 2003; Dinan, 2005; Zafar, 2011). These include, but are not restricted to, adequate structural adjustment, political stability and leadership, conducive international trade agreements, openness to trade, judicious redistribution of rents, foreign direct investment friendly and supportive human capital.

Human capital has often been flagged as being a significant engine of growth for Mauritius, but there is a dearth of studies that have directly investigated this nexus. A large body of literature has been generated, investigating the relationship between human capital and economic growth under different country settings. The empirical evidence generated is highly context-specific and is not necessarily replicable across a small island like Mauritius. Hence, the effect of human capital on economic growth in Mauritius cannot be empirically inferred from the literature. Some exceptions exist, including Neeliah and Seetanah (2016) and Odit et al. (2010). Our objective here is to bring new credence on the role and linkage of human capital with economic growth. The chapter is organized as follows: section two delves into human capital formation in Mauritius, section three describes the theories and empirics underpinning human capital, section four details the empirical model, and section five presents the findings. We offer some conclusions in section six.

Human capital formation

Human capital formation is the process of acquiring and increasing the number of individuals who have the skills, education and experience to increase productivity and who are critical for the socio-economic development of a country. Therefore, the average stock of human capital at the economy level increases productivity at the corporate level. Theoretical models of human capital have been developed and built around this premise. Apart from potentially benefiting individual companies, human capital also exhibits intergenerational externalities whereby younger individuals also benefit from the knowledge and skills accumulated by their elders, and this is expressed at school, in the workplace and in society in general. The private and social returns of human capital (especially in education) are well recognized and acknowledged in Mauritius, both by the government and individuals.

Growth productivity and human capital formation in Mauritius

From a theoretical perspective, human capital is one of the most important components in explaining growth because it has a positive impact on output through various channels. It influences growth through labour productivity (Romer, 1990; Pungpond and Piriya, 2016), the demand for labour (Bergheim, 2005) and the harnessing of innovation and technology. Given that multifactor productivity is measured as the residual part of GDP growth that cannot be explained by changes in labour and capital inputs, it thus covers the effect of changes in innovation management, training, use of knowledge and organizational changes.

Given the inter-relationship between productivity and human capital, it is important to look at the way in which the various productivity indices in Mauritius have trended over the past three decades or so. From 1982 to 2017 there was a 166.7 per cent and a 58.6% increase in labour and multifactor productivity, with annual average growth of 4.8 per cent and 1.7 per cent, respectively. Meanwhile, unit labour costs increased by 466 per cent from 1982 to 2017. As illustrated in Figure 8.1 the unit labour cost trend has been criss-crossing the labour productivity trend since 1993, but from 2007 the unit labour cost index has been trending higher than the labour productivity index. Annual growth in multifactor productivity has been more chequered over the same period. During the period 1982–2007 annual growth in labour productivity averaged 2.1 per cent compared to 2.8% from 2007 to 2017; annual growth in multifactor productivity averaged 1.8 per cent compared to 0.9 per cent during the same period. On the other hand, the average annual growth

Figure 8.1 Productivity indices and unit labour costs for the period 1982–2017
Source: Statistics Mauritius (2018).

rates of unit labour costs were 3.1 per cent and 3.5 per cent, respectively, over the same time frame.

The above qualitative analysis shows that increases in labour productivity have been quite slight since 2007, and have not compensated for the relatively higher increases in factors that comprise unit labour costs (for example wages, salaries, social security and pension payments). Both labour and multifactor productivity need to be systematically improved in order to boost national competitiveness.

Sustained growth in multifactor and labour productivity are reliant on improvements in a population's human capital through education, nutrition and health (Barro and Sala-i-Martin, 1995). On balance, the evidence shows that investment in human capital has a positive and significant effect on productivity.

Education policies

Since independence successive governments have placed strong emphasis on the centrality of education as a prime driver of socio-economic development and have attempted to remodel the education system so that it is more responsive to the emerging needs of the socio-economy. In Mauritius, education is free at all levels, spanning early childhood to university, but public provision is also complemented by private education financed by individuals.

Mauritius has embarked on reform of the primary and secondary education sectors, coined by the nine-year continuous basic education programme, which was implemented in 2017. This reform adheres to the philosophy underpinning United Nations Sustainable Development Goal 4 pertaining to education that aims to 'ensure inclusive and equitable quality education and promote lifelong learning opportunities for all'. It has been designed to provide a more holistic education to children by focusing on developing essential competencies in children aged between five and sixteen years. The education reform process is placing added emphasis on the cognitive development of learners, preparing them to better adapt to an increasingly dynamic and uncertain future. The reform also aims to accord greater recognition to the value of vocational and technical education within the education system.

Over the last 30 years or so there has been a sea change in post-secondary education locally in terms of more generalized access. There is now a myriad of formal public and private institutions offering a wide variety of courses. Higher education is now offered by local and international providers. Given the complexities and intricacies of mobility and articulation in the higher education ecosystem, a Higher Education legislation was enacted in 2017. The legislation and the associated support ecosystem need to foment better regulation, accreditation of courses and equivalence of qualifications.

Given the protracted need for higher skill levels to propel the economy forwards, the realities of youth employment, the expected changes in the world of work, the dire need for science, technology, engineering and mathematics skills, it is not surprising that the Mauritian government is placing added emphasis on the higher education sector.

Human capital expenditure

Government expenditure on education and health

Mauritius has sustainably invested in education over the past few decades, making it accessible for individuals in various age cohorts. This has generally occurred as a result of strong fiscal position and judicious recycling of rents towards human capital formation, including expenditure on education and health services. Between 1972 and 2017 health expenditure as a percentage of government expenditure has averaged 8.5% annually.[1] Education has been established as the main component of human capital formation (see Bergheim, 2005), and respective government expenditures have reflected this fact. Expenditure on education averaged 14.4 per cent during the same period, standing at 13.6 per cent in 2017. Education and health expenditure together accounted for a significant 23.4 per cent of government expenditure in that year. This supports the hypothesis that since the early 1970s successive policymakers and governments have recognized the importance of human capital to the Mauritian socio-economic fabric and have supported it financially.

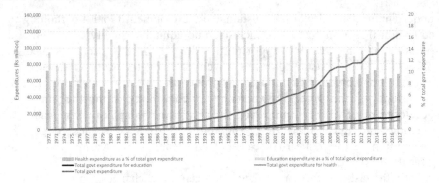

Figure 8.2 Health and education expenditure as a percentage of total government
          expenditure (1972–2017)
Source: Statistics Mauritius (2018).

Primary, secondary and tertiary education

Traditionally, the government has proportionally expended a larger share of its
education budget on secondary education. This is built on the premise that
investment in secondary education is a crucial foundation upon which tertiary
education and subsequent skills development can build upon to foster human
capital formation. The government spent 47.8 per cent and 56.6 per cent in 1995
and 2017, respectively, on secondary education. During the same years expenditure on tertiary education was 11.7 per cent and 8.4 per cent, respectively,[2]
whereas expenditure on technical and vocational education was 1.3 per cent and
3.2 per cent, respectively (Figure 8.3).

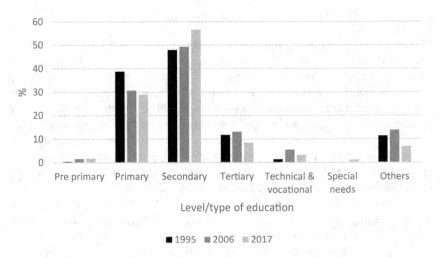

Figure 8.3 Breakdown of government expenditure on education in 1996, 2006 and 2017
Source: Statistics Mauritius (2018).

Human capital: underpinning theories and empirics

Neoclassical theory

The various theories of economic growth account for human capital differently. Solow (1956) and Swan (1956) developed the neoclassical growth theory, positing that the output of an economy grows as a result of increasing input of capital and labour. Under such a scenario, the economy would suffer from the law of diminishing returns and an infusion of technological progress was the only way to minimize the effects of diminishing returns and grow the economy. As highlighted by Awel (2013), the neoclassical theory consequently implied that the long-term growth rate was exogenously determined, thus also directly ignoring the direct contribution of human capital.

New endogenous theory

In the mid-1980s it was acknowledged that there are other factors that could explain economic growth which are not accounted for by the neoclassical exogenous growth models. Romer (1990) stressed that the long-term rate of economic growth is also determined by factors that are endogenous to the economic system. One such factor is human capital. The concept of capital was thus broadened to also include human capital, and the term 'endogenous growth models' was coined. The argument behind this inclusion was that healthy and educated workers would be able to use existing capital and technology more efficiently. This is portrayed as the Hicks neutral technical change in the production function leading to an increasing rather than a decreasing return. Technology and human capital are thus endogenized within the system. Following the conceptualization of the endogenous growth theories in the early 1990s, human capital as a factor in economic growth has been heavily studied both from a theoretical and an empirical perspective.

Evidence from empirics

Different empirical settings

A large number of studies have empirically investigated the link between human capital and economic growth using a myriad of specifications, data sources and modelling techniques. Studies can be categorized as those covering groups of countries or single ones, using cross-section, panel or time series data.

Mankiw et al. (1992) used the Solow growth model with and without human capital as a factor of production and found that the human capital-augmented Solow model better explained cross-country income variations. Barro (1991) found that the growth rate of real per capita GDP was positively related to initial human capital for 98 countries over the period 1960–1985. Human capital in this case was proxied by school enrolment rates. Bils and

Klenow (2000) investigated the human capital-economic growth nexus for a cross-section of countries from 1960 to 1990, and found that an additional year of schooling resulted in faster annual growth of 0.3 per cent during the same period.

A developing country perspective

Several studies have been conducted in developing countries. Abbas (2001) investigated the effect of human capital on economic growth in Pakistan and Sri Lanka during the period 1970–1994, using a human capital production function. Human capital was reported to be positively related to economic growth in both countries. Ganegodage and Rambaldi (2011) also investigated the impact of education investment on Sri Lankan economic growth, and found that the returns on education were positive, but of a lower magnitude. Imputed reasons were that output was negatively affected by war. Seetanah (2009) assessed the empirical link between education and economic growth for the case of 40 African states for the period 1980–2000 and reported that education had been an important factor in the growth process. Using a data-set covering the period 1970–2012, Mercan and Sezer (2014) found that expenditure on education had a positive effect on economic growth in Turkey. Dragoescu (2015) investigated the impact of higher education on economic growth in Romania during the period 1980–2013, using two human capital proxies, namely the number of students enrolled in tertiary education and public expenditure on education, and found that higher education had an important positive effect on economic growth. The returns on human capital investment seem to be significant for developing countries.

Most of the above-mentioned studies have found that human capital is positively related to economic growth; however, in some cases this proved not to be the case during the period under study. Berthelemy and Varoudakis (1996) reported that education investment in Senegal in the early 1990s was wrongly and inefficiently allocated, leading to an inconclusive empirical relationship between education expenditure and economic growth. Some studies have reported disappointing results whereby education variables have been found to be insignificant or even exhibiting the theoretically 'wrong' sign in growth equations. Several reasons have been put forward to explain these counter-intuitive results, including specification issues (Sunde and Vischer, 2015), data quality, increased use of differenced specification in studies using panel data and the use of inappropriate proxies to represent human capital.

Use of proxies for human capital

One of the main challenges in studying the output-human capital nexus is the choice of the proxy indicator for human capital. As highlighted by Pelinescu (2015), whichever is chosen will determine its influence on output. Traditionally, the majority of published studies have used education and health expenditure to measure human capital. Health is an important factor for determining the level of returns from education as a healthier individual can learn more than an unhealthy one, assuming the same education level. Ogundari and Awokuse (2018) showed that both measures of human capital have positive effects on economic growth, although the contribution of health is relatively larger. The health constituent of human capital improves labour productivity and increase an agent's utility (Gong et al., 2012). But some of the studies have also tried to model the impact of human development indices including nutrition. Nutrition is linked to productivity because a person who eats nutritious food is likely to be more productive owing to greater vigour and strength, hence potentially impacting human capital and economic growth.

Wheller (1980), on the other hand, adopted a three-stage least squares method using a large sample of cross-sectional data and found that changes in health, nutrition and education were strong contributors to change in labour productivity and vice versa. Belavi (2017) econometrically modelled the impact of education, health and development expenditure on economic growth in Karnataka during the period 1991–2016 and reported the long-term impact of human capital expenditure on economic growth. Behrman (2000) made a close examination of the interactions between health, education and nutrition and the likely benefits of simultaneously intervening in all three in social development. Studies are emerging, realizing and attempting to consider the intertwining and synergistic factors comprising human capital. Building on the emerging literature, we posit that human capital is an aggregate of health, education and nutrition. These three constituents are positively synergistic and are not substitutes for one another. Bearing in mind the inherent bias of using individual series as proxies of human capital, coupled with the increased recognition that human capital is compositely constituted, we have followed Krueger and Lindhal's (2001) suggestion and have constructed an index of human capital from the information content of three series, namely health, nutrition and education. Exploring new information can considerably improve the results of the impact of human capital on economic growth.

Econometric model, data and empirics

This paper investigates the relationship between human capital and economic growth in Mauritius, with capital, labour, trade openness and private investment as other control variables. We use annual data spanning the period 1970–2017. First, a multidimensional composite index that allows health, education and nutrition to be aggregated is used to represent human capital. A detailed description of the human capital index can be found in Neeliah and Seetanah (2016).

Econometric model

A production function of capital and labour is used as a basis to harbour the human capital variable and allow the examination of the significance of human capital on economic growth. The function is represented as:

$$y = f(K, L) \tag{1}$$

The theoretical foundation of the human capital-growth link has been discussed above and the philosophy is to extend the above Cobb-Douglas production function to include a human capital variable as an additional explanatory variable. Thus equation (1) is augmented into:

$$y = f(K, H, L) \tag{2}$$

The Cobb-Douglas functional form is adopted to represent equation (2), hence:

$$Y = K^a H^b L^c \tag{3}$$

where $a + b + c \leq 1$ to represent constant elasticity of substitution. Taking logarithms on both sides, and where the lower-case variables are the natural log of the respective uppercase variable and t stands for time, (3) becomes:

$$y_t = \alpha + \beta_1 k_t + \beta_2 l_t + \beta_3 h_t + \varepsilon_t \tag{4}$$

where the coefficients measure the elasticity of output with respect to the stocks of the various factors.

Variables and data sources

Output was measured by GDP. Capital was proxied by the gross fixed capital formation, whereas labour was characterized by the labour force. Annual data for GDP, gross fixed capital formation and the labour force were retrieved from Statistics Mauritius covering the period 1971–2017. The current analysis brings an innovation in the characterization of human capital, as we extend the composite human capital index developed by Neeliah and Seetanah (2016) to cover the period 1971–2017. Here, human capital is characterized by a multidimensional composite index that allows the various constituents of human capital to be aggregated. The index comprises an education variable (proxied by secondary school enrolment), a health variable (proxied by life expectancy) and finally a nutrition variable (proxied by calorie intake). Individual human capital variables were indexed over 100 and averaged to constitute the composite human capital index. The data for the education and health variables were collated from Statistics Mauritius, whereas the data for nutrition were retrieved from the Food and Agricultural Organization of the United Nations (FAO). Figure 8.4 presents the time series for the composite human capital index and real GDP during the period under study.

Testing for stationarity and cointegration

Stationary series are those showing basic statistical properties which are invariant with respect to time. It is necessary to for their components to be stationary before making use of such series in econometric modelling. Series can be non-stationary provided that they are stationary in the first difference, and may be co-integrated. If a set of variables are found to have at least one cointegrating vector, then a vector error correction model (VECM) is a suitable technique to be adopted, as it will adjust to both the short-term changes in variables and deviation from the equilibrium. The Johansen (1988) procedure confirmed the existence of a long-term relationship with one cointegrating vector.

Analysing human capital as a determinant of economic growth in Mauritius

The estimated coefficients on the respective growth contributors have the theoretically anticipated signs and are statistically significant (Table 8.1). The results show that there is a significant long-term relationship between GDP, capital, labour, human capital, degree of openness and private investment.

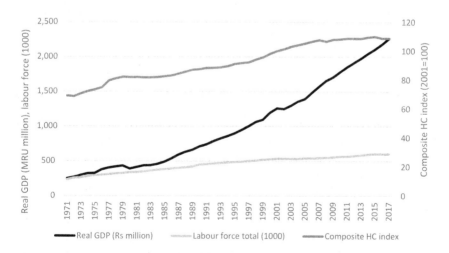

Figure 8.4 Trends in real GDP, labour force and the composite human capital
Source: Statistics Mauritius (2018).

Table 8.1 Estimated long-term estimates

Variables	β *(GDP equation)*
Capital (K)	0.77***
Labour (L)	0.25***
Human capital (HC)	0.47***
Trade openness (TO)	0.37***
Private investment (PI)	0.52***

Note: *** significant at the 1 per cent level.

Long-term growth determinants in Mauritius

Capital has been the most important contributor to economic growth with an output elasticity of 0.77, meaning that a 1 per cent increase in capital formation results in a 0.77 per cent increase in GDP in the long term, holding constant the stocks of the other factors. This finding is in line with Khadaroo and Seetanah (2007) and Neeliah and Seetanah (2012) who found that capital stock was the main growth determinant for Mauritius in the long term. Human capital has an output elasticity of 0.47, implying that a 1 per cent increase in the human capital index would result in a corresponding 0.47 per cent increase in GDP levels in Mauritius in the long term. The human capital elasticity estimated here is slightly higher than that reported by Neeliah and Seetanah (2016), at 0.27, but it provides further evidence for the significance of human capital as a growth factor for Mauritius.

VECM estimates

The variables under study were only stationary in the first difference and were cointegrated; a VECM was consequently formulated and estimated. The estimated error-correction equations pass the residual autocorrelation at the 5 per cent significance level and are presented in Table 8.2 below. The variables in the system are all endogenous, given that the lagged error-correction terms in all the equations of the VECM are generally significant. Cointegration implies the evidence of a long-term relationship among the variables under study.

By construction, the VECM specification forces the long-term behaviour of the endogenous variables to converge towards their cointegrated relationships, which includes short-term dynamics. Estimates from the VECM generally corroborated those presented in Table 8.1, even though, as anticipated, in the short term relatively lower coefficients are obtained. It can be argued that a 1 per cent increase in the growth rate of the human capital index leads to a 0.02 per cent increase in the growth rate of output after one year. It confirms a positive and significant contribution of human capital to output in the short term. It is argued here that human capital is an important contributor to economic growth, even though the coefficient is smaller compared to that in the long term. This supports the argument that human capital investment takes time to fully impact the

Table 8.2 Estimated error-correction equations

Variables (as in Equation 5)	Δ GDP	Δk	Δl	Δh	Δto	Δpi
ΔGDP$_{t-1}$	0.267*	0.129	0.244***	0.074***	1.6**	0.36
ΔK$_{t-1}$	0.27*	0.366*	−0.0946*	0.072	−1.456**	1.64*
ΔL$_{t-1}$	0.119**	−0.71	−0.251	0.016	−2.52*	−2.187
ΔHC$_{t-1}$	0.02*	0.735**	−0.411**	0.364*	−0.868	−0.455
ΔTO$_{t-1}$	−0.1*	0.086*	−0.043*	−0.022	−0.289*	−0.159
ΔPI$_{t-1}$	0.137*	0.0476	−0.092***	−0.0316	−0.601***	0.0332
Ect $_{t-1}$	−0.11**	0.0386	−0.079***	−0.058**	−0.393**	0.194
R^2	0.404	0.52	0.58	0.54	0.48	0.32

Note: *significant at the 10 per cent level, ** significant at the 5 per cent level, ***significant at the 1 per cent level.

economy. Interestingly, the VECM findings show that human capital also has a positive incidence on physical capital indicating possible indirect effects via this channel. A 1 per cent increase in the growth rate of the human capital index leads to a 0.74 per cent increase in the growth rate of physical capital after one year. In turn, we also note that a one percentage point increase in the growth rate of physical capital leads to a 0.27 percentage point increase in the growth rate of GDP in the following year. The estimated error correction equations also allow us to estimate the indirect effect of human capital on GDP in the short term via the physical capital channel, by multiplying the elasticity of human capital on physical capital to the elasticity of physical capital on GDP. It can subsequently be implied that a 1 per cent increase in the growth rate of human capital leads to a 0.19 per cent increase in the growth rate of output after two years. Interestingly, the physical capital variable is an important channel through which human capital can indirectly affect GDP.

Owing to the fact that the variables under study are cointegrated, in the short term deviations from the long-term equilibrium will feed back on the changes in the dependent variables, forcing their movement towards the long-term equilibrium state. The error correction term shows how much the deviation from the long-term equilibrium is corrected gradually through a series of partial short-term adjustments. The coefficient of the lagged error correction term is –0.11 and is highly significant. It indicates that about 11 per cent of the disequilibrium in our model is corrected annually and is a satisfactory rate of convergence to the equilibrium.

Human capital as growth determinant: the past, the present and the future

Romer (1990) highlighted the role of human capital as the main source of increasing returns in growth rates between developing and developed countries. Since independence, Mauritius has adopted this tenet and has significantly invested in its human capital. It has been observed that continuous investment in social welfare and human capital development has fostered and sustained economic development in Mauritius. The country seeks to escape the middle-income trap and to evolve into a high-income economy. Consequently, it must further improve its productivity and boost its economic growth. The role of human capital is fundamental in this endeavour.

This chapter quantitatively shows that during the period 1971–2017 human capital made a strong contribution to economic growth in Mauritius, after physical capital formation. This finding brings additional credence to the existing literature on the link between human capital and economic growth, and also adds to the empirics within the endogenous growth paradigm. More importantly, it also brings confirmatory value to the importance of human capital to economic growth in the island, and also supports the views regarding the macroeconomic pay-off to historical investment in human capital.

The short-term human capital elasticity of 0.02 validates the longer-term one of 0.47. The short-term estimates show that a 1 per cent increase in the growth rate of the human capital index leads to a 0.02 per cent increase in the growth rate of GDP after one year, whereas a 1 per cent rise in the human capital index induces a 0.47 per cent increase in GDP in the long term. The lower coefficient could be explained by the fact that the building of human capital is essentially a long-term endeavour. We argue that it takes time for the effects to fully ripple through the economy and to make a full impact. As highlighted by Neeliah and Seetanah (2016), the human capital index used here is a composite one comprising education, health and nutrition. These factors are synergistic and their interaction towards human capital formation may be complex, with each one operating with their specific lags and differently reinforcing their individual effects, thus achieving their aggregate return over time. The prominence of human capital formation to economic development, and the high returns from investment in human capital, means that it is essential that Mauritius sustains its expenditure on the provision of quality health and education services, while at the same time ensuring access to nutritious food. One can infer from our findings that human capital and broader social development policies and investment need to focus on the synergistic effect of the components making up human capital.

The Mauritian economy is driven by services and future economic growth will heavily rely on adding value to existing services as well as providing new ones. The increased role that knowledge will play within an expanding service sector is acknowledged, but needs to be mainstreamed. Meanwhile, innovation through technological change and digitalization will play an increasingly significant role, and is likely to severely disrupt and disturb established processes and values in the future world of work. Labour adaptability and flexibility will be key. A fitting human capital and human capital formation process will be a strong prerequisite to sustain this evolution. The role of science, technology, engineering, arts and mathematics as fundamental and foundational pre-conditions for instilling innovation capabilities in individuals should be the lynchpin of the education system.

The currently uncertain landscape and the strenuous demands facing the human capital formation system will rely extensively on new information for decisive decision-making. The role of research as a generator of insight in this endeavour should not be underestimated. A relatively new strand of investigation has emerged in the literature, focusing on the impact of the quality of education on economic growth (see, for example, Hanushek, 2013, Ali et al. 2016). Given the increased emphasis being laid on the development of cognitive skills via the nine-year continuous basic education process, it will be interesting to assess its impact on economic growth. Human capital formation is an intricate process, involving a myriad of investment decisions, straddling the education 'on the job' training continuum. This study has uncovered the impact that a composite human capital index has on GDP, but has not investigated the potential impact of training and skills development. Given the crucial importance of up-skilling and re-skilling the workforce with the imminent requisites of a rapidly changing world of work, coupled with the incoming transformation to a knowledge-based economy, the present model should be extended in the medium term to account for and assess the impact of an augmented human capital on economic growth. Such research findings could inform policymaking in human capital formation.

Notes

1 Authors' calculations based on data retrieved from Statistics Mauritius.
2 Authors' calculations based on data retrieved from Statistics Mauritius.

References

Abbas, Q. (2001) 'Endogenous Growth and Human Capital: A Comparative Study of Pakistan and Sri-Lanka', *Pakistan Development Review* 40(4): 987–1007.

Ali, M., Uwe, C. and Ipsita, R. (2016) 'Knowledge Spillovers through FDI and Trade: Moderating Role of Quality-Adjusted Human Capital', *Journal of Evolutionary Economics* 26: 837–868.

Awel, A. M. (2013) 'The Long-Run Relationship between Human Capital and Economic Growth in Sweden', MPRA paper no. 45183, Munich Personal RePEc Archive.

Barro, J. J. (1991) 'Economic Growth in a Cross Section of Countries', *Quarterly Journal of Economics* 106(2): 407–443.

Barro, R. J. and Sala-i-Martin, X. (1995) *Economic Growth*, New York: McGraw-Hill.

Behrman, J. R. (2000) *Literature Review on Interactions between Health, Education and Nutrition and the Potential Benefits of Intervening Simultaneously in All Three*, Washington, DC: International Food Policy Research Institute.

Belavi, S. S. (2017) 'Human Capital Formation and Economic Development in Karnataka: An Econometric Analysis ', *International Journal of Economics and Management Sciences* 7(1): 496.DOI: doi:10.4172/2162–6359.1000496.

Bergheim, S. (2005) 'Human Capital Is the Key to Growth', *Current Issues*, Deutsche Bank Research.

Berthelemy, G. C. and Varoudakis, A. (1996) *Policies for Economic Take-Off*, Paris: Organisation for Economic Co-operation and Development.

Bils, M. and Klenow, P. (2000) 'Does Schooling Cause Growth?', *American Economic Review* 90(5): 1160–1183.

Dinan, P. (2005) 'La république de Maurice en marche 1980–2030: Retrospective et perspective', *Le Mauricien*, p. 126.

Dragoescu, R. M. (2015) 'Education as a Determinant of the Economic Growth. The Case of Romania', *Procedia – Social and Behavioural Sciences* 197: 404–412.

Ganegodage, K. R. and Rambaldi, A. N. (2011) 'The Impact of Education Investment on Sri Lankan Economic Growth', *Economics of Education Review* 30: 1491–1502.

Gong, L., Li, H. and Wang, D. (2012) 'Health Investment, Physical Capital Accumulation, and Economic Growth', *China Economic Review* 23: 1104–1119.

Hanushek, E. A. (2013) 'Economic Growth in Developing Countries: The Role of Human Capital', *Economics of Education Review* 37: 204–212.

Johansen, S. (1988) 'Statistical Analysis of Cointegrated Vectors', *Journal of Economic Dynamics and Control* 12(2/3):231–254.

Khadaroo, A. J. and Seetanah, B. (2007) 'Assessing the Contribution of Land, Sea And Air Transport Capital to the Economic Performance of the Small Island State of Mauritius', *Applied Economics Letters* 14(15): 1151–1155.

Krueger, A. and Lindhal, M. (2001) 'Education for Growth: Why and For Whom?', *Journal of Economic Literature* 39(4): 1101–1136.

Mankiw, N. G., Romer, D. and Well, D. N. (1992) 'A Contribution to the Empirics of Economic Growth', *Quarterly Journal of Economics* 107: 407–437.

Mercan, M. and Sezer, S. (2014) 'The Effect of Education Expenditure in Economic Growth: The Case of Turkey', *Procedia – Social and Behavioural Sciences* 109: 925–930.

Neeliah, H. and Seetanah, B. (2012) 'Energy Use, Emissions, Trade and Economic Growth: Evidence from Mauritius', paper presented at the Second International Conference on International Trade and Investment,24–26 October, Le Meridien, Mauritius. Available at http://sites.uom.ac.mu/wtochair/images/stories/cProceedings12/Neeliah_energy_use_Evidence_from_Mauritius.pdf (accessed 2 October 2014).

Neeliah, H. and Seetanah, B. (2016) Does Human Capital Contribute to Economic Growth in Mauritius?', *European Journal of Training and Development* 40(4): 248–261.

Odit, M. P., Dookhan, K. and Fauzel, S. (2010) 'The Impact of Education on Economic Growth: The Case of Mauritius', *International Business and Economic Research Journal* 9(8):141–152.

Ogundari, K. and Awokuse, T. (2018) 'Human Capital Contribution to Economic Growth in Sub-Saharan Africa: Does Health Status Matter More Than Education?', *Economic Analysis and Policy* 58: 131–140.

Pelinescu, E. (2015) 'The Impact of Human Capital on Economic Growth', *Procedia Economics and Finance* 22: 184–190.

Pungpond, R. and Piriya, P. (2016) 'Human Capital Linkages to labour Productivity: Implications from Thai Manufacturers', *Journal of Education and Work* 29(8): 922–955. DOI: doi:10.1080/13639080.2015.1104658.

Romer, M. P. (1990) 'The Origins of Endogenous Growth', *Journal of Economic Perspectives* 8: 3–22.

Seetanah, B. (2009) 'The Economic Importance of Education: Evidence from Africa Using Dynamic Panel Data Analysis', *Journal of Applied Economics* 12(1): 137–157.

Solow, R. M. (1956) 'A Contribution to the Theory of Economic Growth', *Quarterly Journal of Economics* 70: 65–94.

Statistics Mauritius (2018) *Economic and Social Indicators*, Port Louis: Government of Mauritius. Available at http://statsmauritius.govmu.org/English/Pages/default.aspx.

Subramanian, A. (2009) 'The Mauritian Success Story and Its Lessons', Research Paper RP2009/36, Helsinki: UNU-WIDER.

Subramanian, A. and Roy, B. (2003) 'Who Can Explain the Mauritian Miracle: Meade, Romer, Sachs, or Rodrik?', in D. Rodrik (ed.) *In Search of Prosperity: Analytic Narratives on Economic Growth*, Princeton, NJ: Princeton University Press.

Sunde, U. and Vischer, T. (2015) 'Human Capital and Growth: Specification Matters', *Economica* 82: 368–390.

Swan, T. W. (1956) 'Economic Growth and Capital Accumulation', *Economic Record* 32: 334–361.

Wheller, D. (1980) 'Basic Needs Fulfillment and Economic Growth: A Simultaneous Model', *Journal of Development Economics* 7: 435–451.

Zafar, A. (2011) 'Mauritius: An Economic Success Story', *Africa Success Stories Project*, Washington, DC: World Bank.

9   Tracing the path towards sustainable development in Mauritius through the GDP-CO$_2$ emission nexus

R. Sultan

Introduction

The remarkable economic performance of the Republic of Mauritius in the post-independence era (i.e. since 1968) has been termed by many observers as the 'Mauritian miracle' (Romer, 1993; Subramanian, 2001; Stiglitz, 2011; Svirydzenka and Petri, 2014). In the pre-independence period the island's social and economic situation was based on a low-income monocrop agricultural sector which was subject to the vagaries of a tropical climate, together with significant terms-of-trade and output shocks. With a high population growth rate and ethnic tensions in the 1960s, Mauritius was doomed to failure, as predicted by two Nobel prizewinners, J. Meade (Meade *et al.*, 1961) and V. S. Naipaul (Naipaul, 1973).

From the 1970s onwards Mauritius adopted an economic diversification strategy and a trade liberalization policy, which were tailored to its competitive advantages and weaknesses. With the contribution of sugar exports under the Lomé Convention and the development of the export processing zone (EPZ) (mainly the textile and clothing sector), Mauritius has defied the Meade and Naipaul's prediction of a Malthusian trap. Gross domestic product (GDP) per capita (at market prices)[1] rose more than fivefold from less than US $500 in 1970 to $2,500 in 1990. With the emergence of the tourism and financial sectors in the 1990s followed by a vibrant information, communication and technology (ICT) sector at the turn of the twenty-first century, GDP per capita reached $10,186 in 2017 (see Table 9.1).

The quest for a sustainable development path for Mauritius has been of concern to policymakers for more than a decade. One of the sustainability traits of a country is the 'decoupling' of rising carbon dioxide (CO$_2$) emissions from economic growth. CO$_2$ emissions are a by-product of various activities which are essentially linked to economic growth (Tahvonen, 2000). Decoupling occurs when CO$_2$ emissions grow at a slower rate (relative decoupling) than economic growth or at a negative rate (absolute decoupling). CO$_2$ emissions are a root cause of global warming and decoupling is critical to mitigating climate change (Deutch, 2017).

Table 9.1 Economic transformation 1970–2017

Economic indicators	1970	1980	1990	2000	2010	2017
GDP per capita (US$)	600	1,177	2,506	3,651	7,591	10,186
% share of agriculture sector	31.3	15.1	11.8	6.7	3.6	3.7
% share of manufacturing sector	24.7	25.6	34.1	29.5	20.1	20.4
% share of services sector	44	59.3	54.1	63.8	76.3	75.9

Source: Statistics Mauritius (2017a).

The process of decoupling and the path towards sustainability can be achieved if an economy follows the environmental Kuznets curve (EKC), which hypothesizes that as societies become richer, and reach an adequate level of economic development, improved environmental conditions can be achieved. Economic growth is expected to limit the degradation of the environment created in the early stages of a country's development. The EKC proposes an inverted U-shaped relationship between CO_2 emissions per capita and GDP per capita (Stern *et al.* 1996; Tahvonen, 2000; Kaika and Zervas, 2013), with the decoupling taking place in the falling segment of the curve. If such a relationship does emanate from the Mauritian production and consumption system, it can shed light on the level of income which corresponds to the falling segment of the EKC.[2] Other factors, which are likely to shift the curve monotonically up or down, are equally important.

In Mauritius, CO_2 emissions per capita increased by 455 per cent between 1970 and 2014, with annual average growth of 4.8 per cent (World Bank, 2017). This is indeed a cause for concern since the average annual growth of real GDP per capita in Mauritius for the period 1970–2014 stood at 4.2 per cent.

This chapter traces the linkages between the development path of Mauritius and the consequences of CO_2 emissions over the past five decades. It answers an important question on whether the economy-environment interaction for Mauritius corresponds to the EKC hypothesis whereby economic growth in the initial stage of a country's development leads to rising CO_2 emissions; however, as income increases, this diminishes. A detailed description of the economic transformation from 1970 to 2014 is provided to seek insights on the trend of CO_2 emissions and the extent to which it is coupled or decoupled from economic growth. The EKC is estimated using an autoregressive distributed lag (ARDL) error correction model, pioneered by Pesaran and Shin (1999). Two additional factors are also investigated through the EKC framework, namely the elasticity of CO_2 emissions with respect to total energy consumption and the impact of trade openness.

The two main contributors of CO_2 emissions in Mauritius are the electricity and transport sector. Using the ARDL econometric method, the study also estimates the income elasticity of energy used in the transport sector (diesel and gasoline), and in the electricity sector. Consequently, it connects the information on the demand side with the sources of energy (renewable and non-renewable) in these two sectors to explain the evolution of CO_2 emissions. The chapter concludes with major sustainable policies to decouple CO_2 emissions from economic growth for Mauritius.

Environment-economy interaction: economic transformation and CO_2 emissions

CO_2 emissions are directly linked to economic activities through the use of fossil fuel energy. In Mauritius, the trend of CO_2 emissions per capita for the period 1970–2014 is shown in Figure 9.1. It is observed that after a sharp increase in the early 1970s, emissions decreased continuously until the early 1980s. The decrease in emissions per capita reflects the economic crisis that took place in the late 1970s. After 1983 emissions rose steeply until 1990. CO_2 emissions per capita then increased significantly, especially after 1995, albeit that periodic brief decreases were reported. Economic performance explains a large part of the movement in emissions, with reference to the industrial development in the 1980s, and the shift towards the service sector in the 1990s. Even when major economic activities shifted towards the service sector after 2000, emissions per capita continued its rising trend. The financial crisis in 2008 marked a slight fall in CO_2 emissions per capita, which then moved upward again.

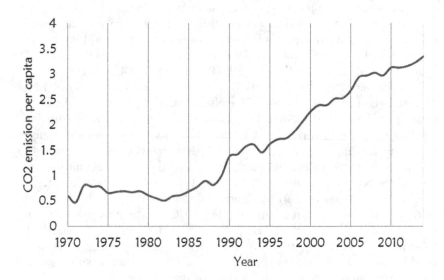

Figure 9.1 CO_2 emissions per capita 1970–2014
Source: World Bank (2017).

There is indeed a close link between growth in real GDP per capita and CO_2 emissions per capita. Figure 9.2 shows the percentage change of the two variables for the period 1970–2014.

Consider the sharp rise in CO_2 emissions in 1972. A closer look at the sector-specific growth rates reveals that the agricultural sector witnessed a rise in value added of 12.5 per cent in 1972[3] compared to 7.7 per cent in 1971, while the mining and quarrying sector recorded growth of 100 per cent. Although the sugar industry is very energy intensive, it is self-sufficient in its energy requirements. Since bagasse is used to produce electricity for the sugar factories, the rising emissions therefore reflect the increase in the value added of the manufacturing sector (the growth rate was 3.4 per cent in 1971 and 12.6 per cent in 1972) and of the electricity, gas, water and sanitary services (growth rates stood at 10.3 per cent in 1971 and at 18.8 per cent in 1972).

The economic downturn in the 1970s, accompanied by increases in oil prices in 1973 and 1975, led to a decrease in CO_2 emissions per capita of 3 per cent and 16.1 per cent, respectively. This coincided with a fall in real GDP per capita of 9.9 per cent in 1975. The economic crisis which confronted the island in the late 1970s also contributed to a decrease in CO_2 emissions. For instance, Mauritius followed with a devaluation of the rupee in 1979 and in 1981.

Although the late 1970s were marked by a period of economic, political and social instability, the economy subsequently recovered. From 1980 onwards,

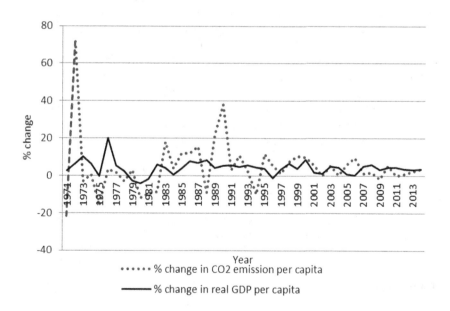

Figure 9.2 Growth in CO_2 emissions per capita and real GDP per capita
Source: Real GDP per capita is calculated at factor cost with 2017 prices. Series data were obtained from Statistics Mauritius (2017a). CO_2 emissions series data for Mauritius were obtained from the World Bank (2017).

Mauritius witnessed positive growth rates. As the industrial sector boomed in the 1980s, the percentage increase in CO_2 emissions per capita was higher than the increase in real GDP per capita. In fact, during the period 1971–2014[4] real GDP per capita in Mauritius grew at an average annual rate of approximately 4.2 per cent, while per capita carbon emissions grew at about 4.8 per cent annually. However, Table 9.2 shows that average annual growth rates of CO_2 emissions for the period 1981–1990 were almost twice that of real GDP per capita, thus reflecting the rise in the share of the manufacturing sector.

The probable explanation emanates from the economic structure in these periods. Table 9.1 shows the evolution of economic sectors from 1970–2017. Indeed, the 1980s and 1990s experienced an increase in the share of the manufacturing sector.

The industrial sector includes all manufacturing industries of the EPZ, the beverage industry, the textile industry and construction. In the late 1970s and early 1980s Mauritius faced massive unemployment which threatened its social and economic well-being. The textile manufacturing sector was consequently promoted to absorb the labour force. It may be concluded that at the time environmental quality was sacrificed at the expense of economic and social development. Textile processes consume significant amount of energy since they involve heavy machinery (Palamutcu, 2010). Electricity is also a major component in spinning, knitting, weaving activities (Martinez, 2010). The wet processes, which include preparation, dyeing and finishing, use high levels of electrical energy since they consume very hot air to remove chemically held water from textiles.

The country's export-oriented strategy also coincided with the rising share of the manufacturing sector in the 1980s. Referring to Table 9.3, the number of export-oriented enterprises increased more than five-fold from 1980 to 1990, up from a mere 3.7 per cent in 1980 to 12.5 per cent in 1990. In this respect, CO_2 emissions are also connected to trade liberalization.

In the 1980s the trend in energy consumption increased with the introduction of mechanical loaders for the sugar cane which further contributed to the rising trend in CO_2 emissions per capita (Figure 9.1 and Figure 9.2)

The 1980s and 1990s consequently coincided with the rising segment of the EKC. As the economy progressed to a post-industrial stage, with the

Table 9.2 Average growth rates of CO_2 emissions per capita and real GDP per capita

	1971–1980	1981–1990	1991–2000	2001–2010	2011–2014
Average growth in CO_2 emissions per capita	2.4	9.5	5.3	3.3	2.9
Average growth in real GDP per capita	7.6	5.0	4.8	3.3	3.9

Source: Series data were obtained from Statistics Mauritius (2017a). CO_2 emissions series data for Mauritius were obtained from the World Bank (2017).

Table 9.3 Export-oriented enterprises in Mauritius

	1973	1980	1990	2000	2010	2017
Number of enterprises	32	100	568	518	372	280
Employment	5,800	21,344	89,906	90,682	55,828	52,172
% share of manufacturing	n.a.	28.5	51.1	50.7	37.3	36.6
% share of GDP	n.a.	3.7	12.5	11.4	6.9	4.9

Source: Statistics Mauritius (2017b).

development of the financial and tourism sector in the early 1990s, an increasing proportion of activities were less energy-intensive. Continued economic growth therefore entailed less energy per unit of additional output and fewer CO$_2$ emissions. Table 9.2 shows that average annual growth of CO$_2$ emissions per capita slowed to 5.3 per cent during the 1990s, while average annual growth of real GDP per capita stood at 4.8 per cent.

The falling trends in average annual growth rates in CO$_2$ emissions per capita continued at the turn of the twenty-first century. In Figure 9.2, it can be seen that Mauritius has been successful to some extent in decoupling economic growth from CO$_2$ emissions. This issue is explored later in the chapter.

Environment-energy-economic growth

CO$_2$ emissions are the direct outcome of the combustion of fossil fuel energy. In Mauritius, the energy sector represents the biggest emitter of greenhouse gases (GHGs) (mainly CO$_2$), followed by the waste sector and the agricultural sector (Table 9.4).

The electricity sector is the main source of GHG emissions, followed by the transport sector. The manufacturing and construction sector represents the lowest share in emissions (Table 9.5).

Mauritius imports all its fossil fuel requirements which includes diesel oil, gasoline, kerosene and liquified petroleum gas (LPG). Diesel oil is used mainly by the heavy transportation sector and for starting up electric generators, while gasoline is used by the light transportation sector. Kerosene and LPG are used for cooking by the residential and commercial sectors.

Table 9.4 GHG emissions in Mauritius, 2017

Energy sector	%
Energy	76.30
Industrial processes and product use	0.83
Agriculture, forestry and other land use	2.63
Waste	20.30

Source: Statistics Mauritius (2017c).

Table 9.5 GHG emissions from the energy sector

Energy sector	%
Energy industries (electricity generation)	60.4
Manufacturing industries and construction	8.2
Transport	25.5
Other	5.9
Total	100.0

Source: Statistics Mauritius (2017c).

The relationship between CO_2 emissions per capita and energy per capita (both in logarithm form) is plotted in Figure 9.3. A linear trend line depicts the relationship with an R-squared of 0.98. The equation shows that the percentage change in CO_2 emissions per capita with respect to a 1 per cent change in energy per capita is greater than 1 (1.9).

An elasticity greater than one is an alarming situation for Mauritius. It implies that each unit increase in energy per capita is likely to bring about a more than proportionate increase in CO_2 emissions per capita. Since the electricity and transport sectors are the main contributors of CO_2 emissions, the explanation lies in the source of energy used in the two sectors.

Energy in the Mauritian transport sector

The demand for travel (resulting in an increase in energy and CO_2 emissions) is expected to expand at the same rate as economic growth. It is observed that either the distance travelled and/or the number of trips are expected to rise in line with higher standards of living. This occurs even though improvements in the mode of transportation lead to time saving. In a small island such as

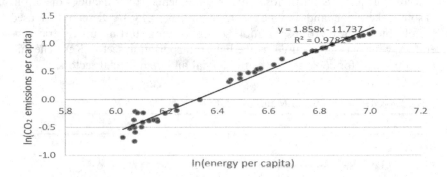

Figure 9.3 CO_2 emissions per capita versus energy per capita
Note: Energy per capita: kg of oil equivalent; CO_2 emissions per capita: metric tons.
Source: Series data for Mauritius were obtained from the World Bank (2017).

Mauritius, the size of the country limits the increase in the distance travelled during a typical trip and hence people have a tendency to compensate for the demand for travelling by making a higher number of trips.

Owing to the growth of the economy, there is currently a rising demand for greater personal mobility. The number of private vehicles increased approximately 20-fold between 1970 and 2017 (Figure 9.4). This is explained by a deteriorating public transport network together with the fact that the residents have greater affluence and prefer to travel by private cars.

The two types of fossil fuel used in the transport sector are diesel and gasoline (Figure 9.5). Diesel is used in bus transport as well in heavy vehicles while gasoline is consumed mainly by private cars. Higher distances, and/or greater trips eventually lead to more fuel being consumed in the sector. Hence, these two fuels provide an indicator of rising mobility.

The two fuels exhibit similar trends up to 1996, after which there is a decrease in gasoline consumption and an increase in diesel consumption. However, the two trends consequently converge and in 2019 gasoline consumption is higher than diesel.

In order to shed light on the travel behaviour and consumption patterns of the two fuels in the transport sector, an attempt is made to estimate the demand function for diesel per capita and gasoline per capita. The long-term equation and the short-term dynamics according to the ARDL error correction model[6] is shown in Equation (1) and Equation (2) for gasoline and in Equation (3) and Equation (4) for diesel.[7]

$\ln GAS_t$ = logarithm gasoline in litres per capita at time t

$\ln DIE_t$ = logarithm diesel in litres per capita at time t

$\ln RPRG_t$ = logarithm of realprice of gasoline per litre at time t

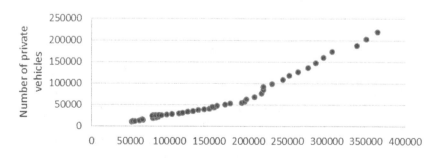

Figure 9.4 Trend ownership of private vehicles in Mauritius
Source: Statistics Mauritius (1984–2017).

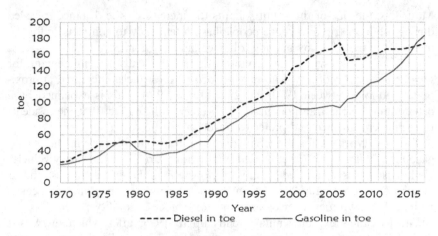

Figure 9.5 Diesel and gasoline consumption in the transport sector (toe)[5]
Source: Statistics Mauritius (1984–2017); Baguant and Manrakhan (1989) for the
period 1970–1983.

$\ln RGDP_t$ = logarithm of real GDP per capita at time t

$$\ln GAS_t = -0.37 \ln RPRG_t + 0.81 \ln RGDP_t$$

Std error	(0.089)	(0.035)	(1)
p − value	(0.00)	(0.00)	

$$\Delta \ln GAS_t = -1.75 + 0.22\Delta \ln GAS_t + 0.36\Delta \ln GAS_{t-1}$$

Std Error	(0.34)	(0.12)	(0.12)	(2)
p − value	(0.00)	(0.07)	(0.01)	

ARDL$(3,0,0)$; Number of observations $= 44$; Sample: $1970-2014$

Adj R − squared $= 0.60$; $Log-likelihood = 75.56$; Lags selection: SBC

$$\ln DIE_t = -0.55 \ln RPRD_t + 0.88 \ln RGDP_t$$

Std error	(0.16)	(0.08)	(3)
p − value	(0.00)	(0.00)	

$$\Delta \ln DIE_t = -0.50 + 0.001\Delta \ln RPRD_t + 0.14\Delta \ln RGDP_t$$

Std Error	(0.50)	(0.19)	(0.23)	(4)
p − value	(0.19)	(0.95)	(0.56)	

ARDL$(1,1,1)$; Number of observations $= 42$; Sample: $1976-2014$

Adj R − squared $= 0.33$; $Log-likelihood = 82.02$; Lags selection: SBC

The price elasticity for gasoline in the long term stands at 0.37 while the income elasticity is estimated at 0.8. Diesel shows a higher price elasticity of 0.6 and an income elasticity of 0.9. The finding shows that a 1 per cent increase in real GDP per capita is likely to lead to an almost equivalent increase in diesel and gasoline.

Can we expect mobility to slow down in the future? Following the theoretical foundation of Becker's theory of allocation of time, transport is intimately related to both consumption and the allocation of time among discretionary activities (Becker, 1965). Hence, travelling (and energy consumption) is a derived demand emanating from consumption and production activities. The causation runs from transport energy to economic growth. With economic transformation, production may become less travel intensive, and the growth in transport and CO_2 emissions may slow down.

However, this fails to account for the fact that travelling can itself be regarded as an activity (Anas, 2007). In recent years, a burgeoning literature on travel behaviour concludes that people derive utility from travelling and hence travelling represents an end product in itself. With economic growth, income increases and consequently consumers engage in recreation or leisure-related activities which are closely connected to travelling as an end product. Car ownership also increases and the availability of multiple private vehicles allows more discretionary mobility to take place. This eventually leads to a rise in transport energy consumption. Based on the above reasoning, the causal relationship runs from economic growth to mobility, transportation and CO_2 emissions.

For the case of Mauritius, it is observed that while gasoline and diesel are both drivers of economic growth, mainly through investment, the causality also runs from economic growth to higher mobility (see Box 9.1). As transportation is totally dependent on fossil fuel, and is likely to remain so, CO_2 emissions associated with the sector are expected to rise.

Box 9.1 Transport energy and economic growth

The causality tests between transport energy (diesel and gasoline) and economic growth were conducted by Sultan (2011), using an aggregate production model with capital formation, labour and energy treated as separate factors of production. The estimation method is an ARDL error correction model. The study concludes that gasoline and diesel lead the change in (Granger-caused) investment in both the short term and the long term, while economic growth takes precedence over (Granger-caused) gasoline and diesel in the long term. Travel behaviour in Mauritius adheres to the concept of discretionary mobility, i.e. that mobility may be an end in itself. Travel behaviour in this respect should not be viewed merely as a derived demand. Economic growth leading to a higher standard of living takes precedence over diesel and gasoline consumption due to discretionary mobility.

Source: Sultan (2011)

Energy in the electricity sector

The main institution for the provision of electricity is the Central Electricity Board (CEB) which was established in 1952 in accordance with the provisions of the first Central Electricity Board Ordinance 1951 (CEB, 2003). In Mauritius, the main renewable sources of energy are bagasse, hydropower, solar and wind. When the national rural electrification programme was launched in 1968, at least 35 per cent of the country's electricity was generated from hydropower. Total energy sales were made to around 91,000 customers. In the 1970s the CEB connected power supply to schools, Central Water Authority pumping stations, housing estates, stone crushing plants, poultry farms, irrigation stations and construction sites.

However, the shortages in rainfall in the 1960s and 1970s which had an impact on the electricity power supply compelled the CEB to invest in thermal power. From the early 1970s onwards the rise in thermal production coincided with the fall in hydropower (Figure 9.6). The CEB expanded its transmission and distribution networks in all directions across the island in the 1980s (CEB, 2003). The EPZ and textile sector, the tourism sector and the construction sector added to the demand for electricity and further increases in electricity consumption were observed.

Power purchase agreements between the private sector and the CEB have been common since 1957 when the St Antoine Sugar Estate (the country's first sugar factory) sold excess electricity generated from bagasse to the CEB. Consequently, other sugar factories followed suit by transferring their surpluses to the

Figure 9.6 Sources of electricity generation, 1970–1983
Source: Annual reports of the CEB (various issues).

grid. The Médine Sugar Estate was the first sugar factory to export electricity to the CEB under contract in 1979. The F.U.E.L. Steam and Power Generation Company signed a power purchase agreement in 1983. The Bagasse Energy Development Programme of 1991 gave a further boost to the sugar industry and provided the necessary incentives to the sugar factories to improve the efficiency of their operations and to encourage the production of electricity using bagasse. The production of the Independent Power Producers (IPPs) consequently rose from 14.6 per cent in 1990 to 38.4 per cent in 2000 and to 60.1 per cent in 2017 (Table 9.6).

The CEB currently has power purchase agreements with three IPPs operating dual-fired coal/bagasse plants and producing electricity on a year-round basis. There are also power purchase agreements with seven IPPs, operating bagasse-fired plants and producing electricity in the crop season only; depending on actual harvest conditions that is nominally July through November.

As more and more sugar-producing activities are centralized, and in an effort to promote the most efficient use of bagasse for energy production, these seasonal power plants will ultimately be converted into year-round electricity production facilities. While competitiveness was the motor for reform in many countries, Mauritius observed that the size of the island was a constraint on the development of a multi-player electricity supply sector. Thus, the government opted to corporatize the CEB as a vertically integrated company and to retain ownership of the company. In 2003 legislation was enacted to provide the legal basis for these reforms.

The gradual decline in hydropower is worth mentioning. In 2017 only 2.9 per cent of electricity was generated from hydropower. The restructuring of the sugar sector led to a decrease in the amount of agricultural land devoted to sugar cane cultivation. Consequently, bagasse as a source of electricity generation fell to 14.7 per cent in 2017 (Table 9.7).

The rise in non-renewable sources of electricity has matched the production of the IPPs since the 1990s. Coal represented 41.6 per cent of total electricity generation in 2017.

The rising trend in coal is clearly visible in Figure 9.7. Since coal is the most polluting source of energy, this trend is likely to contribute significantly to CO_2 emissions in the electricity sector.

Figure 9.8 compares the percentage annual change in electricity production from coal with growth rate in total electricity consumption. From 1997

Table 9.6 Electricity producers GWh (%)

	1990	2000	2017
CEB	574.7 (85.4)	963.7 (61.6)	1214.9 (39.9)
IPP	98 (14.6)	601.2 (38.4)	1827.2 (60.1)
Total	672.7 (100)	1564.9 (100)	3042.2 (100)

Source: Statistics Mauritius (1984–2017).

Table 9.7 Renewable sources of electricity in Mauritius

	1990	2000	2010	2017
Hydro	10.87	5.40	3.84	2.90
Landfill gas	0.0	0.0	0.0	0.5
Wind	0.1	0.0	0.1	0.5
Photovoltaic	0	0	0	2.4
Bagasse	20.20	24.22	17.63	14.67
Total	31.17	29.62	21.57	20.99

Source: Statistics Mauritius (1984–2017).

Table 9.8 Non-renewable sources of electricity

	1990	2000	2010	2017
Gas turbine (kerosene)	4.61	2.41	0.70	0.09
Diesel and fuel oil	58.11	47.56	36.32	37.42
Coal	6.15	20.44	41.50	41.56
Total	68.86	70.40	78.53	79.07

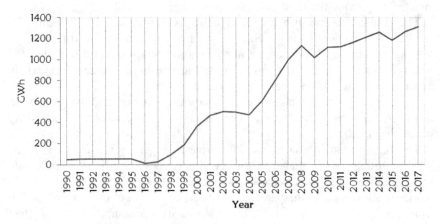

Figure 9.7 Coal as a source of electricity production
Source: Statistics Mauritius (1984–2017).

onwards the rise in coal has been significantly less than the rise in electricity depicting the change in energy mix towards coal. During the past five years or so, the rise in electricity consumption has been matched by rising use of coal, a situation which is far from being sustainable.

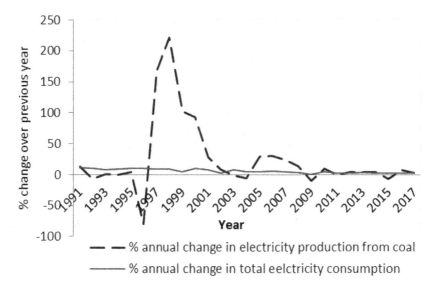

Figure 9.8 Growth in coal-based electricity and total electricity consumption
Source: Statistics Mauritius (1984–2017).

Having described the sources of electricity generation, the next question is the relationship between electricity consumption and economic growth. Two pieces of information are used to provide insight on the relationship: the income elasticity for electricity and the causality tests between electricity and economic growth.

$\ln ELEC_t$ = logarithm total electricity per capita in GWh at time t^8

$\ln RPRE_t$ = logarithm real average price of electricity in Rs at time t

DUM = dummy variable: 1 for 1975 to 1981, 0 otherwise

(treated as exogenous variable)

Long-term equation

$$\ln ELEC_t = -0.39 \ln RPRE_t + 1.05\, RGDP_t$$

Std error	(0.57)	(0.53)	(5)
p – value	(0.68)	(0.06)	

Short-term equation

$$\Delta \ln ELEC_t = -0.20 + 0.53\Delta \ln ELEC_{t-1} + 0.56\Delta \ln RGDP_t - 0.26 \ln RGDP_{t-1} - 0.03 DUM$$

StdError	(0.50)	(0.12)	(0.13)	(0.14)	(0.02)
p–value	(0.69)	(0.00)	(0.56)	(0.07)	(0.07)

(6)

ARDL$(2, 0, 2)$; Number of observations $= 46$; Sample: $1972 - 2017$

Adj R $-$ squared $= 0.76$; $Log - likelihood = 116.9$; Lags selection: SBC

Using the ARDL error correction model,[9] long-term income elasticity is estimated at 1.05. A 1 per cent increase in real GDP per capita leads to an equivalent percentage increase in total electricity. It depicts a close relationship between economic growth and rising electricity consumption.

The second set of information seeks to answer the question of whether electricity is a stimulus of economic growth or whether economic growth drives electricity consumption. The study by Sultan (2012) concludes that electricity is a major stimulus to economic growth, as well as to investment and exports (see Box 9.2). Any attempt to reduce electricity consumption (for example by increasing prices) would have a negative impact on growth. Consequently, CO_2 emissions can be said to be a by-product of economic growth.

Box 9.2 Economic growth, electricity and exports in Mauritius

Is electricity usage a stimulus to economic growth and exports or does economic growth lead to electricity consumption? Using the Johansen cointegration techniques in a vector error correction model, Sultan (2012) shows that electricity takes precedence over (Granger-caused) real GDP per capita, capital formation as well as real exports. However, electricity is not found to be affected by shocks in the cointegrating vector. Hence, the feedback hypothesis does not hold for electricity. However, bi-directional causality is observed for economic growth, investment and exports. The study consequently shows that further economic growth will induce a relatively higher amount of electricity consumption, as an input in the production processes. Thus, a conservation policy to reduce electricity can be detrimental to growth. The importance of electricity provision as an infrastructural service for economic growth, investment as well as for real exports leads to the conclusion that Mauritius might have benefited from the availability of electricity as a source of competitiveness to facilitate its export performance. If the appropriate strategy to generate electricity from renewable energy sources is not adopted, carbon emissions are expected to rise with economic growth.

Source: Sultan (2012)

The environmental Kuznets curve

The EKC is divided into three phases. At low levels of development, the quality and the intensity of environmental degradation is limited to the impact of subsistence economic activity. CO$_2$ emissions and energy use are extremely low. This situation corresponds to the late 1960s when the Mauritian economy was based on sugar. Electricity consumed in the sugar factories originated from bagasse, while electricity from the CEB was generated from hydropower (more than 30 per cent) and thermal power. Many activities in the agricultural sector took place at subsistence level, and mobility was also limited to the low standard of living. The total energy used and CO$_2$ emissions in the economy were very low. With the development of an agricultural sector and industrialization, energy consumption rose leading to an increase in CO$_2$ emissions. This first phase of the EKC corresponds to the process of industrialization in the 1970s and 1980s for Mauritius.

When the island shifted to a service-based economy, CO$_2$ emissions reached a peak (the second phase) before declining again (the third phase) since the associated activities were less energy-intensive. At higher levels of development, structural change and other factors, such as environmental awareness, the use of technology and the enforcement of environmental expenditure, contribute to falling CO$_2$ emissions. This situation is similar to that which occurred in Mauritius in the late 1990s and after 2000. For example, Mauritius enacted the Environmental Protection Act (EPA) in 1991, but then introduced a more effective Act in 2002. The EPA 2002 provides for environmental stewardship, greater transparency and public participation in the Environment Impact Assessment mechanism as well as a streamlining of the EIA procedures.

It is argued that a country is better placed to remedy its environmental problems as its economy develops; moreover, more rapid growth will lead to the swift replacement of its older, dirtier technology with a newer and cleaner version. Since 2008 a number of initiatives and strategies have been proposed to transform Mauritius into a green economy – one that will result in improved human well-being and social equity while significantly reducing environmental risks and ecological scarcities.[10] A series of green economy actions have been designed and implemented at the sectoral level.[11] The strong drive towards resource and energy efficiency and the promotion of clean energy sources through photovoltaic and other renewable sources of energy are currently being prioritized in the energy sector.

However, the chapter concludes that the transport and electricity sectors are expected to consume significant amounts of fossil energy, since in recent years coal has been a major source of electricity. CO$_2$ emissions may be on the rise. Thus, an important question is whether the EKC holds for Mauritius.

In order to test for the existence of an EKC for Mauritius, the long-term relationship between CO$_2$ emissions per capita and real GDP per capita is estimated using an ARDL error correction model. The findings are shown below.[12]

$\ln CO2_t$ = logarithm of CO_2 emissions per capita (metric tonnes)

$\ln TENE_t$ = logarithm of total energy consumption per capita

(kg of oil equivalent)

$XMGD_t$ = ratio of export of merchandised goods plus import

of merchandised goods to GDP

$\ln RGDP_t$ = logarithm of real GDP per capita at time t

Long-term equation

$$\ln CO2_t = 6.86 \ln RGDP_t - 0.28 \ln RGDP_t^2 + 1.59 \ln TENE_t + 0.18 XMGD_t$$

| Std Error | (2.48) | (0.10) | (0.35) | (0.16) | (7) |
| p − value | (0.00) | (0.01) | (0.00) | (0.29) | |

Short-term equation

$$\Delta \ln CO2_t = -26.8 + 0.87 \Delta \ln TENE_t - 0.51 ECM_{t-1}$$

| Std Error | (7.45) | (0.34) | (0.13) | (8) |
| p − value | (0.00) | (0.02) | (0.00) | |

$\mathrm{ARDL}(1, 0, 0, 0, 1)$; Number of observations $= 41$; Sample: $1974 - 2014$

Adj R − squared $= 0.77$; $Log - likelihood = 70.97$; Lags selection: SBC

The ARDL error correction model concludes that there is indeed an inverted-U relationship between CO_2 emissions per capita and economic growth. The turning point is estimated at real GDP per capita of Rs 209,000 (2017 prices). This corresponds to the GDP per capita in 2006–2007.

$$\frac{\partial \ln CO2}{\partial \ln RGDP} = 6.86 - 0.56 \ln RGDP$$

$$\ln RGDP = 12.25$$

The hypothetical relationship is depicted in Figure 9.9.

The main concern is the coefficient of $\ln TENE_t$ (energy per capita). The elasticity is estimated at 1.6 (compared to 1.9 in a simple correlation analysis).

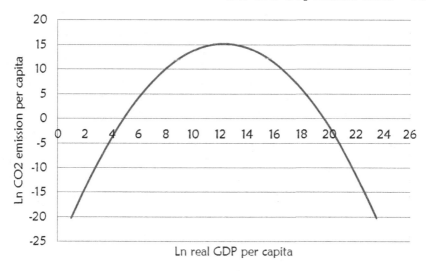

Figure 9.9 The EKC for Mauritius with CO$_2$ emissions per capita
Source: Computed from Equation (7).

This high figure reflects the use of coal and other fossil fuels in electricity production in recent decades as well as the rising mobility in the transport sector.

The degree of openness measured by the sum of exports and imports of
manufactured goods over GDP is a positive link to CO$_2$ emissions per capita.
However, the coefficient is not statistically significant. One possible explanation is that the degree of openness would have a strong influence on total
energy consumption – a variable which has already been controlled in the
equation. Nevertheless, it is included since it improves the fit of the regression.

Discussion and policy implications

Several findings emanate from this study regarding the evolution of CO$_2$
emissions in Mauritius from 1970 to 2017. These are summarized below.

1   The relationship between CO$_2$ emissions and economic growth conforms
    to the EKC. The inverted U-relationship is attributed to the country's
    economic transformation from a monocrop economy in the late 1960s, to
    the period of industrial development in the 1970s and 1980s, and to the
    emergence of a service-based economy from 1990 onwards. The turning
    point is estimated at Rs 209,000 which corresponds to the level of real
    GDP per capita in 2006–2007.
2   The elasticity of CO$_2$ emissions per capita to energy per capita is greater
    than 1 (1.6) – a given percentage increase in energy per capita brings
    about a more than proportionate rise in CO$_2$ emissions per capita. Rising

energy consequently shifts the EKC upwards. The nature of such relationships implies that much of the sources of energy are based on fossil
fuels (coal, diesel and gasoline) in the Mauritian context.

3   Indeed, the sources of energy in the transport and electricity sector show a
rising trend in the usage of fossil fuels, with a decreasing trend in the usage
of renewable energy in the electricity sector (hydropower and bagasse).

4   The bi-directional causality between transport energy and economic
growth (Sultan, 2011) explains the high-income elasticity of diesel and
gasoline demand which approximates 0.9 and 0.8, respectively. This
implies that mobility is seen as an end in itself and it is expected to
increase as the Mauritian society becomes richer. Consequently, a high
demand for transport energy is predicted from the analysis, which may
lead to rising CO_2 emissions.

5   A study on the electricity-growth nexus (Sultan, 2012) concludes that
electricity is a stimulus for growth, investment and exports. Any conservation strategy (through higher prices) will have a negative impact on
economic growth. With a high-income elasticity of 1.5 for electricity
demand in Mauritius, as estimated in this study, electricity is also expected
to rise significantly.

6   Rising demand for electricity has been matched by an almost equivalent
increase in coal in recent years. As a source of electricity generation, coal is
clearly unsustainable and is likely to contribute to substantial CO_2 emissions.

Policy recommendations to bring about further changes in the level of CO_2
emissions will focus on the transport and electricity sectors. Currently, the
government's strategy is to implement an efficient mass transport system
referred to as the 26-km 'Metro Express' project which is expected to connect
Curepipe to Immigration Square in Port Louis. It is hoped that it will help to
curb carbon emissions if it succeeds in reducing the use of private vehicles in
the city of Port Louis. However, it appears that it is more likely to shift pas-
sengers from the public bus transport rather than from private vehicles. It is
unlikely to become an environmentally friendly alternative if it does not
respond to the increasing ownership of private cars and road traffic as a
major source of CO_2 emissions in Mauritius.

Nevertheless, sustainable transport has not been prioritized by the political
decision-makers. Discussions about sustainable practices such as an improved
bus transport system (in terms of networks, information access and quality of
service), bicycle lanes, work shift, and bio-ethanol as a sustainable energy from
molasses or sugar cane, appear in the public discourse but are not really taken
seriously by the relevant departments. Land use planning (for example the
Smart City) which minimizes travel distances has also been considered, but it
lacks a clear vision on sustainable objectives and implementation guidelines.

Increasing the share of renewable sources of electricity is of utmost importance for Mauritius. The newly established Mauritius Renewable Energy
Agency for the promotion of renewable energy technology is worth

mentioning. Indeed, the government is currently emphasizing investment in renewable energy technology (e.g. solar photovoltaic, wind, renewable biomass and waste-to-energy). For instance, in 2010 the government of Mauritius launched the Small-Scale Distributed Generation scheme to encourage households and institutions to install small-scale photovoltaic panels and wind turbines through the provision of a targeted feed-in tariff scheme.

Conclusion

Mauritius provides evidence for the decoupling hypothesis. The transformation of the economy, with the use of technology and energy efficient measures lead to a lower growth of CO$_2$ emissions in recent years. However, it also shows some unsuccessful traits in terms of a polluting electricity and transport sector. In order to further mitigate the increase in CO$_2$ emissions in Mauritius, this chapter concludes that relevant policies and strategies need to be adopted to enhance renewable energy sources in the transport sector (e.g. bioethanol) and the electricity sector.

Notes

1 World Bank (2017).
2 Technically, this income level refers to the turning point of the EKC.
3 Figures were calculated from the real GDP component at factor cost and at constant 1970 prices.
4 CO$_2$ emissions series data from the World Bank Indicators ending in 2014 (World Bank, 2017).
5 Tonnes of oil equivalent.
6 The ARDL error correction model (ECM) involves two steps for estimating the long-term relationship. The first step is to examine the existence of a long-term relationship among all variables in the equation under examination. The ARDL bounds test approach of Pesaran and Shin (1999) and Pesaran *et al.* (2001) is used to test for the existence of the long-term equilibrium relationship. This approach can be applied to series data irrespective of whether they are stationary at the level form (I(0) series) or at first difference (I(1) series) or mutually cointegrated. Conditional upon cointegration being confirmed in the second stage, the long-term coefficients and the short-term coefficients are estimated using the associated ARDL and ECM methods.
7 Data on GDP were obtained from National Income Accounts (various issues) and from Statistics Mauritius. Real GDP was calculated by converting GDP at market prices using a GDP deflator. Figures for gasoline and diesel consumption were obtained from the Digest of Energy and Water Statistics for the period 1984–2017. Data have been converted from toe to litres. The series data for the period 1970–1983 was extracted from the Energy Year Book by Baguant and Manrakhan (1989). Nominal prices of gasoline and diesel per litre were obtained from household budget surveys carried out by Statistics Mauritius. Real prices are calculated using Consumer Price Index with 2017 as the base year. The univariate stationary property of the series data was tested using the augmented Dickey-Fuller and the Phillips-Perron tests. Both tests conclude that the series data are integrated of order one (I(1)).

8 Total electricity and average price of electricity were obtained from the Digest of Energy and Water Statistics (Statistics Mauritius, 1984–2017). Average prices were converted into real values using the consumer price index with the base year 2017.

9 The estimation procedure follows the same steps as the previous ARDL error correction model in this study.

10 The International Labour Organization (ILO) has been supporting the Mauritian government and social partners in designing the strategy and policies towards the creation of green jobs since 2011. Reference is made to the ILO report on green jobs assessment for Mauritius (ILO, 2012) where a number of sectors were identified as potential for green jobs. Further to this initiative is the Skills for Green Jobs Report in 2012 commissioned by the ILO. An update was published in 2018 (ibid., 2018). The United Nations Education Programme (UNEP) has also assisted through the development of a Green Economy Model for Mauritius. Following a multi-stakeholder consultation workshop in 2013 organized by UNEP to define the sectors for transition towards a green economy, seven sectors were identified to drive the green economy: agriculture, energy, waste, water, tourism, manufacturing and transport.

11 These include the programme to transform 50 per cent of agricultural activities to bio-production by 2020, the establishment of bio-farming zones, compost subsidy schemes, the introduction of the Mauritian standard for good agricultural practices (MAURIGAP), sustainable tourism standards, and eco-label standards for the textile sector (ILO, 2018).

12 The econometric analysis follows the same procedure as that used in earlier in this study.

References

Anas, A. (2007) 'A Unified Theory of Consumption, Travel and Trip Chaining', *Journal of Urban Economics* 62: 162–186.

Baguant, J. and Manrakhan, J. (1989) *Energy Data Book, University of Mauritius*, Réduit: University of Mauritius Press.

Becker, G. (1965) 'A Theory of the Allocation of Time ', *Economic Journal* LXXV: 493–508.

Central Electricity Board (CEB) (2003) 'Integrated Electricity Plan 2003–2012' *Central Electricity Board*, p. 13.

Deutch, J. (2017) 'Decoupling Economic Growth and Carbon Emissions', *Joules* 1 (1):3–5.

Enoch, M. P. (2003) 'Transport Practice and Policy in Mauritius', *Journal of Transport Geography* 11: 297–306.

Government of Mauritius (2015) 'Government Programme 2015–2019: Achieving Meaningful Change', address by the President of the Republic of Mauritius, first sitting of 2015 of the first session of the Sixth National Assembly of Mauritius, Port Louis, 27 January.

Kaika, D. and Zervas, E. (2013) 'The Environmental Kuznets Curve (EKC) Theory, Part A: Concept, Causes and the CO2 Emissions Case', *Energy Policy* 62 (November): 1392–1402.

International Labour Organization (ILO) (2012) 'Assessing Current and Potential Green Jobs: The Case of Mauritius', policy brief, Geneva: ILO. Available at www.ilo.org/wcmsp5/groups/public/—ed_emp/—emp_ent/documents/publication/wcms_184298.pdf.

International Labour Organization (ILO) (2018) *Skills for Green Jobs: An Update*, Geneva: ILO.

Martinez, C. I. P. (2010) 'Energy Use and Energy Efficiency Development in the German and Columbian Textile Industries', *Energy for Sustainable Development* 14 (2):94–103.

Meade, J. E. (1967) 'Population Explosion, the Standard of Living, and Social Conflict', *Economic Journal* 77(306):233–255.

Meade, J. E., Foggon, G., Houghton, H., Lees, N., Marshall, R. S., Roddan, G. M. and Selwyn, O. (1961) *The Economics and Social Structure of Mauritius: Report to the Government of Mauritius*, London:Methuen.

Mistry, P. S. (1999) 'Commentary: Mauritius – Quo Vadis', *African Affairs* 98 (393):551–569.

Naipaul, V. S. (1973) *The Overcrowded Barracoon and Other Articles*, New York: Knopf.

Palamutcu, S. (2010) 'Electric Energy Consumption in the Cotton Textile Processing Stages', *Energy* 35(7):2945–2952.

Pesaran, M. H. and Shin, Y. (1999) 'An Autoregressive Distributed Lag Modelling Approach to Cointegration Analysis', in S. Strøm (ed.) *Econometrics and Economic Theory in the Twentieth Century: The Ragnar Frisch Centennial Symposium*, Cambridge: Cambridge University Press.

Pesaran, M. H., Shin, Y. and Smith, R. J. (2001) 'Bounds Testing Approaches to the Analysis of Level Relationships', *Journal of Applied Econometrics* 16: 289–326.

Romer, P. (1993) 'Two Strategies for Economic Development: Using Ideas and Producing Ideas', proceedings of the World Bank Annual Conference on Development Economics, World Bank, Washington, DC, pp. 63–91.

Statistics Mauritius (1984–2017) *Digest of Energy and Water Statistics*, Port Louis: Government of Mauritius. Available athttp://statsmauritius.govmu.org/English/Publications/Pages/Energy_Yr17.aspx (accessed 29 August 2018).

Statistics Mauritius (2017a) *Digest of National Accounts*, Port Louis: Government of Mauritius. Available at http://statsmauritius.govmu.org/English/StatsbySubj/Pages/National-Accounts.aspx (accessed 28 August 2017).

Statistics Mauritius (2017b) *Digest of Industrial Statistics*, Port Louis: Government of Mauritius. Available at http://statsmauritius.govmu.org/English/StatsbySubj/Documents/labour%20-%20digest/Digest_Labour_Yr17.pdf (accessed 29 August 2018).

Statistics Mauritius (2017c) *Digest of Environment Statistics*, Port Louis: Government of Mauritius. Available at http://statsmauritius.govmu.org/English/StatsbySubj/Documents/Digest/Environment/Digest_Env_Yr17.pdf (accessed 28 August 2018).

Stern, D., Common, M. S., Barbier, E. B. (1996) 'Economic Growth and Environmental Degradation: The Environmental Kuznets Curve and Sustainable Development', *World Development* 24(7): 1151–1160.

Stiglitz, J. (2011) 'The Mauritius Miracle, Or How to Make a Big Success of a Small Economy', *The Guardian*, 7 March. Available at www.theguardian.com/commentisfree/2011/mar/07/mauritius-healthcare-education.

Subramanian, A. (2001) 'Mauritius: A Case Study', *Finance and Development* 38(4).

Sultan, R. (2011) 'Dynamic Linkages between Transport Energy and Economic Growth in Mauritius: Implications for Energy and Climate Policy', *Journal of Energy Technologies and Policy* 2(1): 24–28.

Sultan, R. (2012) 'An Econometric Study of Economic Growth, Energy and Exports in Mauritius: Implications for Trade and Climate Policy', *International Journal of Energy and Economics and Policy* 2(2):225–237.

Svirydzenka, K. and Petri, M. (2014) 'Mauritius: The Drivers of Growth – Can the Past be Extended?', IMF Working Paper, WP/14/134, Washington, DC: International Monetary Fund.

Tahvonen, O. (2000) 'Economic Sustainability and Scarcity of Natural Resources: A Brief Historical Review', *Resources for the Future*. Available at www.rff.org.

Wellisz, S. and Saw, P. L. S. (1994) 'A World Bank Comparative Study', in R. Findlay and S. Wellisz (eds) *The Political Economy of Poverty, Equity and Growth, Five Small Open Economies*, New York:Oxford University Press. Available at http://documents.worldbank.org/curated/en/141411468760509368/The-political-economy-of-poverty-equity-and-growth-five-small-open-economies (accessed 28 August 2019).

World Bank (2017) *World Bank Indicators*, Washington, DC: World Bank Institute. Available at: http://data.worldbank.org/indicator (accessed 28 August 2017).

Zafar, A. (2011) 'Mauritius: An Economic Success Story', in P. Chuhan-Pole and M. Angwafo (eds) *Yes Africa Can: Success Stories from a Dynamic Continent*, Washington, DC: International Bank for Reconstruction and Development and the World Bank.

10 Can Africa serve as a trading hub for Mauritius?

An in-depth analysis

V. Tandrayen-Ragoobur

Introduction

In March 2018 44 African nations came together to sign the African Continental Free Trade Agreement (AfCFTA). There are still 11 African nations which need to sign the agreement but it represents a major leap forward, as it forms the largest free trade zone since the creation of the World Trade Organization in 1995. If all 55 African countries join the free trade area, it will be the world's largest by number of countries, covering more than 1.2 billion people and a combined gross domestic product (GDP) of US \$2.5 trillion (SDG Knowledge Hub, 2018). It is expected that intra-African trade is likely to increase by 52.3 per cent by 2020 under the agreement (ibid.). Under this continent-wide accord, nations commit to cut tariffs on 90 per cent of goods with the aim of increasing intra-Africa trade. One of the core tenets of the AfCFTA is the Boosting Intra-African Trade initiative, which indicates the enormous potential for fostering intra-regional and cross-border trade and stimulating opportunities for industrialization and diversification while creating much needed employment opportunities for the continent's growing population (African Export-Import Bank , 2018). Hence, the implementation of the AfCFTA can be seen as the catalyst that can move the region towards high levels of intra-regional trade and development.

Still, the continent accounts for less than 3 per cent of world trade (UNCTAD, 2018). In 2017 Africa's total merchandise trade gathered momentum, growing by 10.6 per cent to US \$907.63 billion, up from \$820.76 billion in 2016 (NBER, 2018). However, in terms of intra-African trade, Africa continues to lag behind other regions. For instance, in 2017 trade with its immediate neighbours was at about 15 per cent, so Africa compared unfavourably to Europe (68 per cent), North America (37 per cent), and Latin America (20 per cent) (African Export-Import Bank, 2018). Furthermore, Africa's export basket is persistently dominated by commodities and natural resources. In 2016 intra-African exports made up 18 per cent of total exports, compared to 59 per cent and 69 per cent for intra-Asia and intra-Europe exports, respectively. The figures for imports are similar. There have been slight improvements in the past 10 years, though, as the share of African countries' exports within the continent has slightly increased while that of imports has remained stagnant. Similarly, the continent's participation in the global value chain has been minimal.

Over the past few decades, the African continent has also experienced a proliferation of sub-regional agreements, with the formation of the East African Community (EAC), the Common Market for Eastern and Southern Africa (COMESA), the Economic Community of West African States (ECOWAS) and the Southern African Development Community (SADC). That proliferation has raised concerns over the potential costs imposed by the fragmentation of the continent's trading system into exclusive blocs, especially in a context of low intra-regional trade performance (African Export-Import Bank, 2018). Given that the share of intra-African trade remains low compared to intra-regional trade in other parts of the world, unlocking Africa's full economic potential is a necessity.

Mauritius, which is a member of a number of African groups including SADC and COMESA, also faces low intra-regional trade within the groupings. It has also multiple bilateral trade agreements across Africa, which means that global investors and traders gain preferential access to a number of key African markets and hundreds of millions of customers. In fact, Mauritius holds treaties with 43 countries (World Economic Forum, 2016). However, trade within the region and within the different regional trade groups remains low. Thus, the objective of the chapter is to examine how Mauritius can boost trade with the African continent. In particular, the chapter investigates the trade potential between the small island economy and the African countries by compiling a series of trade indices. Particular emphasis is placed on countries within SADC and COMESA. The methodology rests on the use of disaggregated trade data from the United Nations Commodity Trade Statistics Database (UN Comtrade) and the World Integration Trade Solution (WITS) database from 2000 to 2017.[1] Using trade indices, evidence-based policy options are proposed to maximize Mauritian trade potential with the continent.

The chapter is structured as follows: section two reviews the literature on regional integration and trade across developing countries. Section three provides an overview of the Mauritian economy with particular emphasis on its trade links with both developed economies and African countries. Section four sets out the methodological approach with particular emphasis on the different computed trade indicators. Section five discusses the findings and we finally conclude with relevant policy options in section six.

Regional south-south trade

The process of regional economic integration has deeply shaped the global economic situation. Different forms of integration driven by political, economic and security considerations and mostly involving developing countries have emerged over the past few decades. Promoting greater trade within regional integration is achieved via the elimination or reduction of barriers to trade such as import tariffs, export duties and quantitative restrictions. Cooperation among developing countries for the expansion of south-south trade (that is trade among equal partners) in general and regional south-south trade agreements has been extensively analysed in the literature but the existing work and thinking still provide a mixed picture.

Proponents of universal free trade have opposed discriminatory trade agreements, in general, and free trade areas among developing countries for the expansion of south-south trade, in particular (Shafaeddin, 2010). Others have argued that south-south trade can have a positive influence on developing countries (Myrdal, 1956; Lewis, 1980; UNCTAD, 1986; Sarkar and Singer, 1991; Oman, 1994; Agatiello, 2007, Rojid and Seetanah, 2010). The potential of south-south trade as a driver of economic development is discussed in terms of the capacity of developing countries to reduce their dependence on northern markets and to overcome bottlenecks related to resource endowments and the small size of domestic markets. Trade integration thus plays a major role in enhancing structural transformation and inclusive growth among developing economies by increasing domestic productive capacity (UNECA, 2015), promoting upward harmonization of standards, improving institutions, introducing technical know-how into the domestic market and increasing preferential access to desirable markets (UNCTAD, 2017). Furthermore, it is also suggested that regional integration can promote higher standards in terms of labour, environment, transparency and other progressive reforms and non-economic objectives, but there are often concerns about policy sovereignty and the balance between commitment and flexibility (ibid.). These are particularly beneficial to least developed or low-income economies whereby trade agreements determine national trade policy and intensify the impact of trade on economic development.

Moreover, there is a large body of literature on the implications of regional integration on developing economies' trade patterns. However, the empirical evidence is not conclusive (Estevadeordal and Suominen, 2008) and the trade-enhancing benefits of regional integration are not straightforward. Viner (1950) was the first to explain the welfare effects of trade agreements in terms of two opposing effects: trade creation and trade diversion. Likewise, Bhagwati and Panagariya (1996) state that preferential trade agreements (PTAs) are two-faced because trade liberalization under these agreements may be achieved at the cost of discrimination or trade diversion. It has been postulated that in addition to direct effects on members within the trading group, such agreements also impact countries that have existing trading relationships with new members (indirect effects). Whether the proliferation of regional trading agreements promotes freer global trade (Summers, 1991; Maggi, 2014) or disrupts the natural process of global liberalization (Bhagwati 1991, 1993, 1995) remains debatable. With the possibility of beneficial or harmful effects, Magee (2008) concludes that the net effects must be guided by country-specific economic structures.

It has been claimed that regional integration among developing countries leads to trade diversion from low-cost to high-cost producers, thus creating welfare losses (Viner, 1950; Corden, 1993; Greenaway and Milner, 1990) so it is better for developing countries to liberalize their trade regimes unilaterally in a non-discriminatory fashion rather than targeting markets in the south. Other arguments hinge on the fact that trade between the south and the north are more advantageous than trading among developing countries as trade potential based on economies of scale among small and poor countries of the south does not have a significant development impact (World Bank, 2000; Subramanian and Tamirisa, 2001; Kowalski and Shepherd, 2006). On theoretical grounds, south-south regional integration is likely to lead to income divergence between member countries (Venables, 1999). Similarly, existing empirical studies show that, on average, low-income countries benefit less from regional integration agreements (de Melo and Panagariya, 1995; Feenstra, 1996; Ariyasajjakorn et al., 2009). According to the World Bank (2000), south-south trade via regional trading groups is quite problematic. On the other hand, trade among equal partners may have a positive impact on developing countries as it is difficult for the latter to access developed country markets (UNCTAD, 1986; Agatiello, 2007). Furthermore, the slowdown in the growth rates of developed economies increases the vulnerability and risks of dependence for developing countries so much that there is a growing need for south-south trade expansion (South Centre, 1993).

Africa is no exception to that regional integration process. Owing to Africa's relatively low share in global trade, trading agreements on the continent are viewed as mechanisms for stimulating trade, evolving commercial links across countries within the region, regional economies of scale, and market access for sustained growth and development (Ogunkola, 1998). Closer economic integration has always been the objective of African countries but the progress achieved so far has been mixed. Divided into 54 economic spaces, Africa consists of 16 landlocked economies and 34 least developed countries (Kingombe, 2017). These countries are scattered across more than 30 overlapping sub-regional and regional organizations and what is often referred to as the 'spaghetti bowl'. Both the scope and depth of economic integration vary considerably, with some regional trading groups doing far better than others (ibid.). The low levels of intra-regional economic exchange and the smallest share of global trade has led to Africa being the least integrated continent in the world. Thus, although Africa has been ahead of the world in terms of the number of existing regional trading agreements, evidence of gains arising from these agreements is mixed. The intensity of trade flows remains very low, showing that the signing of free trade agreements (FTAs) is not sufficient in itself for the development of trade between African countries. In fact, most of the trade flows of these countries are still with other continents. The majority of African exports are still destined for markets outside Africa, namely the European Union and the United States. The last decade witnessed a shift from these traditional partners to the emerging economies of the

People's Republic of China, India and Brazil, among others (Geda, 2013). Such trade patterns thus contradict the predictions of empirical models (e.g. the gravitation model of international trade), according to which the intensity of trade between two countries must be proportional to their economic masses and inversely proportional to their distance.

Numerous explanations are provided to justify the low level of trade flows between African countries, namely the complicated architecture of regional trading groups, the lack of harmonization of policies, regulations and procedures on trade and infrastructure development, poor soft and hard infrastructure which hinders Africa's competitiveness and diversification process and, finally, important constraints such as institutional, administrative and financial capacity and governance among member states (Kingombe, 2017). However, intra-Africa trade still has the potential to raise the level of welfare of the African population through fostering regional economic development (Longo and Sekkat, 2001, Geda and Kibret, 2008). Despite being at low levels, intra-Africa trade may enhance Africa's bargaining power in trade negotiations and help to ensure greater policy credibility. Regionalism coupled with good policies in terms of sound macroeconomic management, lower political tensions, and better physical infrastructure can, therefore, lead to welfare gains (Geda and Seid, 2015). Furthermore, while the measurement of success or failure of regional trading groups has been examined in economic terms, mainly in the form of trade diversion or trade creation, the political, sociocultural and other environmental dimensions have been ignored (Woolcock, 2001).

This chapter thus builds on existing empirical work and the theoretical foundation of south-south trade to discuss how Mauritius can trade more with the African continent, hence promoting trade across developing economies.

Mauritius' trading position

Mauritius' trade links

Mauritius has a liberal economic and trade policy and has been a member of the World Trade Organization since 1995 and was a member of the General Agreement on Tariff and Trade prior to 1995. The island nation is a member of a number of regional economic groupings, namely COMESA, SADC and the Indian Ocean Commission (IOC). It is also a beneficiary of the Generalized System of Preferences offered by Japan, Norway, Switzerland, the United States, and the customs union of Belarus, Kazakhstan and the Russian Federation. Moreover, it has an FTA with Turkey and a PTA with Pakistan. The United States and Mauritius signed a Trade and Investment Framework Agreement in September 2006 in order to address bilateral trade issues and to strengthen and expand trade and investment relations between the two countries. Mauritius is eligible for trade benefits under the African Growth and Opportunity Act (AGOA), which provides for duty-free and quota-free access to the US market for over 6,000 products from eligible sub-Saharan African countries. Export of apparel from Mauritius to the United States made from fabric imported from any country is duty-free under the AGOA Third Country Fabric Provision. In 2015 the United States renewed AGOA until September 2025.

In view of boosting trade with other countries and increasing demand for local products in international markets, in 2019 Mauritius was finalizing the Comprehensive Economic Cooperation Partnership Agreement with India; the FTA with China; and enhancing bilateral cooperation with Saudi Arabia and several Middle East countries as well as renewing its partnerships with the member states of the Commonwealth Group. Mauritius also signed the AfCFTA in March 2018, which promotes the economic interests of the continent as a global player through a single African market. Once known as the 'dark and hopeless continent', Africa is now seen as the 'rising continent'. Various countries across the globe are showing greater interest in African countries including Mauritius, which has had a long-lasting presence on the continent. In 2017, in order to further boost intra-regional African trade and investment, Mauritius supported the Tripartite Agreement between SADC, COMESA and the EAC. The government is aggressively driving forward an African Economic Strategy that will create sustainable economic corridors with African trading blocs, namely SADC, COMESA and IOC and selected economies across the region.

There exist many opportunities in the different African markets for Mauritius. Treaties and free trade access to COMESA and SADC member countries already allow Mauritian exporters to sell to 27 African countries at duty-free rates. Furthermore, with direct air connectivity to six destinations in Africa, it has become easier to export goods. To compensate for its limitations in exporting manufactured goods, Mauritius needs to develop a strategy for exporting services to Africa, such as professional services in the area of accountancy, auditing, consultancy, health, education, construction and information technology (IT).

Mauritius is an open and globally competitive economy and that is fully integrated into the world trading system through its trade policies. Relative to other African economies, customs duties are low and Mauritius does not have any trade barriers. The share of trade to GDP stood at 97.1 per cent in 2017 compared to 98.4 per cent in 2016 (World Bank, 2018). However, Mauritius imports more than it exports, resulting in a trade deficit that increased during the economic crisis and is expected to widen in the years to come. With the exception of 1974 and 1986, the trade balance has always recorded a deficit since 1968. The trade deficit level, which remained quite low until 1975, rose during the difficult period of the late 1970s and early 1980s. After a brief improvement between 1982 and 1986, the balance of the trade deficit has continually worsened over time. In 2017 the trade deficit amounted to Rs 99.7 billion. The trade deficit for the second quarter of 2018 was Rs 27.8 billion, 15.8 per cent higher than the deficit of Rs 24.0 billion for the corresponding quarter of 2017 (Statistics Mauritius, 2018).

Overall export and import trends

The composition of domestic exports is currently more diversified than in previous decades. In 1968 Mauritius depended heavily on sugar as the primary commodity export which accounted for 93 per cent of total domestic exports. Since then, the proportion of sugar exports has dwindled considerably and represented only 16.3 per cent of domestic exports in 2017, while apparel and clothing have emerged as the country's most important exports. The island mainly exports fish and fish products and articles of apparel and clothing accessories. Total exports in goods in 2017 amounted to Rs 81.3 billion, 3.7 per cent less than in 2016. Total exports for the second quarter of 2018 were 0.5 per cent lower than in the same quarter of 2017 (Statistics Mauritius, 2018). However, exports of services have been on the rise with an increase of 2.5 per cent in 2017 relative to 2016. Total exports of goods and services are expected to increase by 7.5 per cent, amounting to Rs 208 billion in 2018. In fact, exports have faced a number of challenges over the past 15 years with large negative terms-of-trade shocks due to the phasing out of the Multi-Fibre Agreement in 2005; reductions in sugar prices guaranteed by the European Union starting in 2006; high global commodity prices, especially for food and oil products; the financial crisis of 2007 and 2008, and increased competition from emerging countries. The trend in total exports and imports of goods and services from 2006 to 2018 is shown in Figure 10.1 below:

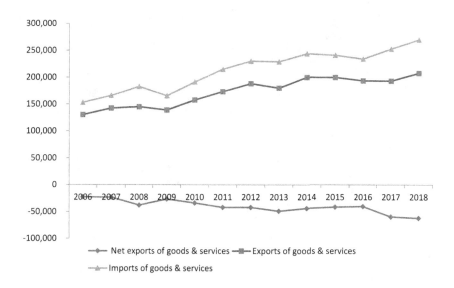

Figure 10.1 Total exports, imports and net exports of goods and services from 2006 to 2018
Note: Figures are in Rs million.
Source: Statistics Mauritius (2018).

In contrast, total imports of goods in 2017 were valued at Rs 180 billion, showing a rise of 9 per cent compared to 2016. Total imports of goods increased by 8.3 per cent to Rs 48.0 billion in the second quarter of 2018, relative to the same quarter in 2017. This was mainly due to increases in imports of mineral fuels, lubricants and related materials. The island mainly imports refined petroleum products, machinery and transport equipment, food and live animals. Imports of services also rebounded by 2.4 per cent in 2017 following a contraction of 8.2 per cent in 2016. Imports of goods and services amounted to Rs 253.2 billion in 2017 compared to Rs 234.1 billion in 2016, representing a nominal increase of 8.2 per cent. Hence, net exports of goods and services resulted in a deficit of Rs 59.7 billion in 2017, representing a deficit of 13.0 per cent of GDP at market prices, higher than the figure of 9.3 per cent in 2016.

Gradually, the landscape of Mauritius' trade destinations has been shifting away from trade with developed regions (the European Union and the United States), and towards trade with emerging nations. Analysis by countries of destination for the year 2017 (see Figure 10.2) shows that the main markets are dominated by the European countries, representing 49 per cent of total exports valued at Rs 35 billion compared to Rs 37 billion in 2016, thus showing a decrease of 4 per cent.

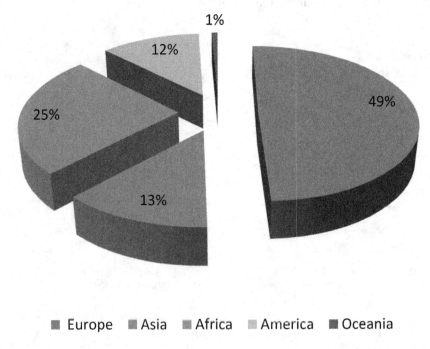

Figure 10.2 Export destinations of goods in 2017
Source: Statistics Mauritius (2018).

The next most important export destination after Europe is Africa which represents 25 per cent of total exports, with South Africa having the largest share of 35.5 per cent of exports directed to the continent, followed by Madagascar with a share of 26.3 per cent. The main imports originate mainly from Asian countries with a share of 51.1 per cent in 2017, followed by Europe at 25.8 per cent and Africa at 14.2 per cent. Within Asia, the two countries which stand out are India and China, having the largest share of 32 per cent each of the total imports from the Asian continent. Within Africa, Mauritius imports mostly from South Africa, Seychelles, Madagascar, Kenya and Egypt.

Mauritian intra-African trade within SADC and COMESA

The chapter focuses on two main regional trading groups, namely SADC and COMESA and investigates where Mauritius stands in terms of its trading potential across countries within both regional trading agreements. COMESA is the largest regional economic organization in Africa, with 19 member states and a total population of about 390 million. It has an FTA with the following countries: Burundi, Comoros, the Democratic Republic of the Congo, Djibouti, Egypt, Eritrea, Ethiopia, Kenya, Libya, Madagascar, Malawi, Mauritius, Rwanda, Seychelles, Sudan, Swaziland, Uganda, Zambia and Zimbabwe (see also Seetanah *et al.*, 2018). Meanwhile, SADC is a regional economic community comprising 16 member states: Angola, Botswana, Comoros, the Democratic Republic of the Congo, Lesotho, Madagascar, Malawi, Mauritius, Mozambique, Namibia, Seychelles, South Africa, Eswatini, the United Republic of Tanzania, Zambia and Zimbabwe. Eight countries are members of both SADC and COMESA.

Overall, Mauritius ranked moderately to poorly within both COMESA and SADC in the overall Africa Regional Integration index in 2016, attaining sixth and ninth place, respectively, with the same score of 0.47 for SADC and COMESA (Koami *et al.*, 2016). Figure 10.3 and Figure 10.4 show the respective Regional Integration index within COMESA and SADC countries. Mauritius compares unfavourably to Kenya and Zambia which have the highest index of 0.57 each but the island fares better than the group average of 0.41 and countries such as Burundi, Swaziland and Comoros. A similar picture is depicted for the SADC bloc where Mauritius is slightly above average but is well behind South Africa (with an index of 0.74), Botswana, Namibia, Zambia and Swaziland, to name but a few (see Figure 10.4).

The composition of Mauritius' trade with the continent is relatively diverse both in terms of exports and imports. In 2017 intra-African exports and imports stood at US $443 million and $747 million, representing 21 per cent of Mauritius' global exports and 14 per cent of the country's global imports, respectively (TRALAC, 2018). The bulk of exports (approximately 86 per cent of total intra-African exports) are destined for South Africa (42 per cent), Madagascar (32 per cent) and Kenya (12 per cent), while the remainder is sent to Seychelles, Swaziland and Zimbabwe. In terms of intra-African imports, Mauritius imports mainly from South Africa (60 per cent), Seychelles (11 per cent) and Madagascar

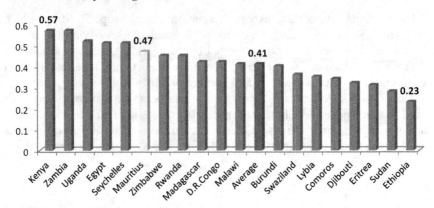

Figure 10.3 The African Regional Integration Index within COMESA countries
Source: Africa Regional Integration Index (2016).

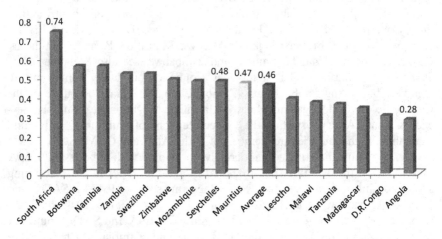

Figure 10.4 The African Regional Integration Index within SADC countries
Source: Africa Regional Integration Index (2016).

(10 per cent) (International Trade Centre database, 2018). The main exported products are articles of knitted or crocheted apparel and clothing accessories (15.3 per cent) and not knitted or crocheted (14.4 per cent) followed by sugar and sugar confectionery (9.9 per cent) (see Table 10.1). Meanwhile, the main imports from Africa are mineral fuels and oils (21.3 per cent), fish and crustaceans (21.3 per cent) and tobacco (11.5 per cent).

In terms of intra-African tariffs, about 90 per cent of Mauritius' tariff lines are duty-free except for clothing which attracts tariffs of up to 56 per cent (e.g. men's suits). Other products which attract tariffs are toilet paper, paper products and suitcases (around 30 per cent) (TRALAC, 2018).

Table 10.1 Top 12 intra-African exports and imports of Mauritius in 2017

Mauritius' exports to Africa: main products	USD (000's) 2017	%	Mauritius' imports from Africa: main products	USD (000's) 2017	%
Articles of apparel and clothing accessories, knitted or crocheted	67,633	15.28	Mineral fuels, mineral oils and products of their distillation; bituminous substances	158,694	21.25
Articles of apparel and clothing accessories not knitted	63,534	14.35	Fish and crustaceans, molluscs and other aquatic invertebrates	158,694	21.25
Sugar and sugar confectionery	43,991	9.94	Tobacco and manufactured tobacco substitutes	85,661	11.47
Knitted or crocheted fabrics	33,322	7.53	Coffee, tea, mate and spices	58,496	7.83
Cotton	32,482	7.34	Cotton	53,285	7.13
Electrical machinery and equipment	27,454	6.20	Vehicles other than railway or tramway	38,493	5.15
Plastics and articles thereof	23,715	5.36	Edible fruit and nuts; peel of citrus fruit	29,734	3.98
Beverages, spirits and vinegar	18,827	4.25	Electrical machinery and equipment	23,515	3.15
Printed books, newspapers, pictures and other products of the printing industry	11,542	2.61	Miscellaneous edible preparations	19,224	2.57
Preparations of cereals, flour, starch or milk	10,888	2.46	Machinery, mechanical appliances, nuclear reactors, boilers; parts thereof	17,504	2.34
Machinery, mechanical appliances, nuclear reactors	10,646	2.40	Live animals	17,390	2.33
Mineral fuels, mineral oils and products of their distillation; bituminous substances; mineral	8,742	1.97	Animal or vegetable fats and oils and their cleavage products; prepared edible fats; animal	16,376	2.19

Source: International Trade Centre database (2018).

Methods: trade indices

The chapter draws extensively on secondary data to explain the trade potential between Mauritius and the African members of COMESA and SADC. Disaggregated trade data is used from the UN Comtrade and WITS databases for the period 2000–2017 to compute a set of trade indices. We use indicators along three different dimensions of Mauritian trade performance in relation to member countries within COMESA and SADC. This framework helps to evaluate the dynamics of the island's exports along different margins of trade and calculates the extent to which Mauritius can gain from African markets, especially members of COMESA and SADC.

Hence, within the first trade dimension relating to potential sources of future growth in exports and imports, two indices are computed, namely the Trade Intensity Index and the Trade Complementarity Index. The Trade Intensity Index indicates with which partners Mauritius has a relatively intense trading relationship vis-à-vis the rest of the world. Next, the Trade Complementarity Index evaluates the extent to which the export profile of Mauritius complements the import profile of each member country of SADC and COMESA. Profiles that strongly complement one another may indicate exploitable sources of growth.

The second dimension relates to the extent to which Mauritius' exports have diversified with respect to products and markets. Three indicators are used, namely the Herfindahl-Hirschman Product Concentration Index which measures the dispersion of trade value across Mauritian products, while the Herfindahl-Hirschman Market Concentration Index does the same across the island's partners. A higher value indicates a greater concentration of value across products or partners, implying a lower diversification of commodities and markets. The third index is the Export Market Penetration index which measures the extent to which Mauritian exports reach proven importers of those products worldwide. A low value indicates potential for expansion. The third dimension covers the level of sophistication of Mauritius' main exports. The sophistication of a country's export products provides an understanding of the island's level of economic development and its position in the global production chain.

Mauritius' trade orientation and growth

The Trade Intensity Index and the Trade Complementarity Index are used to analyse Mauritius' trade orientation and growth. The Trade Intensity Index is computed as follows:

$$100^* \left[\frac{x_{ijk}}{X_{ik}} \Big/ \frac{x_{wjk}}{X_{wk}} \right]$$

where x is the value of exports of product k from origin country i to destination j, and X is the total exports from i of product k, while w indicates the world as origin. The index uses similar logic to that of revealed comparative advantage and indicates whether a reporting country exports more, as a percentage, to a partner than the world does on average. It determines whether the value of trade between two countries is greater or smaller than might be expected on the basis of their importance in world trade. A value greater than 100 indicates a relationship that is more intense than the world average for the partner.

The Trade Complementarity Index considers prospects for intra-regional trade in that it shows how well the export profile of the reporting country matches, or complements, the import profile of the partner. A high index indicates that two countries will gain from increased trade, and is particularly useful in evaluating prospective bilateral or regional trade agreements. The Trade Complementarity Index is defined as:

$$100^* \left[1 - \sum_k \left| \frac{m_{jk}}{M_j} - \frac{x_{ik}}{X_i} \right| \right]$$

where x is the value of exports of product k from reporting country i, and X is country i's total exports. Partner country j's value of imports of product k is given by m, and the total value of its imports value is denoted by M. The index is zero when no goods are exported by one country or imported by the other (perfect competitors) and is 100 when the export and import shares exactly match (ideal trading partners). Strong complementary profiles may indicate exploitable sources of growth.

Mauritius' product and market concentration

The Export Market Penetration Index measures the extent to which a country's exports reach already proven markets. It is calculated as the number of countries to which the reporting country exports a particular product divided by the number of countries that report importing the product that year and this is given by

$$\frac{\eta_{x,ik}}{\eta_{m.k}}$$

where n_x is the number of countries to which country i exports product k, and n_m is the number of countries that import product k from any source. A low export penetration may signal the presence of barriers to trade that are preventing firms from expanding the number of markets to which they export.

Next, the Herfindahl-Hirschman Market Concentration Index is as follows:

$$\frac{\sum_{j=1}^{n_i} \left(\frac{x_{ij}}{X_i} \right)^2 - \frac{1}{n_i}}{1 - \frac{1}{n_i}}$$

where X is the total value of exports from reporting country i, x is the value of exports from country i to destination market j, and n is the number of partner markets to which country i exports. The value of the indicator ranges from 0 to 1, where a higher index indicates that exports are concentrated in fewer markets, whereas a country trading equally with all partners will have an index close to 0. A fall in the index may indicate diversification in the exporter's trading partnerships.

The Herfindahl-Hirschman Product Concentration Index is further measured as follows:

$$\frac{\sum_{k=1}^{n_i} \left(\frac{x_{ik}}{X_i}\right)^2 - \frac{1}{n_i}}{1 - \frac{1}{n_i}}.$$

where X is the total value of exports from reporting country i, x is the value of exports of product k from country i, and n is the number of products exported by country i. It is the sum of squared shares of each product in total exports. A country with a perfectly diversified export portfolio will have an index close to zero, whereas a country which exports only one product will have a value of 1 (least diversified). It is also an indicator of the exporter's vulnerability to trade shocks. Measured over time, a fall in the index may be an indication of diversification in the exporter's trade profile.

Technological sophistication of trade flows from Mauritius

The index used to analyse trade flows according to its technological sophistication is the Technological Sophistication of Exports which provides a percentage breakdown of a country's exports according to five broad technological categories embodied in the final products. These categories are high technology, medium technology, low technology, primary products and resource-based products (Lall et al., 2006). This indicator helps to investigate how a country's export basket has changed over a period of time and thus depicts a clear picture of its pattern of economic development. It is formulated as follows:

$$100^* \sum_{k \in \Omega_{t_{ec}}} \frac{x_{ijk}}{X_{ij}}$$

where x is the value of exports of product k from country i to partner j, and X is the total value of all exports of i to j. Ω_{tec} is the set of all products in mutually exclusive categories: high technology, medium technology, low technology, primary products and resource-based products.

Findings

Our results are based on the different trade indicators computed across the three dimensions of Mauritius' trade performance relative to the trading nations in general and to COMESA and SADC countries in particular.

Trade Intensity and Trade Complementarity Indices

Table 10.2 shows that Mauritius has intense trade relationships with Madagascar, Seychelles, Comoros, Swaziland, Kenya, South Africa, Zimbabwe, Uganda, Mozambique, Zambia, Rwanda and Tanzania. Trade intensity with Zambia, Rwanda and Tanzania has declined over the past few decades. This means that Mauritian trade is intense with some countries within COMESA and SADC compared to its trading pattern with the rest of the world. The natural trading partner theory reveals that countries tend to trade more with their neighbours and close proximate partners. In particular, Madagascar, Seychelles, Comoros, Kenya and South Africa are geographically closer to Mauritius.

Next, the Trade Complementarity Index is analysed for the period 2000–2017 and it can be noted that the index ranges between 19.4 (for Zambia) to 32.4 (for Namibia) in 2017. The index highlights the extent to which the export profile of Mauritius matches the import profile of member states of SADC and COMESA. The index has improved over the past few decades for most countries implying that there are gains from increased intra-African trade for Mauritius and more needs to be done to enable the island to penetrate the African continent and to benefit from both regional trade agreements.

These two indices capture the first trade dimension relating to potential sources of future exports and imports growth, and it can be inferred that Africa represents a potential market for Mauritian products. Africa also embodies a source of valuable resources and inputs to enable local industries to expand and diversify into high value-added activities. In particular, local enterprises must take advantage of the neighbouring markets within the African continent as shorter distances imply lower transport costs which can give them a definite competitive edge. Furthermore, as the government is aggressively pursuing an African Economic Strategy and creating sustainable economic corridors with African trading blocs and selected economies across the continent, local companies will benefit significantly from these preferential market access and agreements.

Similarly, the African market is huge. The regional markets of SADC and COMESA alone represent 500 million consumers and given that many African countries are currently enjoying higher growth rates, there is a burgeoning African middle-class society with a strong demand for goods and services. Mauritius must tap into this segment of the African population and examine its demands for goods and services. The island economy can also contribute to the African supply chain via the special economic zone by drawing on

Table 10.2 Trade Intensity Index with COMESA and SADC economies

	1995	2000	2005	2010	2015	2017
Angola	3.4	2.44	3.07	105.86	31.76	28.11
Botswana	–	884.8	374.0	12.6	3.0	35.1
Burundi	756.0	1,048.8	728.6	2,785.7	530.3	65.2
Comoros	4,571.0	6,968.5	14,810.3	7,521.5	8,252.1	9,276.3
Democratic Republic of the Congo	11.8	17.5	6.7	0.8	5.8	–
Djibouti	14.7	2.0	94.2	2.0	12.3	4.8
Egypt, Arab Republic	8.3	0.9	1.5	8.1	29.8	2.1
Eritrea	–	–	212.1	34.0	11.0	8.6
Ethiopia (excludes Eritrea)	0.3	9.5	160.0	17.5	24.3	21.6
Kenya	202.4	595.2	655.3	864.7	742.3	2640.2
Lesotho	–	3,460.7	1,130.4	816.3	7.9	3.7
Libya	0.54	–	–	3.05	0.19	–
Madagascar	21,123.1	41,129.6	42,156.2	41,328.9	36,948.2	32,696.0
Malawi	381.1	1,117.3	89.6	148.5	50.4	25.9
Mozambique	55.1	314.5	248.7	233.3	82.2	338.2
Namibia		13.3	108.0	21.7	17.6	47.3
Rwanda	1,674.8	4,496.7	1,257.1	1,110.7	2,157.3	229.8
Seychelles	4,165.0	8,181.3	12,570.9	25,225.4	19,548.0	27,864.6
South Africa	89.7	151.5	250.0	813.3	1,729.8	1,951.2
Sudan	–	–	–	17.6	5.0	18.2
Swaziland	–	33.1	309.0	49.8	2.2	3,725.8
Tanzania	228.6	726.3	404.0	305.5	372.9	146.3
Uganda	1,015.7	517.7	183.5	466.2	333.1	356.2
Zambia	83.4	57.2	167.9	221.1	546.7	290.4
Zimbabwe	913.8	1,721.9	430.5	451.5	762.5	906.5

Source: Author's computation from UN Comtrade and WITS databases (2018).

Note: Figures for the Democratic Republic of the Congo are for 2001, 2003, 2006 and 2014; Eritrea: 2006, 2010, 2014 and 2017; Ethiopia: 1994 instead of 1995; Sudan: 2012 instead of 2010; Angola: 1994 instead of 1995 and 2001 instead of 2000; Libya: 2013 instead of 2015.

Mauritius' know-how and capital for production and aiming at exporting the finished commodities to third markets such as Europe, the United States, India and China. In addition, Africa's economy is growing and many sectors are booming, such as the service sector. Hence, Mauritius can develop a strategy for exporting services such as professional services in the fields of accountancy, auditing, consultancy, health, education, construction and IT.

Table 10.3 Trade Complementarity Index with COMESA and SADC economies

	2000	*2005*	*2010*	*2017*
Angola	–	–	19.0	–
Botswana	16.7	26.8	29.2	29.7
Burundi	10.0	20.7	21.3	25.1
Comoros	13.8	19.5	19.4	–
Egypt, Arab Republic	9.2	24.9	22.0	23.2
Ethiopia (excludes Eritrea)	9.5	27.5	18.7	–
Kenya	9.2	19.4	19.6	26.8
Lesotho	15.7	–	27.1	–
Libya	–	–	17.1	–
Madagascar	14.0	23.5	25.1	28.7
Malawi	10.7	21.5	17.2	–
Mozambique	10.2	28.0	25.9	22.4
Namibia	14.9	26.5	28.4	32.4
Rwanda	–	23.3	22.1	–
Seychelles	10.3	19.0	20.6	–
South Africa	11.4	33.2	25.4	30.2
Sudan	–	–	–	25.6
Swaziland	13.7	24.5	–	–
Tanzania	11.5	23.0	17.4	22.8
Uganda	11.2	22.2	19.5	23.1
Zambia	10.3	19.7	24.6	19.4
Zimbabwe	–	20.1	19.0	–

Source: Author's computation from UN Comtrade and WITS databases, 2018.

Measuring the extent of export diversification across products and markets for Mauritius

Based on the trade indices discussed above, the first computed indicator is the index of Export Market Penetration. The trend for the period 1993–2016 is depicted in Figure 10.5. Although the indicator has increased over the past few decades, it is relatively low compared to other emerging nations. A low value also indicates potential for expansion across markets. There is a greater need for Mauritian enterprises to diversify their products as well as to penetrate new markets where they have a competitive advantage.

The Herfindahl-Hirschman Market Concentration Index is computed for Mauritius with respect to all countries as well as for African nations from 2000 to 2017. It can be noted from Figure 10.6 below that the index for all countries has fallen over the years from 0.46 in 2000 to 0.28 in 2017. In fact, Mauritius has gradually been trading more with the emerging economies, namely China and

Figure 10.5 Index of Export Market Penetration for Mauritius from 1993 to 2016
Source: Author's computation from the WITS database, 2018.

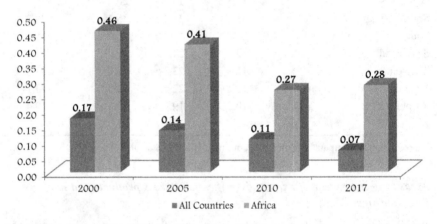

Figure 10.6 Herfindahl-Hirschman Market Concentration Index for Mauritius, 2000–2017
Source: Author's computation from the World Integration Trade Solution, 2018.

India, rather than concentrating solely on the European and US markets. From the African perspective, the market concentration index has also declined from 0.17 to 0.07 implying that there is greater diversification in Mauritius' trading links with Africa. The share of Mauritian trade with non-traditional African countries, namely Swaziland, Zimbabwe, Mozambique and Uganda, has been gradually increasing in recent years. From 2000 to 2010 Mauritius traded with four new African markets, and from 2010 to 2017 three new markets on the continent were tapped. There is a need for extensive market research across

African countries to identify the opportunities that each country can offer to existing Mauritian exporting firms and to potential local exporters who are willing to access the region. By assessing the market potential of different sectors, local firms will be better informed about the markets that they can enter and which are likely to be profitable.

Next, we analyse the Herfindahl-Hirschman Product Concentration Index for Mauritius with member states of COMESA and SADC. From Figure 10.7 it can be observed that Mauritius has a more diversified export product structure with Madagascar, Seychelles, Burundi, Rwanda and South Africa with an index nearing 0, while it has a more concentrated export structure with countries such as Sudan, Namibia, Botswana, Lesotho, Malawi and Ethiopia. Over the past decade there has been a fall in the product concentration index in Comoros, Rwanda, Egypt, Tanzania and Zimbabwe where potential for export product diversification exists. The structure of Mauritian economy is rather concentrated as it can produce only a limited range of manufactured goods for export such as textiles, clothing and apparel, sugar, and seafood and tuna. Hence, in order to compensate for this, Mauritius may have to focus on another avenue, and that is the export professional and financial services to Africa.

Measuring the export sophistication of Mauritius

The third dimension of our analysis relates to the export sophistication of Mauritius' exports. By comparing the sophistication of exports in 2005 and 2017, it shows changes in the island's export basket at all technological levels (see

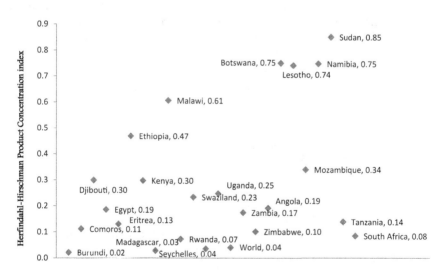

Figure 10.7 Mauritius' Herfindahl-Hirschman Product Concentration Index across COMESA and SADC member states, 2017
Source: Author's computation from the WITS database, 2018.

Figure 10.8). Export sophistication is enhanced by a number of factors, namely capital intensity and engagement in knowledge creation and transfer via investment in education, research and development (R&D), foreign direct investment (FDI) and imports (Zhu and Fu, 2013). An export product is more sophisticated the higher the average income of its exporter (Lall et al., 2006). Over the past five decades, Mauritius has gradually made the transition to an upper-middle-income economy, with GDP per capita improving from a record low of US $ 205.81 in 1960 to an expected GDP per capita of $11,182 in 2018. Both GDP per capita and human capital have played an important role in the country's specialization pattern and the level of sophistication of its exports.

The creation of knowledge capital is also widely regarded as an important element of competitiveness and export sophistication. Knowledge capital embraces indigenous innovation and external technology transfer. R&D and education represent the main sources of indigenous innovation, while FDI and import trade are the two main channels of technology diffusion. In particular, Mauritius has invested heavily in education over the years but innovation and R&D as a share of GDP is on very low at just 0.37 per cent in 2017 (Statistics Mauritius, 2018). The low levels of technological embodiment in Mauritian exports are a cause for concern as exports of sophisticated products are important to economic development. Encouraging signs have nevertheless been reported with the emergence of medium-technology manufacturers (International Trade Centre, 2017). However, there is a need for greater investment in R&D, knowledge creation and innovation to generate higher value-added activities and improve the level of sophistication of exports. Another channel for increasing export sophistication is through imports of large quantities of intermediate goods with a high technology content. The promotion of export-oriented

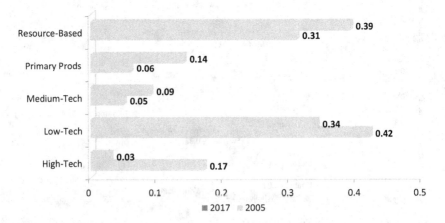

Figure 10.8 Technological classification of exports in 2005 and 2017
Source: Author's computation from the WITS database, 2018.

FDI is also another important factor for improving the export sophistication of Mauritius since it brings with it the knowledge and innovation required to enter foreign markets.

Conclusion

The chapter focuses on the trade pattern and performance of Mauritius and of the member states of SADC and COMESA. Using disaggregated data from the UN Comtrade and WITS databases for the period 2000–2017, three trade dimensions are studied. These dimensions relate first to the potential sources of future growth in exports and imports to the region, then to the extent of Mauritius export diversification across products and markets, and finally to the level of sophistication of Mauritius' main exports. In order to model the three trade elements, various indices are computed, namely the Trade Intensity Index, the Trade Complementarity Index, the Herfindahl-Hirschman Product Concentration Index, the Herfindahl-Hirschman Market Concentration Index, the Export Market Penetration Index and the Technological Sophistication of Exports Index.

Our results reveal that Mauritian trade intensity is higher with its neighbours and close proximate partners, namely Madagascar, Seychelles, Comoros, Kenya and South Africa, all of which are geographically close to Mauritius. Similarly, the Trade Complementarity Index shows that more needs to be done in order for Mauritius to penetrate the African continent and to benefit from both regional trade agreements. Over time, the number of new markets into which Mauritius has diversified within the African continent has increased and as such the number of products reaching the region has also risen. With Mauritius seeking to graduate to the status of a high-income economy, in the event of increased competition and shifts in demand trends, there is a need for the island to further diversify its trade markets and products. The need for diversification must be accompanied by technological innovation and sophistication to facilitate greater export penetration not only in the African markets but also in emerging countries.

Mauritius must endeavour to become a knowledge-based economy that thrives on innovation and value addition if it wants to make the transition to a high-income country. Through greater innovation and ideas Mauritius can then develop a new export strategy for the African region. It is of great importance that local firms should become better informed about existing trade agreements. Market access advisory services should be provided by trade support institutions to potential local exporters, with information about specific sectors that highlights the existing market access preferences, rules and conditions that enterprises can use to enhance trade with the continent. Through greater dissemination of information, the support institutions will be alerted to the difficulties and challenges faced by local producers and exporters who are trying to penetrate the African markets. The government will thus be in a better position to adopt the relevant policy options to improve the trade-related business environment and enhance the competitiveness and penetration of Mauritian exports on the continent. Similarly, in order to strengthen the visibility of local commodities and services, there must be greater participation of Mauritian enterprises at international trade fairs. This can be followed up by regular well-structured economic missions by trade support institutions such as the Economic Development Board, SME Mauritius and the Mauritius Chamber of Commerce and Industry.

However, Mauritius cannot penetrate all the African economies as they are highly heterogeneous with their own specificities and peculiarities. The island's competitive and comparative advantages may thus reside in only a few sectors and clusters; hence, these sectors need to be identified. Greater market intelligence, cultural knowledge, physical presence, finance and collaboration will help in identifying the clusters and sectors where trade can be encouraged. There is a need to identify the opportunities that each market offers to Mauritian exporters and potential exporters, thus extensive market research on each country and its economic sectors will be helpful. As competition intensifies in Africa, entrepreneurs must seek joint ventures in areas of core competence where other exporters have been successful. However, they must also try to find new trade opportunities in areas such as agribusiness, energy, health, infrastructure, human resource development, capacity building, security, IT, banking and finance. Services represent another trading avenue where Mauritius can increase its visibility in African markets.

Mauritius has been relying on the manufacturing sector as a main trade engine for some time but the future of the manufacturing sector lies in its ability to develop a decisive competitive edge while moving up the value added ladder (International Trade Centre, 2017). For this, it needs to continue to invest in more advanced technologies, innovation and R&D as well as enhancing efficiency through the training and development of its human resources. Services also represent an increasingly large share of Mauritius' total exports and Mauritius is rapidly moving away from traditional services to modern, higher value-added services. Innovative and ambitious strategies are now needed to maintain this diversification and drive towards increasing its global market share.

Moreover, in order to ensure fair and equitable treatment of Mauritian exports abroad, the application of burdensome and restrictive trade barriers at the regional level, especially with its SADC and COMESA trading partners, needs to be discussed by the member states. Mauritius must also negotiate and conclude trade agreements at the multilateral, plurilateral, regional and bilateral level to support Mauritian businesses with the necessary market conditions and access. Although Mauritius is part of a number of trading agreements, it is important to know how to make effective use of these agreements as well as maintaining its membership of the different African regional and sub-regional trading blocks. Likewise, Mauritius' traditional exports have been based on preferences and high market concentration, and there is a need to diversify away from that business model and to strengthen the global competitiveness of Mauritian exports. There are several relatively untapped markets that can offer opportunities for Mauritian exports. These countries have a high complementarity for trade with Mauritius and may provide an opening for greater trade.

Furthermore , the AfCFTA will unleash the huge trade potential of the continent and create the requisite conditions to mobilize both African and non-African trade and FDI. Enhanced trade and investment expansion over-seas will play an instrumental role in reshaping the island's economy, ensuring a positive spin on economic development, job creation and the fight against poverty. Mauritius needs to diversify away from being Euro-centric or US-centric and use Africa as an important trading hub by adopting an innova-tion-driven approach. By doing so, the small island can effectively realize its potential as a strategic hub for international trade and investment.

Note

1 United Nations Commodity Trade Statistics (UN Comtrade) database. Available at https://comtrade.un.org/. World Integration Trade Solution (WITS) database. Available at https://wits.worldbank.org/.

References

African Export-Import Bank (Afreximbank) (2018) *Boosting Intra-African Trade: Implications of the African Continental Free Trade Area Agreement*, Cairo: Afreximbank. Available at https://afreximbank.com/wp-content/uploads/2018/07/African-Trade-Report-2018.pdf (accessed July 2018).

Agatiello, O. R. (2007) 'Is South-South Trade the Answer to Alleviating Poverty?', *Management Decision* 45(8): 1252–1269.

Ariyasajjakorn, D., Gander, J. P., Ratanakomut, S. and Reynolds, S. E. (2009) 'ASEAN FTA, Distribution of Income, and Globalization', *Journal of Asian Economics* 20(3): 327–335.

Bhagwati, J. (1991) *The World Trading System at Risk*, Princeton, NJ: Princeton University Press.

Bhagwati, J. (1993a) 'Regionalism and Multilateralism: An Overview', in J. de Melo and A. Panagariya (eds) *New Dimensions in Regional Integration*, Cambridge: Cambridge University Press.

Bhagwati, J. (1993b) 'Beyond NAFTA: Clinton's Trading Choices', *Foreign Policy* (summer): 155–162.

Bhagwati, J. N. (1995) 'US Trade Policy: The Infatuation with FTAs', discussion paper series no. 726, New York: Columbia University Press.

Bhagwati, J. and Panagariya, A. (1996) 'The Theory of Preferential Trade Agreements: Historical Evolution and Current Trends', *American Economic Review* 86(2): 82–87.

Corden, W. M. (1993) 'The Theory of International Trade', *Transnational Corporations and International Trade and Payments* 8: 21.

De Melo, J. and Panagariya, A. (eds) (1995) *New Dimensions in Regional Integration*, Cambridge: Cambridge University Press.

Estevadeordal, A. and Suominen, K. (2008) 'Sequencing Regional Trade Integration and Cooperation Agreements', *World Economy* 31(1): 112–140.

Feenstra, R. C. (1996) 'Trade and Uneven Growth', *Journal of Development Economics* 49(1): 229–256.

Geda, A. (2013) *Africa's Economic Engagement with the Emerging South: Background Study for African Export Import Bank*, Cairo: Afreximbank.

Geda, A. and Kibret, H. (2008) 'Regional Economic Integration in Africa: A Review of Problems and Prospects with a Case Study of COMESA', *Journal of African Economies* 17(3): 357–394.

Geda, A. and Seid, E. H. (2015) 'The Potential for Internal Trade and Regional Integration in Africa', *Journal of African Trade* 2(1–2): 19–50.

Greenaway, D. and Milner, C. (1990) 'South-South Trade: Theory, Evidence, and Policy', *World Bank Research Observer* 5(1): 47–68.

International Trade Centre (2017) *Mauritius National Export Strategy 2017–2021*, Geneva: International Trade Centre.

International Trade Centre database (2018) *International Trade Statistics 2001 to 2018*, Geneva: International Trade Centre. Available at www.intracen.org/itc/market-info-tools/trade-statistics/ (accessed 16 August 2018).

Kingombe, C. (2017) *How Can Transport Infrastructure Promote Trade and Sustainable Development on the African Continent?* Geneva: International Centre for Trade and Sustainable Development. Available at www.ictsd.org/bridges-news/bridges-africa/news/how-can-transport-infrastructure-promote-trade-and-sustainable (accessed 16 September 2018).

Kingombe, C. (2018) *How Can Transport Infrastructure Promote Trade and Sustainable Development on the African Continent?*, Geneva: International Centre for Trade and Sustainable Development. Available at www.ictsd.org/about-us/christian-kingombe (accessed 16 September 2018).

Koami, K. A., Afrika, J. G., Akanni-Honvo, A., Tomen, H. N., Abimbola, O. and Davis, W. (2016) *Africa Regional Integration Index: Report 2016*, Tunis: African Development Bank.

Kowalski, P. and Shepherd, B. (2006) 'South-South Trade in Goods', OECD Trade Policy Papers, no. 40, Paris: OECD Publishing. Available at http://dx.doi.org/10.1787/314103237622.

Laird, S. and Yeats, A. (1986) 'The UNCTAD Trade Policy Simulation Model', in *A Note on the Methodology, Data and Users, United Nations Conference on Trade and Development Discussion Papers*, no 19, Geneva: UNCTAD.

Lall, S., Weiss, J. and Zhang, J. (2006) 'The "Sophistication" of Exports: A New Trade Measure', *World Development* 34(2): 222–237.

Lewis, A. (1980) 'The Slowing Down of the Engine of Growth', *American Economic Review* 70: 555–564.

Longo, R. and Sekkat, K. (2001) 'Obstacles to Expanding Intra-African Trade', OECD Development Centre Working Papers, no. 169, Paris: OECD Publishing.

Magee, C. S. (2008) 'New Measures of Trade Creation and Trade Diversion', *Journal of International Economics* 75(2): 349–362.

Maggi, G. (2014) 'International Trade Agreements', in *The Handbook of International Economics*, Amsterdam: Elsevier, pp. 317–390.

Møen, J. (1998) 'Trade and Development: Is South-South Co-operation a Feasible Strategy?', *Forum for Development Studies* 25(2): 245–270.

Mourgues, T. and Kingombe, C. (2017) 'How to Support African PPPs: The Role of the Enabling Environment', in *The Emerald Handbook of Public–Private*

Partnerships in Developing and Emerging Economies: Perspectives on Public Policy, Entrepreneurship and Poverty, Bingley: Emerald Publishing, pp. 269–310.

Myrdal, G. (1956) 'Trade as a Mechanism of International Inequality', *Development and Underdevelopment, Bank of Egypt 5th Anniversary Commemoration Lectures*, Cairo: Bank of Egypt, pp. 47–51.

National Bureau of Economic Research (NBER) (2018) *IMF: Direction of Trade Statistics (DOTS)*, Cambridge, MA: National Bureau of Economic Research. Available at http://www.nber.org/africa/display/1053 (accessed 16 September 2018).

Ogunkola, E.O. (1998) 'An Empirical Evaluation of Trade Potential in the Economic Community of West African States', papers 84, Nairobi: African Economic Research Consortium.

Oman, C. (1994) *Globalisation and Regionalisation: The Challenge for Developing Countries,* Paris:OECD.

Rojid, S. and Seetanah, B. (2010) 'An Assessment of the Impact of a COMESA Customs Union', *African Development Review* 22(2): 331–345.

Sarkar, P. and Singer, H. W. (1991) 'Manufactured Exports of Developing Countries and Their Terms of Trade since 1965', *World Development* 19(4): 333–340.

SDG Knowledge Hub (2018) *UNECA Regional Forum for Sustainable Development 2018*, Winnipeg, MB: International Institute for Sustainable Development. Available at http://sdg.iisd.org/events/uneca-regional-forum-for-sustainable-development-2018/ (accessed 15 August 2018).

Seetanah, B., Sannassee, R. V. and Fauzel, S. (2018) 'COMESA: A Case Study', in R. Looney (ed.) *The Handbook of International Trade Agreements*, Abingdon: Routledge: pp. 402–413.

Shafaeddin, M. (2010) 'The Role of China in Regional South-South Trade in Asia-Pacific: Prospects for Industrialization of the Low-Income Countries', MPRA Paper No. 26358. Munich: Munich Personal RePEc Archive. Available at https://mpra.ub.uni-muenchen.de/26358/.

South Centre (1993) *Facing the Challenge: Responses to the Report of the South Commission*, London: Zed Books.

Statistics Mauritius (2018) *Statistics Mauritius: Home*, Port Louis: Government of Mauritius. Available at http://statsmauritius.govmu.org/English/Pages/default.aspx (accessed 16 September 2018).

Subramanian, A. and Tamirisa, N. (2001) 'Africa's Trade Revisited', IMF Working Paper, Washington, DC: International Monetary Fund.

Summers, L. (1991) 'Regionalism and the World Trading System', in Policy Implications of Trade and Currency Zones: A Symposium Sponsored by the Federal Reserve Bank of Kansas City, Jackson Hole, Wyoming, 22–24 August, pp. 295–302.

TRALAC (2018) *Mauritius: Intra-Africa Trade and Tariff Profile*. Available at www.tralac.org/resources/our-resources/13407-mauritius-intra-africa-trade-and-tariff-profile.html (accessed 5 July 2018).

United Nations Conference on Trade and Development (UNCTAD) (1986) *Trade and Development Report 1986*, Geneva: UNCTAD.

United Nations Conference on Trade and Development (UNCTAD) (2017) *Trade and Development Report 2017*, Geneva: UNCTAD. Available at http://unctad.org/en/pages/PublicationWebflyer.aspx?publicationid=1852 (accessed 7 December 2017).

UNCTADstat (2018) *Handbook of Statistics, 2018*, Geneva: United Nations Conference on Trade and Development. Available at http://unctadstat.unctad.org/EN/ (accessed 7 January 2018).

United Nations Economic Commission for Africa (UNECA) (2015) *Economic Report on Africa: Industrializing through Trade*, Addis Ababa: UNECA Available atwww.uneca.org/publications/economic-report-africa-2015.

Venables, A. (1999) 'Trade Liberalisation and Factor Mobility: An Overview', in Riccardo Faini, Jaime de Melo and Klaus Zimmermann (eds) *Migration: The Controversies and the Evidence*, Cambridge: Cambridge University Press, pp. 23–47.

Viner, J. (1950) *The Customs Union Issue*, New York: Carnegie Endowment for International Peace.

Woolcock, M. (2001) 'The Place of Social Capital in Understanding Social and Economic Outcomes', *Canadian Journal of Policy Research* 2(1): 65–88.

World Bank (2000) *World Development Indicators*, Washington, DC: World Bank.

World Bank (2018) *World Development Indicators*, Washington, DC: World Bank.

World Economic Forum (2016) *Annual Report 2015–2016*, Cologny-Geneva: World Economic Forum. Available at www.weforum.org/reports/annual-report-2015-2016 (accessed 18 December 2017).

Zhu, S. and Fu, X. (2013) 'Drivers of Export Upgrading', *World Development* 51: 221–233.

11 Running the next development lap in Mauritius

Issues, outlooks and policy priorities

R. Sithanen

From structural transformation and economic diversification to the middle-income trap

In spite of the multiple factors such as a monocrop economy, geographical remoteness, lack of natural resources, ethnic fragmentation, and a rapidly expanding population, Mauritius has experienced a period of significant transformation and substantial economic and human development over the past five decades after gaining its independence in 1968 (Frankel, 2010; Svirydzenka and Petri, 2014). The country has metamorphosed from being a producer of primary raw materials to a competitive export-oriented and broad-based economy with agriculture, manufacturing, tourism, financial services and information and communications technology (ICT) as major growth engines. It has witnessed a remarkable achievement with per capita income rising from US $200 in 1968 to $10,500 at market rates or almost $20,500 on a purchasing-power parity basis in 2017 (IMF, 2018), thereby graduating from low- to upper-middle-income status. Human and social development has also been impressive, with the Human Development Index (HDI) improving from 0.620 in 1980 to 0.781 in 2015 (UNDP, 2016), thereby putting the country into the high human development category.

Mauritius reached a critical crossroad in its development agenda at the onset of the twenty-first century as many policies that had propelled it to success started to lose their steam and relevance and the international environment was changing fast. The resilience that it had historically displayed against external shocks was also wearing out. Since then, the island has found it hard to achieve a high growth momentum and this has had adverse implications for job creation and the quality of life of its people. The old economy has lost its preferential access to some markets, emerging sectors face stiffer competition while new pillars are not taking root fast enough to compensate for the weaknesses of the other drivers of growth. A low technology base, insignificant investment in innovation, research and development (R&D), an acute shortage of skilled labour, an ageing population, a low level of productivity growth, declining investment and savings, a surging current account deficit and public debt, and a shrinking manufacturing base are hindering its capacity to reach a growth rate in excess of 5 per cent and to graduate to high-income status (Mauritius Commercial Bank, 2017). The three main drivers of growth – consumption, investment and exports – show varying levels of weaknesses. Growth in consumption has moderated to less than 3 per cent in the last five years, while exports of goods are declining (Statistics Mauritius, 2017a). Gross domestic fixed capital formation has fallen to around 17 per cent of gross domestic product (GDP) in 2017 while its composition is skewed towards real estate and property development (Bank of Mauritius, 2018)

With the exception of tourism which is performing well, the macro-economic landscape mirrors the challenges at sectoral levels. Manufacturing is underperforming and its contribution to output, jobs, investment and exports is shrinking. Both sugar and non-sugar agriculture are struggling through a combination of external and domestic factors (Mauritius Commercial Bank, 2018). Financial services will need to adapt following the changes in the tax treaty with India and the base erosion and profit shifting initiatives of the Organisation for Economic Co-operation and Development that lay significant emphasis on substantial economic activities and the avoidance of treaty abuses. Growth in the ICT sector has slowed down while the domestic-oriented industries (DOI) continue to face the effects of competition from abroad, falling tariffs and unfair trade practices. The real challenges confronting micro, small and medium-sized enterprises (SMEs) have not changed in spite of good intentions by policymakers over the years.

Reigniting the engines of the old economy

A new economic paradigm is necessary to enable Mauritius to run the next development lap. The island nation must articulate a new development strategy in order to move out of the middle-income trap and to lay the foundations for future growth and shared prosperity in the light of domestic challenges and global constraints. First, it needs to restructure its 'old economy' to make it more dynamic, competitive and sustainable. Second, it must capture more value from the emerging sectors in goods and services. Third, it has to identify new pillars of growth that will facilitate the diversification and transformation of the economy. It must focus on developing a resilient domestic base, a strong manufacturing export sector, a competitive agro-business cluster and a sustainable tourism industry.

The DOI constitute a key pillar of the economy and are an essential component of the manufacturing landscape with strong backward and forward linkages with both the agriculture and service sectors. They represent around 13 per cent of GDP, directly employ 10 per cent of the labour force and comprise around 14,000 firms (Mauritius Commercial Bank, 2018). With the advent of globalization and fierce competition from low-cost manufacturing countries, it has been difficult for these companies to thrive and enhance their contribution to GDP and employment. A multi-pronged strategy is necessary to help the DOI to overcome their constraints and become more competitive. Livestock, fruit and vegetable production and other selected products should be supported through better and more affordable access to land resources, skills upgrading, improved technology, market development and fiscal and financial incentives. Second, sub-sectors such as shoes and leather, furniture and plastic need to become more efficient and sharpen their overall competitiveness in order to better withstand foreign competition. Third, some products such as jewellery, soap, alcoholic beverages and pharmaceutical items should be shored up to enable them to access the regional markets of the Southern African Development Community (SADC) and the Common Market for Eastern and Southern Africa (COMESA) where there are huge opportunities. Policies should aim to develop an adequate skill set to meet market needs, facilitate access to technology and innovation, improve support services and enhance the country's presence in some key export markets, especially in the Indian Ocean and the Southern and Eastern African region.

There has always been a strong, positive relationship between exports and economic growth in Mauritius (see Sannassee *et al.*, 2014). Therefore, industrial development and export diversification of manufacturing activities must remain a major driver of growth and a critical element of innovation, higher productivity and job creation. The export manufacturing sector principally comprises apparel, fish and sugar. All three sectors have been affected by preference erosions. However, there are still opportunities if they are restructured so that they become more efficient and competitive in terms of quality and response time and by investing in technology. They should also climb up the value chain and cut costs to avoid being crushed by low-cost competition from Asian countries. In the apparel industry, the aim is to concentrate on high value-added products with short lead times and to vertically integrate operations, while product and market diversification are key for enhancing the resilience of the sector. The sector must further develop the regional supply chain whereby the actual production of some apparel products is carried out in low cost locations in the region while the other key activities with backward and forward linkages, research and innovation and technology, design and marketing, finance and insurance are undertaken in Mauritius. The opening up of new markets through bilateral free trade agreements with countries such as India, the People's Republic of China and Turkey are crucial as is improving market penetration in existing regional economic communities such as COMESA and SADC and in preferential markets like the European Union and the United States. The objective of transforming the sugar industry into a cane cluster should be consolidated through the production of more refined and special sugars, incremental energy production from bagasse and other biomass and higher value added from molasses and ethanol. The fisheries sector should be further buttressed within an integrated strategy to harness the multiple resources of the ocean.

Mauritius is highly dependent on food imports for domestic consumption. While it will not be economically efficient and viable to aim for complete self-sufficiency, there is a compelling case for revitalizing agriculture by improving the level of food security through higher production capacity of vegetables and fruits, lowering the country's dependence on imports, encouraging specific exports, and promoting a more sustainable agriculture. The diversification and modernization of the sector combined with the adoption of innovative and technology- based agriculture with high-value activities and bio-farming will create new opportunities for entrepreneurs and farmers and support the emergence of a strong, competitive and sustainable agro-processing industry. The domestic agro-processing industry must be re-engineered to improve its productivity and quality. Institutional reforms to enhance farming techniques, encourage the adoption of modern technologies, improve service delivery and empower farmers towards entrepreneurship and professionalism are important. Food crops, livestock, dairy products, agro-transformation, tea cultivation and horticulture should be better supported through incentives and capacity building.

The SME sector, which essentially has been inward-looking, should also embrace an export-oriented strategy, especially in the regional and African markets. Promoting entrepreneurship and encouraging joint ventures and cross-border alliances with foreign investors could open up foreign markets. Access to finance and investment together with support to improve knowledge of markets and business intelligence are instrumental for SMEs' export growth. They should also be supported in quality management, production standards, skills improvement, logistics and transportation and clustering to ensure sustainable growth. Participation at international and regional trade fairs and integrating regional value chains will also foster a culture of exporting.

Tourism is a catalyst for growth and development in Mauritius, representing around 8 per cent of GDP, direct employment and investment. Its expansion has been consistent over the past few years (see Sannassee *et al.*, 2015). The strategy is to maintain Mauritius as an exclusive destination with a high level of services, and to embrace policies and practices to ensure the sustainability and inclusiveness of the sector and the protection, preservation and conservation of its natural environment. Air connectivity is crucial for tourism to continue to act as a major engine of growth (see Seetanah *et al.*, 2019). The country should ensure that the skies are open to cope with the number of new hotel rooms coming on stream and to help it to become a competitive aviation hub between Asia and Africa. It should also protect the reputation of the destination while diversifying products to include eco-tourism, wellness tourism, golf, deep sea fishing, weddings, cruises and the meetings, incentives, conferences and exhibitions market. There is also a niche market for tourists seeking holidays that combine health care and medical procedures at an attractive destination. The industry should also be an integral part of the digital revolution to seize the opportunities offered by technology and social platforms. Consolidating initial gains made in new markets such as

China, India and the Middle East is key for market diversification so as to build up resilience and to reduce an over-dependence on Europe.

Bolstering growth in emerging sectors

Historically, Mauritius has recorded a surplus in its trade in services to compensate for the high deficit in the balance of trade in goods (Bank of Mauritius, 2018). There is a case for broadening the range of goods and services that Mauritius exports so as to narrow the current account deficit. Financial services, including global business, and ICT represent the two main export sectors after tourism. Both are expected to make a considerable contribution to the country's quest to become a high-income economy.

The financial services sector has witnessed impressive development since the early 1990s and has emerged as an important pillar of the economy representing around 12 per cent of GDP, with banking and global business as major contributors (Statistics Mauritius, 2018). Mauritius has become a major financial centre for cross-border investment and corporate banking, especially for private equity and investment funds into India and Africa. The aim is to diversify the geographical footprint of the industry, widen the range of products and services on offer and shift towards activities with substance and high value-added components. The sector should also leverage the vast opportunities for doing business in Africa through a greater presence of banks and other providers of financial services on the continent, the acceleration of cross-border investment and fund administration activities, the supply of wealth and asset management and private banking solutions to high-net-worth individuals and corporations and a greater sophistication of corporate and investment banking services. The cluster should also capture cross-selling opportunities between the capital market, global business, real estate and tourism to generate a deeper impact on the economy. There is a need to attract more global players such as international banks, family offices, global law firms and other providers of financial services in order to provide a critical mass of inter-related services to global and regional stakeholders.

The ICT/BPO industry is also a key driver of economic growth and employment with around 800 companies in various market segments and 25,000 direct jobs (Statistics Mauritius, 2017a). There is a need to build on the current base of the ICT/BPO cluster to propel it to greater heights in terms of contribution to GDP. There are significant opportunities to transform the country into a knowledge-based economy and to position it as a technology hub in the African region by unlocking new prospects in areas such as cognitive computing, big data analytics, cloud computing and the Internet of things that are transforming businesses globally. Mauritius can also tap into the outsourcing industry that is growing exponentially as companies try to contain costs. Digitization, disruptive technologies and innovation will fuel growth and create new opportunities. The country must invest in better telecommunications infrastructure, enhance the competitiveness of connectivity, ensure the availability of diverse skill sets and domain specialists, improve capability in R&D, and upgrade the eco-system and business environment through incentives and flexible regulations so as to further develop the existing base, diversify products and services, and encourage more innovation and value addition. Mauritius should also leverage its well-developed financial services and ICT sectors to capture the opportunities in the financial technology (fintech) sector, blockchain and distributed ledger technology.

Mauritius should also diversify its narrow basket of export goods. It could leverage its current experience in the jewellery sector to position itself as a high-end jewellery manufacturing hub in the Indian Ocean, especially in view of its proximity with Africa and Asia which are the major suppliers of raw materials and finished products for the global jewellery industry. For this to happen, the jewellery sector must be restructured to shift from its current labour-intensive status to a better capitalized industry driven by technology innovation. It should also attract some global players so as to diversify the range of high value-added jewellery products to cater for market trends and buyers' preferences and enhance the reputation and recognition of Mauritian jewellery on international markets. Investment in building capacity in design, modern production techniques and other technical skills will accelerate that transition.

There is also a niche for expanding the country's small but growing medical devices industry that produces some highly sophisticated products such as medical implants, catheters and stents. The competitive tax regime, the stable political and economic environment and a skilled labour force has made it possible to attract some leading industry players from Europe to manufacture medical devices for re-export. Global demand is growing rapidly and Mauritius can seize this opportunity. The sector can develop more rapidly by widening its product offerings and diversifying its export markets, especially to India and Africa, in addition to its current exports to France. It should also vertically integrate some activities such as parts and components to assemble the final products and create greater business linkages so as to create more added value. Investment in R&D and innovation will help. The medical devices sector has indeed the potential to help to reinvigorate the manufacturing industry and transform the economy into one that is driven by knowledge and innovation.

Capturing the opportunities of the blue economy

The ocean and its extensive resources could become critical to wealth creation in Mauritius with its exclusive economic zone of 2.3 million square kilometres, which is more than 1,000 times its land mass. If tourism and related activities and the export of fish and fish products are included, the blue economy currently contributes around 12 per cent of GDP. However, its scope and scale remain below its huge potential as there are significant untapped wealth creation and economic opportunities. Its share of GDP could more than double in the medium term with substantial development opportunities for growing existing activities and pioneering new industries. This is of strategic importance for future growth and prosperity through job creation, food security, socio-economic transformation and a new wave of export-led industrialization. First, the country can expand current activities such as tourism, fisheries, ship-building and repair, and bunkering. Second, it has the scope to broaden economic value added with new clusters such as aquaculture, renewable marine energy, seaweed transformation, cosmetic, medical and pharma-ceutical products, petroleum storage, deep sea mining of hydrocarbons, minerals and polymetallic nodules, and a regional logistics and ware-housing port. Third, prospects exist for the country to become a centre for R&D, technology and innovation in ocean-based activities. There is also scope to create significant synergies among the three pillars of the ocean economy.

Sustainable ocean development necessitates a balance between resources, people, the environment and the economy. The country should boost the growing opportunities provided by the blue economy while ensuring the management of the ocean in a responsible and sustainable way. This requires the creation of an enabling environment that protects, develops and supports an effective, efficient and sustainable ocean economy while enhancing the institutional, human and technological capacity in that sector. This should include regional and international cooperation, sound and comprehensive regulatory frameworks, research capability, large capital investments, infra-structure development and innovative financing, knowledge transfer, public and private partnerships and multinational partners injecting capital, tech-nology and expertise, in order to implement and manage the project. For instance, aquaculture represents huge economic opportunities for Mauritius as an export activity, not only in terms of fish farming but also for species such as oysters, abalone and other crustaceans. Its processing and other activities in the supply chain could also contribute significantly to a new dawn in manufacturing exports.

Accelerating the shift to a circular economy

Mauritius faces all the challenges and vulnerabilities of a small island developing state and as such must accelerate the transition to a green and circular economy as an innovative pathway to foster sustainable growth, generate new jobs, boost competitiveness and shore up industrial renewal. This strategy will also support new business models with green industries, avoid environmental damage, lower dependence on imported raw materials and reduce greenhouse gas emissions so as to facilitate the emergence of a regenerative and restorative economy. It is already among countries adopting circular economy principles to guide economic and environmental policies and practices as it charges for plastic bags, converts muni-cipal waste to energy, produces around 20 per cent of its energy from renewables and transforms furnace fly ash and bottom ashes into additives for cement. The country should go further to ensure that resources circulate more by promoting natural and organic farming in agriculture, generating a higher share of electricity from renewable energy, encouraging water and energy efficiency in manufacturing and tourism, and a greater use of low-carbon vehicles and bio-fuels for public transport, as well as reducing , reusing and recycling waste.

The circular economy must become an integral part of the national development strategy so that Mauritius emerges as a resource-efficient, green and competitive low-carbon economy. It should proactively address the transition from a linear to a circular economy by adopting policies that include fiscal incentives, financing facilities, and institutional support and investment in recycling infrastructure. It must also focus on developing regulations and standards, public procurement to support the demand for circular products and services, education, training and capacity building, research and development, collaboration among companies and transparency across global supply chains regarding the origins and content of circular products and materials. Targets should be set to manage the life cycle of natural resources and change the design and manufacture of products so as to turn outputs from one manufacturer into inputs for another. Such targets should include waste management, water and energy efficiency, agribusiness and manufacturing supply chains.

Strengthening growth through deeper trade and investment links with Africa

The country depends heavily on exports to Europe and the United States for its growth. It has started to reduce this over-reliance by tapping into trade and investment opportunities in Africa. It is also emerging as a gateway for businesses and a transhipment hub for goods between Asia and Africa while integrating further with the African continent. The surge in foreign investment in Africa has triggered a race among regional and international financial centres to become a platform for such cross-border flows. Mauritius' growing financial sector already channels a reasonable share of this capital and investment to Africa.

The strategic shift to broaden and deepen the country's footprint in Africa and to play the south-south cooperation card should accelerate with policy initiatives that recognize the growing importance of sub-Saharan Africa for the export of goods and services, investment and the economic benefits of faster integration. With its track record, credibility and capabilities, Mauritius is committed to becoming a robust and viable platform for regional investment with prospects in financial services, fintech, wealth management, logistics and distribution, agri-business, tourism, manufacturing, education and health and professional services.

Mauritius has a small domestic market and hence faces a major barrier to economies of scale. Regional integration offers a solution as enlarged markets will stimulate national production, trade and investment. Access to markets is key for the export of goods and services. Mauritius is member of the Tripartite Free Trade Area that constitutes a merger of three regional economic communities in Eastern and Southern Africa with a population of over 630 million people with harmonized trade regime and duty-free access. Such integration will spur greater efficiency, productivity gains and competitiveness by lowering border barriers, reducing costs and minimizing trade and investment risks.

In addition, the country is helping some African countries to set up special economic zones (SEZ) and industrial parks that are intended to open up investment opportunities, strengthen regional cooperation and foster greater trade and investment. The SEZ initiative could become a value proposition for international investors to use the Mauritian platform for their investments in Africa. A Mauritius-Africa equity fund has been set up to provide capital for companies investing in these industrial parks while special purpose vehicles are being created to facilitate the funding of large projects in these countries. There are many joint commissions being set up to enhance economic and commercial partnerships with African countries. Given its limited resources, it is desirable for Mauritius to focus on countries with good potential in Eastern and Southern Africa with emphasis on some selected sectors where it has built competitive advantage and competence over the years and also in areas which are strategic and where it cannot afford to be absent.

Mauritius should also expand its sugar, garment, banking and hospitality industries into Africa in order to grow beyond its limited domestic market size. It has the potential to help countries in their quest for development as it has been through several growth phases to reach its current upper-middle-income status. Given its educated workforce, there are also opportunities for the export of professional services while its sophisticated financial services and its good ICT infrastructure could make the country a fintech and blockchain hub for Eastern and Southern Africa. The Stock Exchange of Mauritius is setting up an international capital market to attract governments and corporations from Africa to issue multicurrency bonds in Mauritius. The country could also become an effective platform for an African dollar market, especially with the excess of US dollar liquidity generated from global business activities. Potentially, Mauritius could also emerge as a renminbi clearing centre for Africa in the light of the internationalization of the Chinese currency and higher trade and investment in the China-Africa corridor

Air, sea and digital connectivity between Mauritius and Africa must be improved to facilitate trade, investment and greater economic cooperation. The country must attract more airlines and shipping lines while digital communications should be faster and more affordable. This would help to increase the attractiveness of Mauritius as a tourism destination, a centre for regional headquarters, and foster people-to-people contacts. It would also enhance the competitiveness of exports for locally produced goods and the freeport as a hub for breaking bulk and assembly of goods destined to the regional market under the preferential trade regime. Greater diplomatic presence on the ground will help to consolidate cooperation with key African countries. It is important to work on building human resource capacity to sustain the regional expansion effort and train, coach, groom and motivate middle and top management cadres to work in Africa while reaching out to the Mauritian diaspora on the continent.

Leveraging science, technology and innovation for better growth

Science, technology and innovation (STI) will be the lynchpin for improving productivity and sustaining strong economic growth and global competitiveness. Growth accounting explains the determinants of growth by allocating the expansion in output to the growth in capital, labour and total factor productivity (TFP). Growth in TFP stems from improvements in the way in which capital and labour are combined in the production processes for greater efficiency. While better managerial practices and organizational improvements contribute to such progress, STI in the production of goods and services is crucial for sharpening competitiveness and delivering quality growth. In its quest to attain high-income status, the country must allocate more resources to STI and R&D. It also has to embrace technological changes that are having profound consequences on both the economy and society as they will create new industries, transform existing ones, as well as offer businesses, especially SMEs, an effective means of reaching global markets. The setting up of a sovereign fund for seed capital, knowledge-based investments and a strategic partnership between the public and the private sectors and academia are key to commercializing innovations across sectors, thus contributing to higher and better growth.

There is a need to focus on a wide array of disruptive technological advancements linked to the fourth industrial revolution that the global community is intently focused upon in innovative areas such as big data analytics, the Internet of things, artificial intelligence, 3D printing, distributed ledger and blockchain technology. They have a multitude of applications in different sectors that range from financial intermediation, manufacturing, agriculture, energy, education, health, environment, transport, governance and IT. The objective is to cut costs, enhance efficiency, grow customer loyalty, improve business processes and innovate new products and services. For instance, fintech has the potential to foster innovation and unlock a wide range of activities, including viable disruptive solutions to provide greater access to financial services. Significant income in the financial sector run the risks of being displaced by fintech, while a substantial share of world trade in services is already digitalized allowing small companies and start-ups that were previously excluded from mainstream business to participate directly in globalization.

Mauritius has the required resources to become an attractive regional platform for distributed ledger technology and to deliver competitive services to the African region. In addition to its skilled labour force, good infrastructure, a competitive and reputable financial centre, a sound and respected regulatory and institutional framework, many tax treaties and investment promotion and protection agreements with several African countries, there is also both government and industrial will to emerge in that space. The country has started to strategically assess the emergence of new technologies, consider their regulatory implications and provide for an enabling environment and incentives to emerge as a key player in the innovation space and become a regional fintech and technology hub for Africa. The regulatory framework needs to be flexible in order to accommodate the development and adoption of new technologies and for the establishment and operation of start-up activities. The country must also build strategic partnerships to overcome some of the binding constraints while industry professionals and researchers should collaborate with reputable global institutions to boost capacity and talent to create a much broader innovation culture in financial and technology services, facilitate knowledge sharing, and keep up to date with the latest advancements in that ecosystem. There is a need to encourage global players in fintech to set up in Mauritius in order to capture the huge opportunities in Africa.

The reform agenda as a base for structural transformation

In order to run the next development lap and become a high-income economy, Mauritius needs to implement structural reforms in many sectors such as education, training, human capital, labour force, infrastructure, technology acquisition, innovation, institutions and factor markets. A new generation of deep-rooted and coherent structural reforms is essential to reverse the declining trends in competitiveness, productivity, investment and exports and to ensure that global challenges can be converted into opportunities. It is impossible to remain competitive in global and regional markets without massive investments to improve the quality of human resources and the economy's capacity to innovate. Given the country's ageing population, economic growth increasingly will be spurred by expanding productivity.

In addition to investment in quality physical infrastructure in transport, energy, water and sanitation, port and ICT to remove supply-side bottlenecks and a clear, predictable and transparent policy environment, there is need to boost labour, capital and TFP and sharpen global competitiveness, increase the labour force participation rate, especially that of women, and facilitate the transfer of resources from low to high productivity sectors, nurture innovation, R&D and encourage industrial upgrading and build scientific and technological competence. The country must design new institutions or reform existing ones to support the technological development and upgrade of companies in order to improve competitiveness. It should also attract technology through FDI, improve efficiency, use scarce resources more effectively, and make education, training and skills fit for the economy by resolving the mismatch in the labour market with a focus on technical and vocational education and apprenticeship. Labour market reforms should ensure flexibility and security so that people can move across sectors. The emphasis should be on protecting people rather than jobs. The country must continuously improve the ease of doing business and the investment climate, reduce inefficient government bureaucracy, and attract foreign skills and talent, technology and capital in promising sectors in order to accelerate the transition to a high-income economy. It should end the bias in the tax incentives for land development as it is crowding out investment in the productive sectors of the economy. It should also revisit the investment incentive framework to support the development and growth of new pillars that have potential for exports. The public sector should be re-engineered to reduce its inefficiencies and strengthen its capacity to design, implement and monitor major public infrastructure projects in a timely and a cost-efficient manner and to make key institutions not only stronger but also more independent, transparent and accountable. Mauritius should also ensure the sustainability and equity of the pension systems and revisit the welfare system to make it fairer for the poor. Tax expenditure on rent-seeking activities should be lowered to protect the fiscal base, reduce debt and generate revenue to invest in physical and social capital.

The role of institutions and infrastructure

High-quality and effective institutions are key to making the transition to an era of sustained high growth (Acemoglu and Robinson, 2010). At an earlier level of economic development with an abundance of cheap labour, low technology and unsophisticated physical capital, it is not absolutely necessary to have quality institutions because policy formulation and implementation is quite straightforward. However, graduation to high-income status requires a different set of institutions which are both sophisticated and of high quality. This includes but is not limited to effective governance and accountable public institutions, corporate governance, transparency, rule of law, good partnership and cooperation among various stakeholders such as policymakers, businesses, academics and employees' representatives, an efficient and transparent relationship between the public and the private sector, a responsible, reliable and capable government, strong leadership, a competent civil service and an entrepreneurial and globally competitive private sector.

Infrastructure, both economic and social, plays an important role in economic growth as it increases the country's productive capacity and sustains development (Knack and Keefer, 1997). It is also an essential ingredient to build a competitive modern economy. Mauritius has invested in both physical and social infrastructure to create the necessary conditions for growth and development. If it is to achieve high-income status, the quality of infrastructure will be important in raising the productivity of human and physical capital. Improvement is required in energy, water, transportation, sanitation, telecommunications, air, sea and digital connectivity and in education and skills in order to cope with an insufficiently equipped labour force, an ageing and dwindling population and low productivity. There is need to upgrade and expand the country's human capital infrastructure to make it more resilient and adaptable. The country should also adopt a more flexible immigration policy and attract the

Mauritian diaspora so as to bridge the skills gap and improve competitiveness and facilitate the transformation to a knowledge-based economy. This would help to address the current disconnection between the supply of skilled workers and the demand for jobs.

Shared prosperity and inclusive growth

While the country has made progress on absolute poverty (Statistics Mauritius, 2017b), major challenges persist. Pockets of deprivation and social exclusion, relative poverty and rising incomes, asset and wealth inequality remain significant developmental challenges. Poverty is high among the unemployed, women, those who are outside the labour force and the working poor. The rapidly rising economic inequality represents a great risk to social cohesion and national harmony. As the depth of poverty increases, Mauritius run the risks of lagging behind in terms of many shared-prosperity indicators. The HDI that measures life expectancy, education and GDP per capita declines on average by 15 per cent when adjusted for inequality.

Effective poverty and inequality reduction must be an integral part of the development strategy. The poor should be integrated in the growth process as there are institutional, policy and political factors that can both cause poverty and impede its alleviation. A faster and deeper poverty reduction strategy should be developed and it should recognize the multidimensional nature of poverty, focus on outcomes that will benefit the poor and ensure better coordination and alignment of all partners. Mauritius requires a combination of faster growth, investment in human development, redistributive policies and an effective empowerment programme, combined with an improvement in the social safety nets so that benefits accrue more to the poor. Evidence shows that focused social assistance, cash transfers and income support work much better in curbing poverty than universal subsidies that benefit disproportionately the non-poor. Fiscal policies to lower inequality and foster greater redistribution should be reviewed. There is still room for raising more tax revenue by improved tax administration, reducing tax expenditures that mainly benefit some unproductive sectors and considering the merit of imposing taxes on some passive income and wealth. Furthermore, policies such as broad-based employees' ownership schemes, meaningful profit sharing and citizens' funds for workers and the wider public could help to lower economic inequality.

While strong and sustained growth is not enough on its own to fight poverty and inequality, it is very important (see also Ravaillon, 2001). There is a clear growth-employment-poverty nexus. Growth and structural changes that generate productive employment can decrease poverty and bring about greater inclusiveness. However, more could be done to generate jobs for the poor. Additional investment is essential in physical infrastructure and support that will contribute to socially inclusive development. A strategy that provides greater access of the poor to education, training, skill development and human capital, health, decent housing, water and sanitation, micro-credit, and markets will go a long way in broadening the circle of opportunities and help to remove the 8 per cent of people from the poverty trap. Equally, support for entrepreneurship is vital to encourage and enable young people and women in particular to have their own micro enterprises.

Redistribution and comprehensive social policies are vital to successfully fight exclusion at one end of the income spectrum and to curb income and wealth inequality at the other (see also Baye, 2006). Mauritius currently has a combination of many universal benefits and very few targeted programmes in its social assistance architecture. The share of universal benefits that disproportionately accrue to the non-poor accounts for a significant share of close to 85 per cent of social welfare expenditure. As a result, the poor have to shoulder the burden of the social assistance policy as they are being sacrificed to make the benefits universal. The few programmes like social aid that have a significant impact on poverty alleviation are too few and have too little resources. The predicament is worsened by the fragmented approach adopted and the lack of coordination which affects the efficiency and the effectiveness of the poverty reduction strategy. An effective poverty reduction strategy has to rebalance transfers and subsidies between universal benefits and targeted support in favour of the latter.

Even with good macroeconomic performances, redistribution policy is key to prevent rising inequality in income and wealth. Growth usually increases the absolute incomes of the poor, but it does not always have a systematic effect on their relative shares in total income. Fiscal policy – taxes and transfers – can have a large, significant impact on lowering inequality and reducing poverty. There is thus a strong case for policies to alter the unfair distribution of income and wealth, especially in the light of the huge inequality that has arisen from the globalization, liberalization and financialization of the economy, the consequences of technological progress and the structural transformation of the country. Market forces on their own seem incapable of curbing these excesses. The objective is not to retreat from globalization and shun technological progress but rather to design the right fiscal policy mix to ensure fairness and lower inequality.

There is an absolute necessity to rethink the Corporate Social Responsibility/ National Empowerment Foundation programme so that most of its resources are deployed to fight poverty and empower the vulnerable groups. It should focus on poverty alleviation, empowerment and social inclusion as opposed to being all things to all people which it has turned out to be. It should restrict its core interventions and funding to a narrow set of five or six key areas that will support the poor and facilitate their integration in the socio-economic mainstream. Its emphasis should be on education, training, capacity building, skills upgrading and development so as to reduce the importance of socio-economic background in life outcomes, investment in social housing and related basic infrastructure and amenities for the poor, employment access and job opportunities, self-employment and the informal sector which have the potential to create both jobs and wealth.

Conclusion

The success of a small island economy depends to a large extent on its ability to adjust to shifting economic circumstances. Due to globalization, trade liberalization, preference erosions and technological innovations, Mauritius is now competing with many countries. It has lost most of its trade preferences. There is no quick formula for exiting the middle-income trap and attaining high-income status. The factors that differentiate countries that have made the transition to high-income status from others are mostly linked to the quality of economic policies. Policies, mutually reinforcing strategies, good execution, disciplined stewardship, coherence, consistency and hard work are crucial. A coherent strategy must be embedded on clear macro-economic policies that give direction and milestones to all participants. It should lift productivity, sharpen competitiveness and adopt the right mix of structural, budgetary, fiscal, monetary and exchange rate policies to reignite the engines of growth, foster shared prosperity and protect the environment. It must enable the nation to unleash its full potential by investing in people, technology, infrastructure, environment, institutions and society to overcome the challenges, remove binding constraints and deal with structural weaknesses. The history of Mauritius is one of adaptability, innovation and anticipating global changes. Its success is attributable to its people, and the future also depends on its people, its ability to cope with changes, to reinvent itself and to seize new opportunities.

References

Acemoglu, D. and Robinson, J. (2010) 'The Role of Institutions in Growth and Development', *Review of Economics and Institutions* 1(2), Fall.

Bank of Mauritius (2018) *Annual Reports: June 2018*, Port Louis: Bank of Mauritius.

Baye, F. M. (2006) 'Growth, Redistribution and Poverty Changes in Cameroon: A Shapley Decomposition Analysis', *Journal of African Economies* 15(4): 543–570. Available at https://doi.org/10.1093/jae/ejk010.

Frankel, J. A. (2010) 'Mauritius: African Success Story', NBER Working Papers 16569, Cambridge, MA: National Bureau of Economic Research.

International Monetary Fund (IMF) (2018) *International Financial Statistics*, Washington, DC: International Monetary Fund. Available at http://data.imf.org/?sk=4C514D48-B6BA-49ED-8AB9-52B0C1A0179B.

Knack, S., and Keefer, P. (1997) 'Does Social Capital Have an Economic Payoff? A Cross-Country Investigation', *Quarterly Journal of Economics* 112(4): 1251–1288. Available at https://doi.org/10.1162/003355300555475.

Mauritius Commercial Bank (2017) 'Post-Budget Outlook', no. 69, *MCB Focus*, Port Louis: MCB Publications.

Mauritius Commercial Bank (2018) *Local Entrepreneur in Mauritius*, SME Report, Port Louis:MCB Publications.

Ravaillon, M. (2001) 'Growth, Inequality and Poverty: Looking beyond Averages', *World Development* 29(11): 1803–1815.

Sannassee, R. V., Seetanah, B. and Lamport, M. J. (2014) 'Export Diversification and Economic Growth: The Case of Mauritius', in M. Jansen, M. S. Jallab and M. Smeets (eds) *Connecting to Global Markets—Challenges and Opportunities: Case Studies Presented by WTO Chair-Holders*, Geneva: World Trade Organization, pp. 11–23. Available at www.wto.org/english/res_e/booksp_e/cmark_full_e.pdf.

Sannassee, R., Seetanah, B. and Rojid, S. (2015) 'The Impact of Relative Prices on Tourism Demand for Mauritius: An Empirical Analysis', *Development Southern Africa* 32(10). DOI: doi:1080/0376835X.2015.1010717.

Seetanah, B., Sannassee, R., Teeroovengadum, V. andNunkoo, R. (2019) 'Air Access Liberalization, Marketing Promotion and Tourism Development', *International Journal of Tourism Research. DOI*: doi:10.1002/jtr.2242.

Statistics Mauritius (2017a) *Annual Digest of Statistics 2017*, Port Louis: Statistics Mauritius.

Statistics Mauritius (2017b) *Household Budget Survey 2017: Preliminary Results & Updated Weights for the Consumer Price Index*, Port Louis: Statistics Mauritius.

Statistics Mauritius (2018) *Annual Digest of Statistics 2018*, Port Louis: Statistics Mauritius.

Svirydzenka, K. and Petri, M. (2014) 'Mauritius: The Drivers of Growth. Can the Past be Extended?', IMF Working Paper No. 14/134, Washington, DC: International Monetary Fund. Available at https://ssrn.com/abstract=3014022.

United Nations Development Programme (UNDP) (2016) *Human Development Indices and Indicators*, New York: United Nations Development Programme. Available at http://hdr.undp.org/sites/all/themes/hdr_theme/country-notes/MUS.pdf.

Index

Page numbers in *italics* and **bold** indicate Figures and Tables, respectively.

Printed in the United States
by Baker & Taylor Publisher Services